The Orga

OTHER WRITERS & ARTISTS TITLES INCLUDE

Writers' & Artists' Guide to Writing for Children and YA by Linda Strachan
Writers' & Artists' Guide to How to Get Published by Alysoun Owen
Writers' & Artists' Guide to How to Hook an Agent by James Rennoldson
Writers' & Artists' Guide to Self-publishing
Writers' & Artists' Guide to How to Write by William Ryan

ABOUT THE AUTHOR

Antony Johnston is an award-winning, *New York Times* bestselling author and creator of *The Coldest City*, adapted to film as *Atomic Blonde* starring Charlize Theron. His work spans books, film, graphic novels, videogames, music, podcasts, and more, with titles translated throughout the world. He lives and works in England – and is highly organised.

Follow Antony on Twitter @AntonyJohnston

Organised-Writer.com

The Organised Writer

HOW TO STAY ON TOP OF ALL YOUR PROJECTS AND
NEVER MISS A DEADLINE

Antony Johnston

BLOOMSBURY YEARBOOKS
LONDON · OXFORD · NEW YORK · NEW DELHI · SYDNEY

BLOOMSBURY YEARBOOKS
Bloomsbury Publishing Plc
50 Bedford Square London WC1B 3DP UK

BLOOMSBURY, BLOOMSBURY YEARBOOKS, WRITERS' & ARTISTS' and
the Diana logo are trademarks of Bloomsbury Publishing Plc

First published in Great Britain 2020

Copyright © Antony Johnston, 2020

Antony Johnston has asserted his right under the Copyright, Designs and
Patents Act, 1988, to be identified as Author of this work

All rights reserved. No part of this publication may be reproduced or transmitted
in any form or by any means, electronic or mechanical, including photocopying,
recording, or any information storage or retrieval system, without prior permission in
writing from the publishers

Bloomsbury Publishing Plc does not have any control over, or responsibility for, any
third-party websites referred to or in this book. All internet addresses given in this
book were correct at the time of going to press. The author and publisher regret any
inconvenience caused if addresses have changed or sites have ceased to exist, but can
accept no responsibility for any such changes

A catalogue record for this book is available from the British Library

ISBN: PB: 978-1-4729-7718-2; eBook: 978-1-4729-7717-5

2 4 6 8 10 9 7 5 3 1

Typeset by Deanta Global Publishing Services, Chennai, India
Printed and bound in Great Britain by CPI Group (UK) Ltd, Croydon, CR0 4YY

To find out more about our authors and books, visit www.bloomsbury.com
and sign up for our newsletters

For Benjamin Read;
where others saw pedantry, he saw a book.

CONTENTS

INTRODUCTION
Becoming an organised writer 1
A productive timeline 3 | Assumptions and caveats 5 | *Clean mind* theory 6 | How to use this book 7

PART I: *Get organised*

CHAPTER 1
FASTEN your seatbelt 13
Buckle up! 15

CHAPTER 2
Clocking in (and out) 21
A day in the life 26 | Use your calendar 27 | Multiple projects in one day 42 | Get smart with email 45 | Use a task manager 57 | Learn to say 'no' 65 | Work to a quantity, not time 67 | Productive procrastination 70 | Invest the time to set up your system 72 | Organise your personal life 74

CHAPTER 3
Taking notes and making lists 79
Taking notes 80 | Making lists 89 | Job sheets 91 | Files and archives 102 | Packing lists 106

PART II: *Write!*

CHAPTER 4
Five pages after breakfast 117
Words, not time 120 | Just write 133 | Writing on the move 140

Contents

CHAPTER 5
From scribbles to script 151

Initial notes 151 | Initial plot 151 | Bullet-point outline 153 | Treatment/Pitch 155 | Breakdown 156 | Manuscript 157 | Rewriting 159

PART III: *Non-writing stuff*

CHAPTER 6
Money matters 165

Hire an accountant 167 | How I learned to stop worrying and love the spreadsheet 168 | Invoicing 182 | Find your price, and stick to it 183

CHAPTER 7
It's a set-up 189

Take a weekend 191 | ... and relax 208 | Hardware 209 | Software 215 | Taxonomy 232 | Gadgets 236

CHAPTER 8
Conclusion: Living as an organised writer 241

AFTERWORD 243
ACKNOWLEDGEMENTS 244
APPENDICES 245
Summary checklists 247 | Job sheets 252 | Further reading 257
INDEX 259

INTRODUCTION

Becoming an organised writer

'Be regular and orderly in your life, so that you may be violent and original in your work.'

Gustave Flaubert, Letter to Mme Tennant, 1876

I'm a novelist and short-story writer, graphic novelist, screenwriter, videogame scriptwriter and consultant, musician, and podcaster. I attend conventions, talk at conferences, and make regular public appearances. I was first published in 1996 while holding down a day job, and since 2002 I've been a full-time professional author.

I tell you this not to brag, but to explain why this book exists and why I'm qualified to write it.

All writers get stressed out over plot, characters, conflict, resolution, backstory, timelines, world-building, consistency, editors' notes, cover art, titles, book blurbs, good reviews, bad reviews – you name it. If it's related to writing, we get stressed over it. That's not the problem; writing isn't easy, and no book can help you with that – especially if you're trying out new things all the time, as any good author should. Sweating over those things is what makes you a writer.

But you *shouldn't* be stressing out over missed deadlines; reaching the end of another day and wondering where all the time you'd intended to spend writing has gone; trying to remember where you put your notes, your contract, or your cat; discovering you should have filed your tax return two weeks ago; worrying about office and admin tasks piling up; or being unable to relax when you should be having fun with friends and family, because your writing is behind schedule.

That kind of stress will send you to an early grave, make you no fun to be around and even prevent you doing your best work. It's a self-imposed tyranny that prevents you being able to focus on writing, because you're too distracted by all the other tasks you haven't yet started, let alone finished.

You can change that – if you're willing to put in the work. The first five years of my life as a full-time writer were spent playing endless games of 'Where on earth did I put that contract? Oh God, the deadline for this script was last week! How can this many unread emails even exist?' before I finally realised managing your work isn't something that magically happens around you while you type. It takes practise. It takes discipline.

It takes being an *organised writer.*

This book is for writers of all kinds. You might be established, or just starting out; a working professional, or an enthusiastic amateur; writing fiction, or non-fiction; have a traditional contract, or prefer to self-publish; write full-time, or part-time; be a novelist, poet, screenwriter, playwright, historian, games writer or something else entirely. Whatever kind of writer you are, whatever your personal situation, *The Organised Writer* can help you. It's not a book on how to write (see Further reading on page 257 for some useful resources in that direction), but it is a practical guide designed to help you with all the other aspects of a writer's life: getting organised, managing your time, making better use of the time you have, and keeping track of your work and business affairs.

The Organised Writer draws on more than a decade of my own career and working life, during which time I've successfully juggled dozens of different projects without ever missing a deadline. It describes a holistic system that helps you achieve a structure and routine, freeing you to immerse yourself more fully in creative work by rewarding consistency while boosting creativity.

To that end, first I'll explain the concepts and thinking behind the system, which will help you understand and implement the practical advice that follows. And if you do find something within these pages that absolutely, positively won't work for your situation… why not take the raw material as inspiration, use that inspiration to craft something that uniquely suits your style, and finally polish it to make it as useful as possible?

After all, that's what writers do.

A productive timeline

I used everything in this book to write this book.

The truth is, I didn't set out to create a productivity system. When I became a full-time writer, I assumed all I'd have to do was write, answer a few emails, and send an invoice every once in a while. What else could a writer possibly have to worry about? I was laughably wrong, but also far from alone; the same error is made by many writers, and other freelance creatives. It's especially common among those of us who are leaving a corporate environment, as we often don't appreciate the sheer amount of administration hidden from our daily working life because our employer took care of it.

After a few years of freelancing my career was taking off, and I had more work than ever – but along with more creative work comes ever more non-creative work, boring stuff like invoicing and accounts and tax and office supplies. Sure, we all want to see how much money is coming in. But who wants to take time away from creative writing to deal with office admin and file taxes?

That reluctance to take care of non-creative affairs is how, after about three years of working like this, I found myself drowning in a sea of unanswered emails, unsent (and therefore unpaid) invoices, lost project notes, mislaid schedules, and – worst of all in my eyes, the cardinal sin – missed deadlines. I *never* missed deadlines. Except suddenly, I'd missed two.

That was the jolt I needed to understand that this lackadaisical approach was untenable; that I needed to implement some kind of structure to properly keep track of my schedule and business.

(Is it ironic that it took an adverse effect on my writing work to make me finally decide to get my *non*-writing work organised? Perhaps, but I'm guessing the same could be said for most of you reading this.)

My first port of call was, naturally, the internet. I don't recall the exact search terms I used, or the precise path I took when looking for help in the resultant cascade of search results, but I was soon awash in a sea of 'productivity systems', a term I'd never even encountered before. GTD, Pomodoro, Midori, Nozbe, Kanban; such baffling acronyms and neologisms, all promising to hold the key to a better life, a more organised existence where stress and chaos were banished to the past.

I began reading up on these systems… and quickly realised most of them were not for me, or writers of any stripe. I don't just mean in terms of attitude or outlook, but also because of their target audience: corporate leaders, business executives, lawyers and managers and supervisors, oh my! There's nothing wrong with that, but it makes those systems terribly ill suited to creative workers. Few of us are fortunate enough to have an assistant, let alone an office full of employees. More importantly, productivity systems aimed at corporate managers and workers make assumptions about how a typical day is structured that are way off the mark when it comes to creative work.

I found this out the hard way, by trying to implement those systems and failing terribly. But I persevered, because I could see there was *something* to be learned from them; under the assumptions about staff and schedules and resources was a glimmer of light, one I felt could be nourished and cultivated into something that would illuminate my own situation. I had to figure out what a creative professional *needs* from a productivity system, and to do that meant looking (with rather brutal honesty) at my own situation.

The Organised Writer began with a single short article I published on my website way back in 2007, outlining the very first version of this system after a year of successfully using it myself. I expected it would be read by a few friends and colleagues, who might take away one or two useful tips, before it would be forgotten. When it racked up half a million hits in the first six months, though, I realised I had, in fact, struck a nerve. I went on to write other short articles and blog posts, about my notes-to-story process, how I use writing software, and more. All were popular, and people told me I had a good voice for making this sort of thing useful and easy to read. People who *weren't even writers* told me how much they enjoyed reading these articles.

Eventually friends began to ask when I would write a book about getting organised; something to expand on the system, and go into more depth on both administrative and creative matters. I said I'd think about it... but I was too busy to give it my full attention and, ironically, could never find the time to write it.

Now, at last, here it is.

Assumptions and caveats

For the sake of simplicity and clarity, I'm going to make certain assumptions. I apologise in advance if they're not true for your situation.

I assume you're a writer of some experience, whether published or not, whose working life is chaotic and disorganised. I assume you use a computer, that you have internet access, and are comfortable performing basic online tasks even if you're not technically-minded. I also assume that you input text through a keyboard, and are generally able-bodied and neurotypical.

But everything here can be used and adapted by writers of different circumstances (and maybe even by non-writers; artists, musicians, designers, anyone engaging in a creative endeavour) either as-is or with only minor modification. Because the main assumption I make is that you're *smart*. Smart enough to see how a specific method or usage may not fit your own situation or working style with absolute precision – but it would only take a tweak here, a poke there, to make it fit. Smart enough to see the underlying philosophy that permeates these pages, and figure out how you can use its principles in ways that are relevant to you and compatible with your life.

If you're able to, begin by following everything in here to the letter. You'll find complete routines and instructional methods, and if you're completely at sea in terms of organisation, adopting these practices will give you a stable base from which to develop your own personalised habits. But if for some reason you're unable to follow my advice to the letter, with only a little extra work *The Organised Writer* can be a template which you can adapt in order to build your own system.

Clean mind theory

I subscribe to something called *clean mind* theory, so allow me to briefly explain what that means (relax, it has nothing to do with morals). I admit it's unscientific; I have no quantifiable evidence beyond my own experience, and that of friends and colleagues, but my experience backs it up.

What do I mean by a clean mind? Quite simply, it's the state we find ourselves in when we first wake up, before we allow the demands of our daily life to begin taking up space in our thoughts. I firmly believe that most creative people, especially writers, are more productive when our mind is clean. The more we allow the real world to barge its way into our consciousness and take up space, the less able we are to lose ourselves in the state of imaginative creativity necessary for us to work. Thus, messy-minded people struggle to get work done, and the quality of what they do achieve is below their best.

Now, those of you with children or other dependants are probably throwing your hands up in despair, but hear me out. If you need to get your kids ready for school, or walk your dogs, or attend to any other family matters first thing, then of course those duties must be carried out. But such tasks don't require you to continue thinking about them *after* they're done; once the kids are sent off or the dogs are in their beds, you can mentally check them off and forget about them for the time being. And whether or not you have dependants, you may also have a day job, a situation I'll touch on later. *The Organised Writer* is nothing if not pragmatic, and understands that life often dictates your schedule. That's okay, because you can still put its principles to use. Even if your schedule doesn't allow you to follow the system exactly, you can still practise many of its methods such as note-taking, time management, and ubiquitous thought-capture.

No mind can ever be perfectly clean, because such a mind would be one without personality, or much of a life. Nevertheless, the cleaner it is while we work – the more distance we put between ourselves and everyday mundanities trusting that they'll be dealt with at the right time – the more we can get done without being distracted by ordinary concerns, and the better our writing will be as a result.

How to use this book

The Organised Writer is divided into three main sections.

Part I: *Get organised* – explains how to organise your time and schedule, making the most of both your writing sessions and any spare time you might have. It promotes the value of taking good notes, shows how best to use and make to-do lists, and explains why you should adopt a simple task management system.

Part II: *Write!* – is all about what to *do* with the time you allot to writing; how best to optimise those sessions so you can write more, and better, on any given day. It gives advice on incorporating travel without ruining your schedule, and explains why 'just write' is not a flippant hand-wave, but in fact a valuable part of every writer's self-improvement. This section walks you through my own 'scribbles to script' process, to show you how

The Organised Writer's principles and practices help me to develop an initial idea into a fully-fledged work.

Part III: *Non-writing stuff* – deals with all the tasks other than writing that you must take into consideration; finances, spreadsheets, and office admin. It walks you step-by-step through the process of stripping down, assessing, and then re-organising your work space, to put the system into practice. Finally, it describes what to look for in the equipment, hardware, and software you use.

At the end of each chapter is a summary of its main points; checklists of their contents are included at the back of the book for easy reference. You can use these as 'cheat sheets' when you begin practising the system – but I strongly suggest you read the relevant chapter before using them, to avoid confusion. The chapters describe the reasoning and motivation behind each part of the process, and explain *why* the system encourages you to do things a certain way. Absorbing this detail will help you use the system, and summary sheets, more effectively.

The good news is, you won't need the summaries for long. The methods and practices of *The Organised Writer* are natural and intuitive, and after a short time you'll find they become habitual.

RECOMMENDATIONS DISCLAIMER

Throughout this book I sometimes recommend software, tools, and products. These are all my own independent and unbiased opinion, derived directly from personal experience. No company, brand, or product mentioned has paid or compensated me in any way for inclusion or recommendation. I have no partnerships, arrangements, sponsorships, or quid pro quo with anyone for equipment, software licences, computers, stationery, or anything else that might influence my opinion. 'Neither a borrower nor a lender be', as Stratford's favourite son wrote.

I suggest you read the whole book through once, cover to cover, without taking any action. Then read it a second time, with the perspective of having now seen the whole picture, and begin to plan how you can implement the system.

Next, take a weekend (literally; see Chapter 7) to sort out your working space, and on the following Monday, begin putting the system into practice. Don't worry if you falter along the way. You'll be making a lot of big changes, and slipping back into bad habits occasionally is natural. Keep the book handy and refer to it as necessary to get yourself back in the saddle. Over time you'll develop and cement new, better habits, and find yourself needing the book less often.

Eventually you'll reach a place where you're practising the system without consciously thinking about it – which is the ultimate goal. As counter-intuitive as it may sound, nothing would make me happier than for you to read this book, put its methods into practice, then pass it on to a friend or colleague who might need it!

PART I

Get organised

CHAPTER 1

FASTEN your seatbelt

(×) A ***disorganised writer*** is not consistent in how they conduct their working life from day to day, and lives in perpetual panic mode.

(✓) ***The organised writer*** has a system in place to deal with all aspects of their working day, while staying flexible enough to apply common sense.

If *The Organised Writer* could be summed up in a word, it would be *focus* – everything here is designed to increase that focus and remove the possibilities for you to succumb to its natural enemy, *distraction*.

We gain focus when we 'lose ourselves' in a task; when it's all that we're thinking about, with our conscious brain power fully devoted to it. Every writer knows this feeling. Some call it *flow*, *being in the zone*, or *getting on a roll*... there are many different terms for it, but they all mean the same thing – reaching a state where you forget about everything except the work in front of you.

How do we achieve this blissful, elusive state? The answer is as simple to describe as it is difficult to implement: by *eliminating distraction*.

I'm not necessarily talking about things like a noisy environment, music playing or people chatting around you. Some writers are able to focus perfectly well in such circumstances – in fact, the environment in which you most easily find your focus is almost certainly different to that of other writers. For some, the ideal working set-up is a noisy, anonymous place like a coffee shop or diner; for others it's a completely quiet and disconnected room, silent and windowless; and for most of us, it's somewhere in between.

I prefer a dedicated room, to reinforce the idea that I'm 'going to work' when I step through the study door; but far from needing silence, I actually prefer to have music playing while I work, and my window looks out over a local park.

By contrast, I know one very successful writer whose first years of freelance writing were spent at a corner of her kitchen table, banging away on her laptop in between bouts of wrangling infant children (or at ungodly pre-dawn hours, to give herself some uninterrupted time). I know another who wears headphones, but instead of listening to music through them he plays computer-generated white noise, to shut out the real world. Ask ten writers to describe their ideal writing environment, and you'll get eleven different answers.

That's not what I mean by distraction. What I'm talking about – what I'm confident every writer in history would agree is the mortal enemy of our art – is something I call *memory distraction*.

Memory distraction is sabotage from within. It's what happens when you're trying to remember everything that you need to do, and keep this list in your mind because you fear that if you forget about it for a moment, it will be gone forever (and you're probably right).

How many times have you sat down, ready to work, but just a few words in you suddenly remember that you need to call a client this week? You mentally file it away, resume writing – but by the next paragraph you're thinking about the email you got from your editor this morning, and how you'll reply to it. Shaking that off, you return to your work document, but two sentences later you remember a story idea you had last night that still sounds pretty good… and don't forget you still need to call that client, and reply to your editor's email… and on, and on. Filled with this ever-mounting detritus, your brain becomes an obstacle course of time-wasting hazards and energy-sapping anxiety which you try in vain to negotiate. Before you know it the day is over, your stress levels are through the roof, and you *still* haven't finished that chapter.

Sound familiar? You're not alone.

This section is about getting yourself, and your work environment and practices, organised in order to eliminate as much memory distraction as possible, leaving you free to focus on your writing.

Buckle up!

If focus is the ultimate aim, then the path by which we achieve it is filled with a host of preparatory work, all of it based around the simple principle of reducing the amount of effort and energy you have to spend on thinking about anything that isn't writing. If your mind is occupied by questions like this...

Where should I file this letter?
Where's that bank statement I received last week?
When's that call with my editor, again?
What do I need to work on tomorrow to stay ahead of deadline?
Wait, are my accounts due yet?
What was that great idea I had yesterday?

...then you're going to have a hard time concentrating on writing. That's memory distraction in a nutshell.

The human brain can hold, on average, seven items in its short-term memory, and each will only stay in our memory for about 30 seconds unless we 'rehearse' them – i.e. repeat the list of items regularly, to maintain them.

In 1956, the famed psychologist George Miller codified this principle in his paper 'The Magical Number Seven, Plus or Minus Two: Some Limits on Our Capacity for Processing Information', and it came to be known as Miller's Law. As with all things relating to human cognition, it's difficult to draw universal or absolute conclusions, and studies continue to this day on the nature and abilities of human memory. But Miller's Law is compelling and aligns with what many of us feel instinctively. How many times have you been so preoccupied trying to remember the half-dozen things you need to do that you just can't bear to take on another item?

That's because item rehearsal places a large cognitive load on our mind, forcing it to the forefront of our thoughts. Doing this while trying to write leads directly to memory distraction, because it clashes with precisely the kind of mental juggling in which we're already engaged for our work.

When writing, we're attempting to hold and organise in our memory a large number of things related to what we're working on; the next word, the next sentence, the reason we're writing this sentence at this point, the conclusion we want to make at the end of the paragraph, how the viewpoint character relates to their current situation, why something from their character history makes this moment important, how the current scene will affect the following scene, how this chapter relates to those around it... we hold all these things, and more, in our memory without much conscious thought because they're all connected to the matter at hand and relevant to our writing.

But what if we're also trying not to forget the calls we need to make, admin tasks we have to perform, filing that must be done, this evening's shopping list, and more? Now all these other thoughts – none of them relevant to what we're writing – are fighting for a place in our short-term memory. If we focus on them, we risk forgetting everything else we're trying to remember that actually *is* relevant to our writing. If we focus entirely on writing instead, we forget the other tasks we were supposed to do. Phone calls don't get made, groceries don't get bought, accounts don't get filed.

Most of the time we wind up somewhere in between, remembering part of each group, but neither of them as a whole.

Not only does our writing suffer, but we also forget to buy milk while picking up the kids. It's a lose/lose situation.

How do we fix this problem? How do we eliminate, or at least significantly reduce, memory distraction without the risk of forgetting the tasks we need to perform?

We remove unnecessary things from our memory, and put them in a safe place.

You may think I'm speaking metaphorically, but I'm not. Removing things from memory isn't something you can consciously do, of course; you can't 'make' yourself forget something, any more than you can prevent yourself thinking of an elephant when you read this sentence.

What you can do is *off-load* an item, out of your memory and into a 'safe place' – a place where you know you'll be reminded of it at the right time, but not before. If you do that, and you completely trust the system to remind you of the item in question at a more appropriate time, you'll forget it naturally; your brain will relax, subconsciously aware that it doesn't need to rehearse the item to hold it in memory, and thus let it slip away.

You might think you could do this with a simple to-do list; just write everything down on a piece of paper. In theory, you could. But a piece of paper won't hold all of your bank statements, or deal with your tax return, or remind you when it's time to send your mother a birthday card. This system isn't about simply making lists of things to do; it's about establishing a system of habits, patterns, and delegation (whether to a person or a computer) that allows you to perform this off-loading of tasks, to make your actual writing time as productive as possible.

Eventually this off-loading will become a habit, the default method you use to organise your life, and that elusive focus on your writing will be easier than ever to achieve. There's no greater feeling than sitting down at your keyboard and knowing – without any nagging doubts – that you can work for several solid hours, free from worry that you might have forgotten something important you need to do.

If it's about more than writing lists, how do we off-load these items from our memory? How do we build a simple system that ensures we don't forget anything, don't lose anything, are reminded of time-sensitive tasks at the right time, and write more productively?

We do it with the help of a handy acronym, FASTEN:

Filing
Assistance
Say 'no'
Time
Equipment
Notes

- **Filing.** Filing everything, both short- and long-term records, in a simple and comprehensive way means you're never worried about where to put something, or where to look when you need to retrieve it.

- **Assistance.** Employing people to whom you delegate tasks for which you have neither the time, expertise, or inclination – accountants, contract agents, lawyers – frees you to work without worrying that your legal and business affairs aren't being taken care of.

- **Say 'no'.** Being mindful of which projects you take on, and which you turn down, allows you to work without being distracted by mounting apprehension about all the jobs you don't really want to do but to which you've mistakenly committed yourself.

- **Time.** Managing your time properly, and using your calendar as a flexible planning tool, means you're not worried about missing deadlines or appointments.

- **Equipment.** Investing in good-quality equipment – be it hardware like a great chair or computer, or software for writing or record-keeping – puts your mind at ease and prevents you becoming frustrated with your tools.

- **Notes.** Taking immediate and comprehensive notes of story ideas, revision thoughts, people to email, places to research and anything else that comes to mind frees you from the distraction of trying to rehearse thoughts and ideas in your memory.

Rest easy; simple though it may be, this acronym isn't a mnemonic you have to remember, or a mantra for you to chant each morning. After all, the point is to clean your mind, not clutter it with jargon. Nevertheless, the FASTEN principles permeate what you're about to read. Referring to them will help you assess your performance as you put *The Organised Writer* principles into practice, and refresh your knowledge of the system after you've been using it for a while.

You might still be asking: *how does this help?* Even if you can achieve all of the above, and your mind becomes a perfectly clean slate free of memory distraction, how will that help you write more productively?

It helps by allowing you to place your focus entirely on your writing – but now without any concern that you'll forget the other tasks you need to carry out. Phone calls *do* get made, groceries *do* get bought, accounts *do* get filed. You pick up the kids from school, *and* you remember to buy milk. Knowing that you don't need to rehearse these tasks while you work allows your mind to call freely on the resources of your imagination, instead of fighting for space in your short-term memory.

That focus – the ability to imagine creatively, free from distraction – will in turn allow you to write better and more freely, be more productive when writing, and increase your output while actually spending less time writing.

These are bullish claims. In fact, it's the dream of every writer who ever lived; 'Oh, I could get so much done if only I could spend a few hours doing nothing but writing, with no distractions or interruptions!' There isn't a writer in history who hasn't had that dream. My aim is to help you realise it by practical, achievable means.

When you're able to write in that way – better and faster, because you've eliminated distraction – it also helps you carry out your other tasks. You can deal with non-writing matters at a sensible pace, instead of running around in a blind panic and doing them all at the last minute. Best of all, this is a virtuous cycle; handling those non-writing tasks further reduces opportunities for memory distraction, which helps you write more effectively… and around and around it goes.

CHAPTER 2

Clocking in (and out)

(×) A *disorganised writer* never knows from one moment to the next what they should be doing; they miss deadlines, lose notes, and forget appointments, because they try to remember everything they must do.

(✓) *The organised writer* knows exactly what to do at any given moment; they hit deadlines, never lose notes, and keep appointments, because they don't rely on their memory to keep track of tasks.

If the purpose of any system is to increase and maintain efficiency, then one made specifically for writers has two primary goals:

1. meet your deadlines;
2. don't forget anything.

I'll deal with the second aim in Chapter 3, *Taking notes and making lists*, as it encompasses both writing matters and administrative tasks. For now, let's focus on the first; how to ensure you meet deadlines, with the side benefit of allowing you to better enjoy the extra time you'll gain as a result.

Douglas Adams, author of *The Hitchhiker's Guide to the Galaxy*, was notorious for turning in his work months – sometimes years! – later than originally agreed, and famously once said, 'I love deadlines; I love the whooshing sound they make as they go by'.

But that was Douglas Adams, whose hem we mortals are not fit to touch.

You and I, by contrast, want – and need – to meet our deadlines. How do you do that? By ensuring you write enough at the times when you should be working. How do you do *that*? By managing your time effectively. Relax; I'm not about to turn you into an inveterate clock-watcher. In fact, my purpose is the opposite. I want to help you reach a place where you can not only reduce the amount of time you spend watching the clock, but for the majority of your working day simply render it unnecessary.

Time management was one of the major problems I ran into when I first started trying to apply traditional productivity structures to my own work. Many popular modern systems are based around the twin concepts of *contexts* and *sprints*, which are useful in traditional office environments, but not for our purposes. To confuse matters, you may also know these terms from project management, but their meanings in productivity jargon are quite different.

Working with *contexts* means building your to-do list around different situations, and only concerning yourself with tasks that apply when you're in those situations. For example, a *computer* context might contain tasks like 'Answer emails' or 'Check calendar'; a *phone* context might find you writing out items like 'Call client X' or 'Arrange meeting with Y'. When you find yourself sitting at your desk in front of the computer, you can therefore begin working through the *computer*-context tasks on your to-do list. On the other hand, if the only thing you have easy access to is your phone, you can check off items on your *phone* list.

I know your eyes are already starting to glaze over, because this is the sort of corporate stuff I had to wade through in order to create my own system, and my eyes were practically crystallised by the time I finished.

You're also likely having the same realisation I did; that this sort of task-arrangement is nonsense for writers, especially fiction writers. We're almost always at our desks, which means the computer is right there, as are our phone and calendar, and pretty much everything else we need to work. We're not generally running to and from meetings, living off our phones, and only grabbing 30 minutes a day in front of a screen (although, if you are, Chapter 4 will discuss best practices for working while travelling). Contextual task lists simply make no sense for a writer.

Then there's the *sprint*, sometimes called the *interval* or, after the technique that popularised the term, a *pomodoro*. They all share the same basic concept; you work on a task for a short amount of time, generally less than 30 minutes, then interrupt yourself to take a break, before returning to either continue that task or begin a new task.

Read that part again: you *deliberately interrupt yourself every half-hour.*

The thinking behind this is that people have terribly short attention spans, so forcing ourselves to focus on a single task for more than thirty minutes will only lead to disaster as we inevitably lose interest; and besides, nowadays we work in 'interrupt-driven' environments where, even if we want to work on something for more than 30 minutes, we can't because someone will interrupt us with a new task, or our phone will ring, or we'll have to run to a meeting, and so on.

This may all be true for people who work in an office, particularly managers. And I do know some writers who use *sprints* to focus on a short block of writing, as it allows them to set an arbitrary period in which they give themselves permission to ignore interruptions. But *The Organised Writer* system is expressly designed to remove those distractions in any case.

Writers spend most of our working day desperately trying *not* to be interrupted; to find a continuous stretch of time, one as long as possible, in which to work without distraction. It's been shown that artists and creators need a short amount of time to 'get in the zone'; to reach a point where the outside world fades away and we can be truly creative, finding ourselves in what renowned psychologist Dr Mihaly Csikszentmihalyi first coined a state of *flow*. The exact period of time required differs from person to person and day to day, but the average seems to be around 15 minutes.

If you want to read further on the concept of flow, *Frontiers in Psychology* published a piece on 8 August 2017, 'Creative Flow as a Unique Cognitive Process', which is both itself informative and also contains many links to sources, including papers by Csikszentmihalyi himself. Find it at www.frontiersin.org.

Being in a state of flow is wonderful, but fragile; any interruption removes us from it. To resume work we must regain flow all over again, and while it may not take another 15 minutes, it certainly doesn't happen instantly. Not only that, but while we're writing we're thinking several lines ahead, using our short-term memory to hold phrases and structures that we intend to solidify over the next few sentences. Interrupt us, and *poof!* All those potential turns of phrase, lines of dialogue, and waiting concepts vanish in an instant, with a very real chance they'll never reappear.

If deliberately interrupting ourselves is a non-starter, and working according to situational context is functionally useless, how *can* writers get organised in a way that makes sense for the work we do, and the way we do it?

This is where we open the door to time management.

Writers are often very sceptical of managing their time. Yet here it is, right at the start of the book. What a hurdle to clear!

I understand the adverse reaction, I really do. *Time management* sounds a lot like *time tracking*, used by office workers to keep minute-by-minute records of how much time they spend on different tasks, often so clients can be billed accordingly. In my experience there is little writers hate more, because what we do is by its very nature not centred around person-hours. Take a dozen writers, set them to work for three hours each, and by the end of it every single one will have written a wildly different amount to the others. You don't even need more than one; take a single writer, put her to work for exactly three hours every day, and the chances are she'll write wildly differing amounts each time. Plus, this doesn't even begin to address the thorny issue of *thinking time*; those periods we spend staring into space as we turn things over in our head, wrestling with a plot or searching for the right words. Just because we're not typing, doesn't mean we're not working.

So don't worry. I hate time tracking as much as you do – perhaps more! – and I'm not going to ask you to do it. But even if you acknowledge that *time management* is not the same as *time tracking*, you may still think it's unnecessary. As long as you get a good few hours' writing in every day, what's the problem? Why get all stuffy about it?

In fact, *The Organised Writer* is entirely about that principle; helping you to make good use of your daily writing time. You're right that 'getting in a few good hours of writing every day' is all you really need to do. But be honest and ask yourself: how often do you achieve that? How often do you accomplish your writing goals for the day, *and* then deal with all the other tasks you need to take care of, without being distracted, without forgetting things you need to do, without becoming frustrated at how slowly things are going?

The truth is that all of us on some level *already* manage our time, or at least try to. We have deadlines, chores, family, friends, and responsibilities that must be taken care of, and somehow those commitments must be juggled. If you don't have a system, then you're probably doing it all on instinct; and, again, because you're reading this I'm willing to bet that's not working as well as you'd like.

This is the simple, boring truth: the best way to be a more productive writer is to become a creature of routine and habits – to be 'regular and orderly', as Flaubert put it. An author who writes at the same time, in the same place, every day is more reliably productive than one who is constantly in upheaval or on the move. I believe every writer already knows this, deep down; but not all of us are able to put it into action, or know where to start in our attempt.

A day in the life

My ideal working day goes something like this:

- 07.30: Wake up, brush my teeth, have a quick breakfast, and take my dogs out.
- 08.00: Head to the gym, work out for an hour, return home for a snack and shower.
- 09.30: Make myself a coffee, sit at my desk, and begin writing.
- 10.30: Take a short break to feed my dogs and make myself another coffee.
- 10.45: Return to writing.
- 12.30: Take my dogs for a lunchtime walk.
- 13.00: Return to my desk. By now I may be done with 'real' writing for the day. If so, I attend to my email and office admin; filing documents, entering items into my accounts, and so on.
- 14.00: If anyone is waiting on me for proofreading, now's when I deal with it. If not, I work on any outlining/note-making related to other projects – this includes reading for research.

    If I've scheduled any phone calls for the day, this period of the afternoon is also when I prefer to make them.
- 16.00: If nothing else urgent needs attending to, I spend some time reading for leisure.
- 17.30: By now the old brain cells are starting to flag, so I might spend some time on social media, and doing online promotion.
- 18.30: Finally I give in to my dogs' collective demands for their evening food, and call it a day.

This is an *ideal* day; in reality, every day is different because every job, and every medium, is different. If I'm working on a videogame, for example, the creative writing part of my day will often continue well into the afternoon because of the sheer workload, and that naturally affects how many other tasks I can perform later in the day. Even working on a novel, there are days when I'm still banging away at the draft come four o'clock. Or if proofreading is urgently needed, that might take up most of my day instead. Plus, I might need to have a phone conference mid-morning, or take a late night call with someone in a different time zone... etc, etc. So being flexible is important, but nevertheless I hit the kind of day described above more often than you might imagine.

You'll have noticed how much of my schedule is structured around my dogs' routine, which of course won't map exactly to your own situation. But the need for *some* kind of structure and routine is universal. Where possible, you should build yours around existing home and family commitments.

Use your calendar

Some of my methods might send traditional productivity gurus into fits of apoplexy, but make perfect sense for a writer. We'll begin with one such piece of advice.

> *Plan ahead, and block out which project you'll work on each day for the next four weeks. Where possible, restrict yourself to working on just one project per day.*

The traditional productivity approach is to never use your calendar for planning general work, saying it should be reserved for 'hard appointments', while work tasks are carried out according to *context* as described previously. But the situational context approach is nonsense for a writer. We live and die by our deadlines; the most important decision when we sit down to work every day is not whether we should write, but what project we should be working on to meet those deadlines.

(A 'hard appointment' is anything you can't reschedule, or afford to miss, without notifying or co-ordinating with someone else: a meeting with your agent, a train booking, a doctor's appointment. That doesn't mean you can't change it, but that doing so requires coordinating with others. Its opposite is a 'soft appointment'; an informal arrangement or reminder that, if necessary, you can let slide and reschedule without consequences.)

This is why *The Organised Writer* system advocates making, setting, and keeping to your own self-imposed schedule wherever possible – because that decision is so important, it's better to make it weeks ahead of time when you're objective about the project, and can make a dispassionate estimate of how long you'll need to complete whatever work needs doing. Otherwise there's a risk you may overlook necessary work, and one day suddenly realise you have two competing projects that should both be finished by tomorrow – but you only have time to complete one of them. Hands up everyone who's ever done this?

(Almost everyone, including your humble author, raises their hand.)

Setting your own deadlines is a way to prevent this happening. Blocking out work in advance allows you to assess how long you think you'll need for a particular piece of work, find space for that amount of time in your calendar, and reserve it. Things don't always go to plan, of course, and I'll address shifting days around and being flexible in a moment. But as with writing itself, it's easier to revise than to create from scratch; having a schedule planned to begin with makes being flexible, and allowing for unforeseen problems, that much simpler.

Exactly what calendar you use is a matter of taste. I use my Mac's built-in Calendar app, while I know people who use an online calendar like Google's, or the Outlook software built into Windows. Most calendars these days perform all the same basic functions; however, the one thing you should ensure it does reliably is *synchronise* across all your computers and devices, such as your smartphone, so you can make and rearrange hard appointments on the fly, while you're away from your desk.

Syncing in this way is critical, especially nowadays, to being able to plan your time. You should be able to look up your schedule wherever you are, on whatever device you have with you, in order to use it efficiently.

That being the case, you may wonder if you could use a paper calendar, like a planner diary or Filofax-style system. After all, you can carry one of those with you everywhere, and it doesn't even require synchronisation. Which is true, and if you think it'll work for you, I won't advise against it – but the big downside to a paper calendar is that you can't search it. One of modern computing's greatest usability breakthroughs is the principle of 'search everywhere'; Google's Gmail service is entirely founded on the principle, and most computer systems are now designed around the assumption that it's easier to search for something than to locate it in your personal file taxonomy (or, as many creative people call it, 'the desktop'. That's a rant for another time). Whether or not you agree with that philosophy, being able to search your calendar for both future and past appointments is invaluable. You may not need to do it often, but when you do, paper is no substitute. Therefore, I suggest you go digital.

Full-time novelists, by the way, are probably smiling bemusedly right now and wondering how having the same project blocked out for weeks, even months, on end will make them any more organised. If you're the fortunate (not to mention rare) novelist who writes only one book at a time, with no other work requirements, it's true that this part of the system may not fully apply to you. But the rest of the book will, and while you're skipping ahead spare a thought for the 99.9 per cent of novelists who are proofreading one book while drafting another, and outlining a third to boot. If that sounds more like you, getting organised in this way will help a great deal.

Let's get visual. I'll use two imaginary projects as samples to demonstrate. Let's say it's 3 January 2022, and after the holiday break I've returned to my desk, with two things on my plate for the new year. One is a novel featuring my spy character Brigitte Sharp, with the working title *The Encrypted Bookshelf* and a deadline of 1 May for the first draft due to my publisher

Awesome Novels. I've also been hired to write for a videogame, *Project Gamepad*, which will require some work at my desk but also occasional visits to the London-based developer, Awesome Gamez (no relation). One such visit has already been scheduled, a three-day trip to meet the team and hammer out the scope of work I'll be doing.

The majority of January is taken up with the novel, with a short block of time devoted to the game-studio visit. These calendar events are 'all-day' rather than time-based, because as I mentioned above, in an ideal world I'm only working on one project per day (the world isn't always ideal, of course, and I'll address working on multiple projects per day later).

The illustration below is an abstraction, of course, printed in black-and-white. In reality each group in my calendar's sidebar

	JANUARY 2022			MONTHLY VIEW		
CALENDARS:	☐ Writing	☐ Agenda & Admin		☐ Personal & Leisure		

Mon	Tue	Wed	Thu	Fri	Sat	Sun
27	28	29	30	31	**JAN 1**	2
3	4	5	6	7	8	9
The Encrypted Bookshelf						
10	11	12	13	14	15	16
The Encrypted Bookshelf						
17	18	19	20	21	22	23
Project Gamepad on-site			**Encrypted Bookshelf**			
24	25	26	27	28	29	30
The Encrypted Bookshelf						
31	FEB 1	2	3	4	5	6

Figure 2.1 Example blocked-out weeks.

has a different colour, but the principle is the same. The time blocks here are dark grey, because they've been created within the *Writing* calendar. There are three main calendar groups:

1. Writing
2. Agenda & Admin
3. Personal & Leisure

I have another two groups: *Design*, because I also design some of my own books, and *Dogs*, for vet appointments and recurring medical treatments. You probably won't need those specific calendars, but you may have other additional needs for family business, club meetings and so on. We'll just concern ourselves with the main three; let's define them.

WRITING

Mainly used as described above, to block out which project you're going to work on at any given time. It's also the place for time-based appointments, such as phone calls you need to make, interview appointments with the press, and even emails you absolutely must send at a certain time that relate *directly* to a writing project.

AGENDA & ADMIN

Used for all other tasks, appointments, and administration that relate to work, but not a specific project. If you need to call your agent for a general discussion, or take an hour to file your expense receipts, or even just remind yourself to tidy up your office files, it should be entered in this calendar.

(Certain admin items may be better served in your task manager. We'll get to that shortly.)

PERSONAL & LEISURE

This is for everything non-work related: a family dinner, a trip to the beach, going to the cinema, etc. It all goes in here, and I'll deal with the perhaps unconventional notion of putting personal items on your calendar in a moment.

Once you become used to using your calendar in this way, maintaining it takes very little time and effort. The only time I have my calendar open for more than a minute is when I'm arranging travel and, for example, need to have convention dates to hand while booking flights. On a day-to-day basis I rarely open my calendar more than two or three times a day, and each of those instances is usually for less than a minute – enough time to check an existing appointment, or create a new one, before closing the app again.

You may be wondering how to deal with *alarms* and *notifications* from your calendar.

Work blocks should be set with no alarm, because they're for reference only; either when planning your week, or if you're unsure what you should be writing when you sit at your desk in the morning.

Alarms for hard appointments vary according to the appointment type. I like to give myself enough notice to finish anything I might be doing, gather my wits, and prepare for the appointment. If that involves travel, I'll take it into account.

For example: if I have a phone call scheduled with my agent, I'll normally set the alarm to warn me fifteen minutes beforehand. That's enough time for me to pause whatever I'm doing when the alarm sounds, take a comfort break if necessary, and be ready to hop on the phone. For calls with a client, however, I'll give myself thirty minutes' notice – enough time to refresh my memory and make agenda notes where necessary, especially if the call will involve in-depth discussion of a project. On the other hand, a dentist's appointment requires taking travel time into account, so for those I give myself an hour's notice.

My default notification style is a pop-up window on my computer, accompanied by a sound in case I'm not facing the screen. The notification is also set to remain on-screen until snoozed or dismissed, so that even if I'm out of the room making coffee when it goes off, it'll be waiting for me upon my return. That's another reason I use calendars that sync across my devices – even if I don't return to my computer, my phone will buzz me anyway.

You'll notice in the above illustration that I didn't block out anything more than a week after that scheduled visit to the game studio. That's partly because I don't yet know what work might arise out of that meeting. The most likely outcome is that nothing will be required of me immediately upon my return home, or if they do require work it can wait a couple of weeks. However, it's equally possible the developers will ask me to produce material for the game straight after the meeting. If that happens, I'll make room by shifting the following novel block, currently assigned 24–28 Jan, to the week after, 31 Jan–4 Feb.

I try to never commit more than a month ahead, in order to remain flexible. Like everyone, I have some idea of what I'll ideally be doing in a few months' time, and in cases where it's already fixed – the proofreading period for a book, an on-site marketing meeting, a period working in-studio – I'll of course mark it in my calendar. But otherwise, I like to keep my options open in case things change.

Again, if you're the kind of writer who works strictly on only one project at a time, you may not have these concerns (though you should still create the three calendar groups, to divide and identify task and appointment types). If you're working on several projects at once, though, flexibility is important. At the end of each week, I look ahead on my calendar and block out the first 'blank week', normally three to four weeks ahead of the current time, with whatever project I think will be best to work on at that point.

Things inevitably change over the course of time. Let's say that by 14 Jan I've worked on *The Encrypted Bookshelf* for a couple of weeks, and heard nothing further from the *Project Gamepad* developers in the meantime. I'll take a risk and block out the two weeks following the studio trip to continue writing the novel (see Figure 2.2 overleaf).

Then 17 Jan arrives, the day of the studio visit, and I travel to London. Over the next couple of days with the developer, I realise things are moving faster than anticipated. After several meetings

The Organised Writer

	JANUARY 2022			MONTHLY VIEW		
CALENDARS:	☐ Writing	☐ Agenda & Admin		☐ Personal & Leisure		

Mon	Tue	Wed	Thu	Fri	Sat	Sun
3 *The Encrypted Bookshelf*	4	5	6	7	8	9
10 *The Encrypted Bookshelf*	11	12	13	14	15	16
17 *Project Gamepad on-site*	18	19	20 *Encrypted Bookshelf*	21	22	23
24 *The Encrypted Bookshelf*	25	26	27	28	29	30
31 *The Encrypted Bookshelf*	FEB 1	2	3	4	5	6
7	8	9	10	11	12	13

Figure 2.2 Adjusted schedule.

about aims and scope, I now have a work assignment from them that will take me four days to write, and they want it sharpish.

This is exactly the scenario I knew was possible, and demonstrates why it pays to remain flexible. So I go into my calendar, select the *Encrypted Bookshelf* block that had been assigned to 24 Jan–4 Feb, and move it all onward to the following week. In its place I create a new four-day block for *Gamepad* starting 24 Jan, followed by an 'admin day' for Friday 28 – I know my own habits well enough that trying to resume work on a Friday, especially on a manuscript with which I now won't have spent any serious time for almost two weeks, is folly. Instead I put that day aside for admin: invoicing, filing receipts, going through my in/out trays to make sure everything there is dealt with, handling any phone calls I need to make, maybe even have a general clean and tidy of my study.

			JANUARY 2022		MONTHLY VIEW		
CALENDARS:		Writing	☐ Agenda & Admin		■ Personal & Leisure		

Mon	Tue	Wed	Thu	Fri	Sat	Sun
10	11	12	13	14	15	16
The Encrypted Bookshelf						
17	18	19	20	21	22	23
Project Gamepad on-site			Encrypted Bookshelf			
24	25	26	27	28	29	30
Project Gamepad				Admin day		
31	FEB 1	2	3	4	5	6
The Encrypted Bookshelf						
7	8	9	10	11	12	13
The Encrypted Bookshelf						
14	15	16	17	18	19	20

Figure 2.3 Adjusted schedule featuring admin day.

Note that I *moved* the novel writing block to begin the following week, rather than just deleting it from the week I'll now be working on the game. It's a small difference, but a kind of psychological trick that reinforces my commitment to the work – which was made when I committed it to the calendar. One way or another, one week or another, that novel work needs to be done.

DEALING WITH PROBLEMS

This is a good time to answer the inevitable question, 'What if things go wrong?' Because plenty of things *can* go wrong, as any writer knows only too well. What if you've planned out your working week, and suddenly someone falls ill; or you realise you forgot about a dentist's appointment; or a particular job is simply taking you much longer to complete than you expected?

First look at the time ahead, and assess if you're able to move other work blocks around to make things fit as in the above example. That's always the easiest solution, so if you can do it without causing a big upheaval, go right ahead and be thankful for staying flexible. The next best option is to shuffle things around with only minor upheaval, such as working over a weekend, or shortening the work block for another project by an amount of time that might make delivery tight, but not impossible. This solution isn't ideal, but for a one-off occurrence, it's manageable.

A more extreme way to deal with tightening of deadlines is to work on two projects per day for a while. It's not for the faint of heart, but if it's the only solution to the problem, see the following section on scheduling half-days.

Finally, the least favoured option – though sometimes the only solution – is to re-negotiate your deadline/s. Nobody wants to do this, on either side of the equation, but there are times when it's the only workable route. If that's the case, get in touch with your editor/publisher/client *as soon as possible* and work something out. Don't delay or put it off, because the client or publisher can't help you if they don't even know there's a problem, and these things are always easier to work out the farther away from a deadline you are. Conversely, if you have mere days till deadline and your editor still thinks everything is peachy, calling them at the last minute to explain something happened two weeks ago and you suddenly need an extension probably won't go over well. When it comes to deadlines, honesty is always the best policy.

(Also, spending days or weeks fretting because you know you're going to miss a deadline, but you haven't yet squared it with your editor, will contribute directly to memory distraction. The only way to off-load that 'item' from your memory is to re-negotiate the deadline as soon as possible.)

Whichever solution you're able to implement to solve the problem in the short term, you should then assess whether this situation was a one-off, or likely to recur. If it's going to persist, you must make changes to allow for those future instances; increase the amount of time you block out for certain types of job, for example, or perhaps work on increasing your daily quota (see below).

> **TAKE TIME TO SOLVE PROBLEMS**
>
> Sometimes the changes necessary to deal with a persistent problem can't be made quickly, and will require taking time away from work to focus on their resolution. Block out that time as you would any other work commitment, allowing you to focus on it. A little short-term disruption now, to find an ongoing solution to a chronic issue, will pay dividends. By contrast, having to resolve a problem anew over and over again will drain your energy and sap your morale.

In some cases with recurring issues, the solution may be to completely ring-fence a particular day of the week for personal reasons. Don't apologise for this – the health and wellbeing of you and your family must take priority, even over your Great Novel. Besides, even four days a week is enough to get plenty of work done if you follow the advice in this book.

HOW LONG IS A PIECE OF STRING?

Most of the above is common sense. The ability to stay flexible is one of the main advantages of being a freelance writer, and you should draw on it fully when you're able to – but where possible, block out your schedule and stick to it as tightly as you can. In the example we're using, if nothing else interrupts me then I'll be writing that *Encrypted Bookshelf* manuscript for three, maybe four weeks solid as we move from January into February; enough time to get a serious chunk of work done.

That brings us to figuring out how long a job will take you, and like the proverbial length of string, the answer is 'it depends'. Only you can really know your own pace and working speed, and being able to estimate accurately is something that often comes only with time and experience. One thing I can tell you is that once you've made a mental estimate of how long something will take you to write, when you block out the time on your calendar you should add a certain amount of 'problem time' to allow for any unforeseen issues that may arise.

For example, let's say I've been asked to contribute an article to a magazine, and the deadline is the end of February. It will mean taking time off from *The Encrypted Bookshelf*, but the magazine is widely read and they only want 1,500 words, so I figure it's worth it. As it happens, 1,500 words is my daily quota, so in theory I could get the whole thing done in a single day. But I also have to allow for revision, not to mention the possibility that I might get halfway through and realise

FEBRUARY 2022 — **MONTHLY VIEW**

CALENDARS: ■ Writing ☐ Agenda & Admin ■ Personal & Leisure

Mon	Tue	Wed	Thu	Fri	Sat	Sun
31	FEB 1	2	3	4	5	6
The Encrypted Bookshelf						
7	8	9	10	11	12	13
The Encrypted Bookshelf						
14	15	16	17	18	19	20
The Encrypted Bookshelf						
21	22	23	24	25	26	27
Magazine article		The Encrypted Bookshelf				
28	MAR 1	2	3	4	5	6
The Encrypted Bookshelf						
14:00 Article deadline!						
7	8	9	10	11	12	13

Figure 2.4 Schedule adjusted for article.

I need to start over. So I block out two days for the article, and schedule them a week *before* the deadline, giving me some breathing room in my schedule to shuffle things around if major problems arise. I also create a time-based appointment for 2pm on 28 Feb, the deadline day, to remind me to turn the article in to the magazine editor.

By planning for two days, a 'worst case' scenario, I'm staying flexible; if I do in fact complete the article in a single day, I can simply strike off that second day and resume work on the novel sooner than anticipated. Better to find myself with an unexpected extra day than to only assign one day to the article, then panic when I realise halfway through that it really needs two.

Another reason to write small jobs like a column or article ahead of deadline is to compensate for the *hindsight effect* – that moment three days after finishing a piece when you inevitably think of a better way to connect the last third to the opening, or a real zinger of a closing line, or a better metaphor for the middle section. In those cases I'll make a quick note of the revision idea, then make a time-based appointment on my calendar for time in my 'non-writing' schedule – probably late one afternoon, or maybe a weekend morning if I can spare it – to make those revisions and punch up the piece.

For longer projects, like novels or scripts, a good rule of thumb is to estimate how long you think it will take you to write, then add another 25 per cent for contingency time to deal with unforeseen problems. That may seem like a lot, but would you rather have a schedule long enough that you might finish the project a week ahead of time… or one so short that when you hit a snag in the middle it renders your deadline impossible?

Again, part of scheduling well is about knowing your own pace, and sticking to it. Veteran writers should already have a pretty good idea of what they can achieve per day without over-taxing themselves. Less experienced writers might still be figuring out their pace. It will come, with time and experience, and you can always tweak your daily writing quota to suit.

Wait, 'daily writing quota'? Ah, yes. Now we're getting to it. This is how a structured routine helps you meet deadlines.

My personal daily writing quota is an amount I know I can force myself to write, even if I have to grind it out because I'm not really feeling it that day. On the other hand, it's not such a large amount that writing it will exhaust me. That's important, because it leaves open the possibility to be over-productive on good days; the days when I meet my quota with ease, and still have enough energy to keep going and write more. On days like that, sometimes I'll write the same amount all over again, and those are very good days indeed.

You'll notice I haven't specified what those amounts are, and that's because it will differ from one writer to another. We all write at different speeds, to different levels of polish. What matters is knowing your *own* figure, nobody else's.

I'll talk more about how to meet that daily writing quota in Chapter 4, *Five pages after breakfast* (um, spoiler alert?), and elaborate further on why it's so central to *The Organised Writer* system. Let's address a common complaint I hear from disorganised writers; that they're too slow to work like this, and they 'need' to push themselves to exhaustion every day or they'll never meet their deadlines. I say, hogwash. I've known and worked with such people, and if you think you're one of them, listen up; I'm going to blow your mind.

It doesn't matter how slow you are. If you write regularly and to a quota, you will meet your deadlines.

I know you don't believe that, but here's why you're slow: some days everything else you have to deal with gets out of control, and there are all those fires to put out, and before you know it you've only got half an hour left to get any actual writing done, and you know it takes at least fifteen minutes just to get into the zone and start writing anything of use... and now you've psyched yourself out of getting anything productive done today, so you put it off till tomorrow. Which more than likely repeats the previous day, and before you know it the deadline is looming closer than ever and you've barely written a word all week.

Or: you try to write, but get distracted while staring at the blank page and check social media for a while, then go back to the blank page, but the words still aren't coming so you do some research online, then check social media again, then go back to the blank page... and suddenly the day is over and you haven't written a thing. Rinse and repeat.

There are a thousand permutations of this problem, but they all boil down to the same thing; you think of yourself as a slow writer, because you struggle to maintain any level of consistent productivity. The only way you seem to get anything done is right at the last minute when you're in a deadline panic. It's a classic tortoise vs hare situation, and at the moment you're the hare. It's exciting, exhilarating, and maybe even feels a little bit dangerous. By contrast, being the tortoise is dull, boring, and safe.

All true. Now remind me, who wins that race?

This is where the daily writing quota will help – even if you're a slow writer. Let's imagine you're writing a novel, and you set yourself a quota of 500 words a day. 500 words! That's less than the last few paragraphs in this section. It's barely a double-spaced side of typing paper. It's a sidebar column in a tabloid newspaper, a letter to the editor, a couple of half-considered emails. 500 words is *nothing*. Who can't manage 500 words in a whole day? It's hardly even worth bothering. You'll never finish a novel at that pace!

Actually, you will.

I'm as allergic to mathematics as the next author, but let's run the numbers. If you start on 1 January and write 500 words every weekday – that's five days a week, Monday through Friday – by 31 December you'll have written a 130,000 word draft. You'll also have taken every weekend off.

That's pretty incredible. In fact, the most unrealistic part is the suggestion that you'd *only* write that much each day. It's far more likely that on most days, when you hit the 500-word target, you're going to keep on going and write another 500. Maybe even more.

Let's be conservative, and suppose that on half those days you write 1,000 words instead. Even if that's the most you ever write in a single day, and it only happens every other day, the time reduction is still huge. Now that same 130,000 word draft, which previously took a year to write, will be finished in mid-September. And if you only need to produce 100,000 words, you'll be done by the end of July.

Remember: this is with a self-imposed daily writing quota of just 500 words, *and* you get to take every single weekend off – which is the other unrealistic part of this whole thought experiment, because let's face it, you're a writer. The chances of you going three months, let alone a whole year, without ever working at the weekend are somewhere between zilch and zip. The point is you *can* take weekends off if you want to – and merely knowing that will help reduce your working stress.

I'll talk more (a lot more) about the daily writing quota in Part II. For now, let's summarise everything we've discussed in a more logical order.

1. Figure out your daily writing quota.
2. Work out the number of days you'll need to finish the project at that pace.
3. Add 25 per cent problem time to account for unforeseen issues.
4. Block out that many days in your calendar.
5. Stick to your daily writing quota.
6. That's one big weight off your mind.

Multiple projects in one day

The Organised Writer assumes you only work on one project per day, for a couple of good reasons.

First, it allows you to approach each day with our proverbial clean mind. I'm an advocate of beginning work with as little as possible intruding upon your thoughts, and the simplest way to achieve this is by only working on one project per day. That way, every time you sit down and begin to write, your mind is 'clean' because it reset itself overnight and is ready to begin a new day. Second, if you plan your schedule well and meet your daily writing quota you simply shouldn't have to work on more than one project per day to make a living.

But no system is perfect, and neither is anyone's life. Clients happen, as do unforeseen problems, and sometimes working on only one project per day simply isn't an option. If that's what it will take to meet your deadlines, go ahead and block out two jobs for the same day/s on your calendar.

> **ONE PROJECT PER DAY**
>
> If you're reading this for the first time, the idea you shouldn't work on more than one project per day may sound outrageous. Stay with me, and when you revisit these pages you'll find yourself nodding along instead.

The important question is this: in what order will you work on them?

Remember, I'm talking here about making progress on *two separate writing tasks* in a single day. This isn't about admin, phone calls, proofreading or story outlining. It's expected that you'll do such tasks in addition to and after your writing work. Generating ostensibly usable/final text for two different projects in a single day is a different beast altogether, and requires discipline.

When I have to adopt this kind of dual schedule, the first thing I figure out is which of the two jobs will require the most focus, the most imagination, the most raw energy to tackle. That's the project I work on first – when my mind is cleanest, my energy levels are highest, and the chances of me being distracted are at their lowest.

Some productivity systems tell you to prioritise the task to which you're *least looking forward*. The theory goes that once you've done that task, you'll feel such overwhelming relief that you'll positively look forward to any remaining, more desirable tasks.

I don't believe that works for writers. It's true that we sometimes need a bit of a downhill push to get going, and there's no shortcut for that; it takes willpower and commitment, and nothing can force those things upon you. Once your fingers begin moving, though, you're likely to enter a state of flow and keep going in a creative burst. Like a marathon runner, each time you stop you'll find it increasingly difficult to start moving again; thus, your concentration span shortens as the day goes on. That doesn't have much effect if you follow the normal daily schedule I've already described – by the time your concentration is flagging you've moved on to the afternoon's admin tasks, which don't require a fully active creative mind. But on days where you need to tackle two jobs in succession, if you leave the job requiring the most creative concentration till last, you risk approaching it with less creative energy than is necessary to do the job... and thus blowing your deadlines all over again.

Working two jobs in a single day also requires working *fast*. On these days I begin as normal, working at the first task in the morning, with an expectation that I'll hit whatever quota or deadline is necessary by lunchtime.

At lunch, I take a break. Not just for a couple of minutes, but a good solid break to eat, maybe go to the gym or do some household chores... anything unrelated to work that will help clear my mind (note that this does *not* include things like checking my email, going on social media, etc. Stay offline!).

Suitably refreshed, I begin work on the second task – the one I expect will require less energy – with an expectation that I'll finish somewhere around mid-to-late afternoon, leaving a short amount of time to carry out admin tasks for the day. Even on days where you're working flat out on multiple projects, it pays to put aside half an hour at the end of the day to at least go through your emails.

> **FOR SUPERHUMANS ONLY**
>
> I know of one incredibly prolific writer whose regular day consists of working on his current novel in the morning, then writing his current comic script in the afternoon. He is the only person I know capable of doing that every day without fail, and I do not recommend you follow his example; merely admire the concept of him from afar, like a shining and inimitable unicorn.

One big question remains; what if each of these writing tasks is too big to finish in half a day… but you still need to get both of them done today?!

Sadly, that dilemma has no good answer. Somewhere, somehow, you've screwed up your scheduling and must now dig yourself out of the hole you've created by powering through and working beyond whatever your normal schedule dictates.

On the bright side, once you begin putting *The Organised Writer* system into practice, scheduling howlers like this will become a rarity (I can't promise they'll *never* happen, but they won't be the norm). Until then, there's no alternative but to grit your teeth and get through it.

Get smart with email

An email arrives. You read it, and realise it contains some form of request or instruction that means you now have one or more new tasks to carry out.

What do you do?

If you're an *Organised Writer*, you mark it 'unread' and move on to the next email.

Again, this is heresy to traditional productivity systems. They will tell you to never use your inbox as a to-do list. Their advice is typically to read the email; isolate and identify whatever action/s must be taken before you can consider that email dealt with (e.g. 'look up a reference and then reply with that information to the sender'); open your task manager and create this new action within it, adding a deadline date if necessary; and, finally, archive the email so it disappears from view. If you've ever seen the phrase *'Inbox Zero'* used around the internet, what I just described is a broad overview of how it works. Inbox Zero is both a state of achievement – *I have zero unread emails in my inbox!* – and a method of reaching that state, by transferring tasks from within an email into your task manager, so you can mark the email as completed and remove it from your inbox.

You may think that surely this is a good thing. It removes the email's ability to distract you and instead gives you a clear action to perform, logged in a centralised location (i.e. your task manager). What's wrong with that?

Several things, from a writer's perspective.

For a start, you've added several extra steps that must be performed without getting any closer to actually completing the task. Not only are you reading and processing the email itself, but now you also have to open your task manager, consider how to reword the email's contents as one or more tasks within the manager, add any appropriate tags so you know the task's context and can find the email again if necessary, then finally switch back to your email application and archive the message. Oh, and if it's a hard appointment (i.e. something that must be done at a particular time), you also need to open your calendar and enter it there.

Is that too much to ask for a single email? Perhaps not, but traditional systems expect you to do it for every single email you receive. It's all too easy to suddenly find yourself spending longer rewording and recording the tasks found in your inbox than it takes to read the emails in the first place.

Then consider what happens in the future, when you carry out the task. Now you have to open your task manager again, check off the item, switch to your email, search the archives to find the original message – and by now you've probably forgotten the exact date and subject line, so you'll inevitably have to open half a dozen before you find the right one – then send a reply to inform the sender you've completed the task.

Doesn't that seem like a lot of extra work?

Here's a simpler way: you read and process the email, realise the tasks within it can't be done immediately, mark it unread (or flag it) and move on to the next email.

MANAGING EMAILS

Whether you mark emails unread, flag them, star them, or use some other labelling method depends on your own preference and your email application of choice (also called an email 'client', which can lead to all sorts of confusion). If you use Gmail in a web browser, there's an option to show your unread emails above all others, regardless of date; and another one to show only starred emails. In the Mac Mail application, and in Outlook for Windows, you can view all your flagged or unread emails together in a single view. The details don't matter; any modern email application will let you mark or flag emails in some way that allows you to later see them all at a glance. Find out what that view is in your own software, because it will become part of your regular daily routine.

The Organised Writer is nothing if not pragmatic, and the fact is that nowadays we live in our inboxes. When we're not writing, there's a very good chance we're checking email instead. For better or worse, we look at our inboxes far more often than we open task managers or to-do lists. If our email is right there in front of us, why not do something useful with it?

The traditional argument against using your inbox in this way is that it increases the risk your inbox will get out of control. Heck, your inbox may *already* be out of control. Perhaps you're currently staring at hundreds of unread emails, appalled that I'm not providing you with a method to handle them.

But I am. It's just not the method you might expect.

First of all, stop and think. Are you actually receiving hundreds of emails every day, *and all of them are relevant and important to your current work*? If that's truly the case, I would venture to suggest that by definition you're in-demand enough to warrant hiring an assistant to deal with them and apply some serious triage before they ever reach your inbox.

I know one writer whose 'unread count' is genuinely in the thousands! But he's both very successful, and spent years working as a high-profile journalist. Consequently, much of the high-volume email he receives is a combination of fan mail, and PR/marketing from companies in the industry he used to report on – neither of which is vitally urgent. Personally, I'd take a few minutes to set up a massive filter which sends the fan mail into a separate folder, and the PR emails into a black hole…

FILTERS AND LABELS

Let's assume you're not receiving thousands of emails every day – but you *are* receiving dozens, from all sorts of sources. Some are work-related, some are personal, and some are just email lists you've never got round to quitting. The first step of triage is something your computer can do for you, by *filtering* your email.

All modern email clients can do this, though they may use different terms, like 'rules', 'categories', or 'tags'. The principles are the same; a *filter/rule* is an automated process to check every email you receive and automatically do something to it according to the contents, such as place it in a folder separate to the inbox, flag it, or apply a label to it. A *label/category/tag* is something that marks an email out from others; a coloured label, a three-letter acronym to identify its sender, a gold star, and so on. Labels can be applied automatically by filters, or manually by yourself.

I use filters and labels extensively. Emails that I know in advance won't require me to perform an action – conversational mailing lists, retailer offers, confirmation of online payments – are filtered, automatically given a label, and filed away; they never see my inbox. They're still unread, so when I look at email folders besides my inbox I can see there are emails waiting for me, but I know there's no urgent need to read them.

Work emails that come from particular clients are filtered by sender's address, and labelled with an abbreviation of the client's company name, e.g. all my videogame clients have blue labels with three-letter abbreviations, so if I regularly correspond with a producer at, say, Sony, I'll set up a filter to automatically tag their incoming emails with a blue label that reads 'SNY'. If they work at Ubisoft it's a blue 'UBI', while Microsoft is a blue 'MSF'. Film and TV producers get green labels, so this time Sony gets a green 'SNY', Universal is a green 'UNI' and TGIM has a green 'TGIM' (no point trying to condense that down to three letters). Book and graphic novel publishers get a red label; Marvel Comics becomes a red 'MVL', Eye & Lightning gets a red 'EYE', Bloomsbury is a red 'BLM'… you get the idea. (Note that while such work emails are automatically labelled, the filter leaves them in my inbox.)

This level of filtering and labelling may be overkill for some writers, especially novelists who focus on one or two books a year. But if you hop about from job to job like me, or if you're a journalist who receives dozens of marketing and PR emails every day (or vice versa; perhaps you're a marketer who receives dozens of emails from journalists every day…), then filters and labels are a great way to prevent your inbox from overflowing, and to keep track of what goes where.

You've set up all your filters, you're labelling everything that comes in according to client… but naturally, you still have an inbox full of emails. So now it's time to figure out how and when to deal with them. Every email you receive belongs to one of three broad categories:

1. Read and archive
2. Deal with it now
3. Deal with it later
4. Ignore and delete

Read and archive emails contain no tasks for you to perform; all you have to do is read them.

Deal with it now is any email containing requests/reminders for you to do something that can be dealt with quickly, in no more than a couple of minutes.

Deal with it later means an email containing requests/reminders for you to perform one or more actions that will take longer to complete (sometimes much longer, if it's writing-related) or can't even be started until a future date.

Ignore and Delete is a category I trust you can identify easily enough! Don't hesitate to be ruthless.

Learning to recognise and act upon these different types of email is an important part of dealing effectively with your inbox, and is the main reason I advocate for making your 'email time' a solid block of your day that doesn't even begin until you've finished writing.

Let's break the types down further:

- **Read and archive.** *Conversations or notifications with no 'actionable items', e.g. a conversation, a mailing list, an acknowledgement of receipt, a marketing or PR email from a contact.* This is everyone's favourite kind of email. By definition, you don't need to take any action; just quickly reply if you want to, then archive the email and move on.
- **Deal with it now.** *Requests/reminders for you to do something that can be dealt with in a couple of minutes, e.g. a simple query, a document to file, an appointment to confirm.* With these you have to do something, but it's not much, and can be completed quickly. You should therefore carry out the task

in question right away, before you do anything else. Reply if necessary, archive the email, and move on.

- **Deal with it later.** *Requests/reminders for you to do something that will take longer than a couple of minutes, or can't be done until a future date, e.g. a detailed query, a document to complete and return, confirmation of an event.* These emails ask you to do something that will take time, require thoughtful consideration, and may be complex. These are the ones we're mostly concerned with; the emails you should mark as 'Unread', to be dealt with whenever you can actually perform the task required. In the case of tasks that can't be started until a certain date, as well as marking them 'Unread' you should also make a hard appointment in your calendar to begin work on them at an appropriate future time.

Each day when you come to deal with your email, first work from the *top down* to deal with everything new that's come in since yesterday. Reply to the task-less emails if you want; deal with the quick/simple tasks immediately; delete spam; and mark as 'unread' any emails that contain longer tasks.

Once you've done that – and by definition it shouldn't take too long, because all you're doing is reading, assessing, and performing short actions – you're ready for the second part. For that, go down to the end of your unread/flagged list, and work from the *bottom up* applying the same criteria. You won't even need to open half of them; just reading the subject line will often be enough to remind you what particular task is associated with an email.

Consider the email at the very bottom of your Unread list, and decide: *is this task something I can or should work on now? Or can it/must it wait?* If it does indeed merit working on right now... well, then get to it. If it doesn't, leave it there (mark it Unread again if necessary), look at the next unread email above it, and go through the process again.

Not all of these 'long' tasks will be gargantuan. Anything that takes more than a few minutes to do will fall into this category. Let's look at two examples.

EXAMPLE 1: EMAIL INTERVIEW

I recently agreed to an email interview for the *Lovely Author Interviews* website, to talk about *The Encrypted Bookshelf.* Now the interviewer has emailed me her list of questions.

First: I read the email, process what it is, and realise it's the question list. That means there's a long task in here – *write my answers to the questions* – which also necessitates a short task – *copy the questions into a text document.*

(Some people prefer to write interview answers directly into an email reply, but I'm old and craggy enough not to trust network connections. I always draft my answers in a separate document, so there's no risk of them being lost to a server or database error. Also, most email clients have lousy spellcheck.)

The short task can be done immediately, so I copy and paste the questions into a new text document.

The longer task of writing my answers will take a while, and I may not have time to even start on them for a day or two. So I reply to the email saying, 'Got the questions, thanks, will reply soon', mark it Unread, and move on to the next email.

I now have two ways of approaching this task in the future. If the interview is time-sensitive, immediately after marking the email Unread I'll make a hard appointment in my calendar – for a future time when I know I'll be able to devote myself fully to the task – to write those answers. For example, I might set an appointment for 3pm in two days' time, which simply says *Write Lovely Authors interview.* When that alarm goes off, I'll open the text document I just created and begin writing my answers.

If it's not time-sensitive, and I'm okay with answering whenever the mood strikes me, then instead I'll rely on my daily bottom-up email check to remind me that it's waiting to be done, until the point where I see that email in the list and figure now's a good time to begin.

(Note to journalists: this is just an example. I don't really leave interviews to be done whenever the mood strikes. Honest.)

In either case, at some point in the future I'll write out my answers; revise them a dozen times, because I can't help myself; and send them back to the journalist. I then return to my unread list, open the email, write a short note ('Here are my answers, let me know if you need anything else'), attach the text document, and hit Send. Then I archive the conversation. Done, and all without having to trouble my task manager.

A few hours later, the journalist replies to acknowledge receipt. That's a new email, so I come across it during my next round of top-down email processing; but it's a purely conversational email, with no action required, so I can simply archive it.

EXAMPLE 2: CALENDAR APPOINTMENT

My publicist emails me, asking if I'm free to make an appearance at Lovely Book Festival on either 29 or 30 May.

Again, I read the email and process its contents, deciding that this is a 'Deal with it now' situation. It contains one simple task that will take me less than a minute – I just have to check if I'm available on those dates.

I open my calendar and check 29–30 May, which is a weekend. It turns out I have no other commitments on those dates, so I could attend on either day.

I close my calendar, return to the email, and reply, 'Yes, I'd love to, and I can make either/both days'.

There's nothing more I can do at this stage, so I leave the email marked as read. However, I don't archive it because now I'm waiting for a specific reply to confirm a time and date. I therefore want to leave it visible in my inbox, in case I need to chase that reply.

However, my publicist is no slouch, and replies within minutes to ask if 3pm on 29 May works for me. It does indeed, so I open my calendar again and add an appointment at 3pm on that day, with a reminder set to buzz me a few days prior to the fair, then an hour beforehand. I return to the email, reply with, 'Sounds great! I'll book a train soon'.

I've now given myself a new task, which is to book a train to get me to the festival. I can do that immediately – I make train bookings often enough that I could easily complete the task in less than a couple of minutes – and once it's booked, I can then archive the email thread and consider everything completed.

Or, I might have a reason to want to leave the booking until a future time; in which case I'll mark the email Unread, so that I'll see it on my future bottom-up inbox checks and be reminded to book my journey when it's appropriate.

The above examples are incredibly laborious, not to mention laboured, blow-by-blow accounts of how I deal with a task that comes through in email. Most of the time you won't need to consciously think about these steps; they're second nature to anyone who deals with email, which these days is pretty much all of us.

But I've gone into such an absurd level of detail here because I *want* you to read the above and think, 'Well, that's obvious'. It really is, and yet many of us can only see that clearly by observing someone else's situation; when it comes to ourselves, we often have difficulty identifying the so-called obvious course of action, no matter how self-evident it might be. The same can happen when dealing with email, especially as these days we're surrounded by people telling us email is a 'nightmare', some terrible horror that should never have been unleashed upon the world.

Poppycock. Email is the *most* user-friendly of all online communication methods, especially for a freelancer. It's asynchronous (you can read and reply at your leisure, rather than in real-time), it's omnipresent (who doesn't have an email address?), and for someone who earns a living typing, it's convenient.

Email only becomes a problem if you *let* it; if you let it interrupt your regular work, if you let emails fester instead of dealing with them, if you don't put filters and sorting rules to judicious use, if you feel some strange obligation to answer every email you receive from random people.

On that point, here's a crucial thing to remember that creators of all kinds too often forget: *you don't owe strangers a reply*. The Delete key is your friend, and you should never feel bad for using it on emails that arrive unsolicited from people you don't know who want you to read their book/answer a question/fill out their term paper questionnaire/etc. If you're lucky enough to get fan mail, by all means reply to it when you have time – but even that can sit for a while if you have other, more important emails to deal with. Prioritise.

You also shouldn't feel you have to respond to every work email immediately. Take a moment to think: when does this person *need* to see a reply from you? Consider the impact of replying immediately against waiting a while. You're a freelancer, and the most important thing you have to sell besides your talent is your time. The more often you reply to someone immediately, the more they'll come to expect it – and, on the day you *don't* reply immediately, possibly take unintended offence.

Don't let others define your schedule for you, or demand your time when you're not ready to give it.

Finally, on the matter of letting things sit for a while... some of your 'long task' emails will be more complex than simply writing answers to interview questions, and may therefore take weeks to act on fully. Those emails will be in your Unread list for a very long time, so should you handle them differently? No. The principle remains the same, because this is all about trying to keep things as simple as possible.

Again, some people will tell you this is a bad idea because you're increasing your cognitive load every time you see that email in your inbox, reminding you that you haven't finished the task. But *merely looking at your inbox* is a massive cognitive load in itself, enough to occupy most people's minds entirely and push out all other concerns. Any further load increase you get from looking at a specific email is incrementally tiny – and offset by the value of knowing, at a glance, which emails you still have to deal with.

The Organised Writer

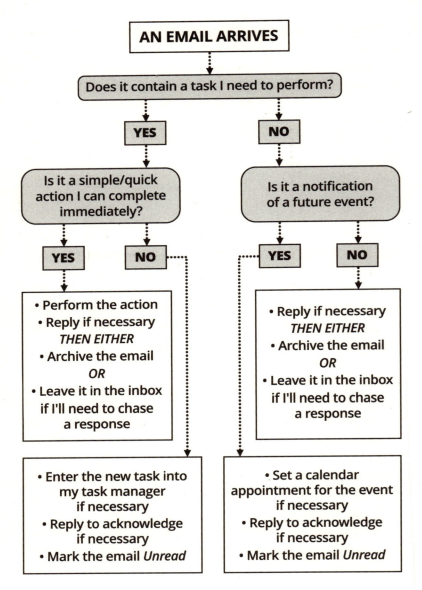

Figure 2.5 Reacting to email.

That doesn't mean you won't get overwhelmed from time to time – no system is a panacea – but the risk is no greater than that of being overwhelmed by any other demand on your time.

My general rule is that if I have more than fifty emails marked Unread in my inbox, I block out a solid amount of time to deal with them and their various tasks. The length of that block will differ according to the situation and my energy levels, but if things have become this bad then I'm probably going to need at least a couple of hours, maybe even a whole afternoon, to clear out a bunch of tasks.

I should emphasise, though, that such a situation is rare. As I write this, my own Unread list is currently quite long, maybe half as long again as on an average day. But it still only contains 26 emails, and a quick glance over the list tells me that when I come to deal with it later, at least half a dozen of those are either simple notifications or 'Deal with it now' tasks.

Contrary to what you may have heard, email is not the enemy; but you mustn't let it dictate your schedule. Learn to deal with it on your own terms, and in time you can dispel the dread of facing up to your inbox.

Use a task manager

I've just railed against converting tasks from your email inbox into a to-do list, so you might justifiably think I'm also against using task managers, but that's not the case. I simply dislike using them to track tasks for which your inbox (something you look at every day anyway) serves equally well.

If you're not converting email tasks into to-dos, what are you using a task manager for? Simple: *everything else*.

All your writing projects, whether commissioned or self-initiated, should go into a task manager. The self-initiated ones *have* to go in there, because there are no emails from other people asking you to do them. But you should also enter commissioned projects into a task manager, to have an at-a-glance record of their progress.

Like your calendar, a task manager isn't only for work purposes. If you have personal, family, or leisure projects you want to complete, you should put those in too. As with everything in this system, never rely on your memory alone; if it's important, mark it in the appropriate place, whether that's your calendar, a task manager, or job sheet (more on those later). Projects like 'build treehouse', 'organise birthday party' and 'clear out garage' may not be work-related, but it's still important to know what stage they're at.

Some task managers are very complex; their methodology seems to expect you to hold a flowchart in one hand while clicking around a multi-level interface with the other, vainly fretting over whether your task is *suspended*, or *pending review*, or *requires nested action*, or… for heaven's sake, what are you doing? Stop this madness. Use something simpler.

Your specific choice of task manager is your own. I have my own suggestions (see Chapter 7), but ultimately it just needs three basic qualities.

First, you must be able to use it while you're away from your desk. This can mean it synchronises through an online cloud system between your main computer and your laptop, and/or phone. Or it can mean your task manager is paper-based, like the 'bullet journal' system growing in popularity at time of writing (which, for all its flourish and fancy name, strikes me as little more than a big to-do list that you rewrite every day… but that's no bad thing, as long as it works for you).

A paper-based system has its downsides. You have to remember to carry it, and a pen, with you; if it's a large notebook it might be unwieldy to take out at a moment's notice; it uses up a lot of paper and ink; and you can't automate recurring or scheduled tasks. On the other hand, a paper-based task-management system will never need an internet connection; never run out of battery power; and won't annoy people too much if you suddenly whip it out to set yourself a task you've just realised needs completing (which is still a danger with smartphones, although as the world becomes more and more reliant on them, it seems increasingly acceptable in both work and social settings to take one out, even mid-conversation, and perform a quick task).

Second, your task manager mustn't be so unwieldy that you can't use it for small things. Some projects may only have two or three necessary steps, and if it takes you ten minutes to set up that project and enter three tasks, I'd suggest you're using the wrong system. Like I said, some software is too complex for our basic purposes; if you spend longer organising your task manager than actually carrying out the tasks, something has gone wrong.

Third, a task manager must be fast and simple to use. While I've placed this last, it's undoubtedly the most important, and reflects a notion that has become increasingly clear to me over the years: the easier and more convenient something is to do, the more likely you are to make it a habit. Or, to state the inverse: the more difficult, annoying, and inconvenient something is to do, the less likely you are to do it even once, let alone adopt it as part of a regular system.

Every part of your system, including your task manager, must be something you can use without much conscious thought, as this will enable you to make it into a habit. This philosophy will come to the fore in Chapter 7, It's a set-up, as it relies heavily on designing your physical space to ease workflow. It's also vital to remember in technical matters, especially software. We can be drawn in all too easily by marketing bullet points, impressed by promises of technical wizardry, only to wind up wrestling with something so complex it almost becomes a full-time job in itself to maintain.

This is why I recommend the Things task manager for Mac and iOS; it's startlingly simple, and the developers have actively resisted adding unnecessary complexity over the years, even though a small (but very vocal) segment of their customer base continually cries out for a thousand bells and whistles. I'm thankful for this resistance, because it means I can open Things, add a new task, place it in a project at the correct order-of-task position, and get out in ten seconds flat. The cognitive load is almost zero.

There's one caveat to the issue of complex task managers; there's nothing wrong with using one, if you can do so in a simple manner. While it's not a task manager, a good example of this principle is Scrivener, my favourite writing application. It's extremely powerful and feature-rich, and to learn how to use every single feature would take a lot of time... but you don't *have* to learn them all. Scrivener satisfies the needs of many different kinds of writer – novelists, screenwriters, journalists, academics, playwrights, lawyers, and I even know of a forensic consultant who uses it for case notes – so most users only have to learn its core functionality, plus maybe a further 20 per cent of its specialist features. The catch is that every writer learns a *different* 20 per cent according to their specific type of work. Even two straightforward novelists using the application will do so in different ways. The important thing is that we all find it easy to use in our own particular fashion, rather than struggling with complexity as we write. The same might be true of your favourite complex task manager – I have friends who swear by an application called OmniFocus, for example. OF's workflow makes my brain melt, but it works for them, and that's what matters.

So find a task manager you can get your head around with ease. Look for an application with core features designed to be used quickly and simply, that syncs reliably with your laptop/phone; or a paper system that doesn't take two hours to rewrite every day, and which you understand instinctively.

TASK MANAGER VS TO-DO LIST

What's the difference between a task manager and a to-do list? As far as I'm concerned, they're two different things – but at the same time it's largely a matter of nomenclature. You can call them whatever you like. What matters, and makes a difference to your workflow, is how you use them. This is how I define them:

A task manager is a permanent fixture in your workflow, containing projects (which in turn contain tasks) that might take days, weeks, or more, to carry out.

A to-do list is a short, temporary checklist of (often related) minor tasks – small enough that the entire list can be completed in a single day – which must be checked off to call something 'done'.

Your grocery shopping list is a kind of to-do list. It's a catalogue of connected small tasks, i.e. each item you want to purchase, that must be fulfilled to complete your shopping. It may also include things that aren't strictly groceries – 'pick up dry-cleaning', or 'buy stamps' – but which you intend to carry out as part of the same trip.

A more potentially work-orientated example is my own most common use for a to-do list: preparing to travel. Let's say I'm going to London on 10–12 June to attend meetings. In my calendar I block out those three days as 'London', and make time-specific hard appointments for the meetings I've arranged, e.g. 'lunch with agent' at 1pm on 11 June.

In my task manager I create a single item in the Agenda ur-project: 'Pack for London' (see below for how the Agenda project works). I then create a separate to-do list of all the things I need to pack for London; not just clothes and toiletries, but any documents I need to take, gifts for people, pens in case I'm asked to sign books, and so on. The to-do list is temporary, designed only to make sure I don't forget to take anything; when I've finished packing, I can check off 'Pack for London' in my task manager and know that I'm ready to travel. (For a more in-depth look at packing lists, see Chapter 3.)

PRIORITIES

You may have heard the saying, 'If *everything* is a priority, then *nothing* is a priority'.

I understand the sentiment – if the point of marking things as High Priority is to ensure you carry out those tasks before any others, then what good is having 50 High Priority items? Maybe you now need a *Higher* Priority list, but if you put too many things on that, you might need a *Highest* Priority list... and so on. It gets rather silly, and is the same mentality that leads to a file list like this, with which we're all too familiar:

> *Great Manuscript Final.doc*
> *Great Manuscript Final REV.doc*
> *Great Manuscript Final Final.doc*
> *AAA Great Manuscript REALLY FINAL.doc*
> ***** *Great Manuscript FINAL THIS ONE.doc*

As with all dogma, the opposing puritanism – that a High-Priority list must contain only one or two tasks at a time – can also be taken too far, and such a 'lean' list is equally unwieldy and unusable. If you follow the 'if everything is, then nothing is' mentality too strictly, you reach a place where your task manager contains only a single High-Priority item, and every time you complete that High-Priority task, you have to go back through your list of non-High-Priority projects to select the next task to promote as the single High-Priority item...

...Which doesn't sound much better than just having 50 items on your High-Priority list.

My own Priority list (called the 'Today' list in Things, but it's the same principle) has around a dozen tasks on it, from multiple projects – in fact, every item in the Priority list is from a different project.

But wait! How can several different projects all be top priority?

They're not, of course. Where it helps is when I've decided which project I'm going to work on at any given time. Then I can look down that list and know exactly which task related to the project is waiting to be carried out.

My Priority list has two simple rules:

1. any project may have only one to-do item in the Priority list at any one time;
2. the exception is a 'project' called Agenda & Admin, which actually contains a list of business errands.

The purpose of Agenda & Admin is to be a catch-all repository of things I need to do that *aren't* time-sensitive, *aren't* linked to a specific work project, and *don't* relate to an email in my inbox (otherwise I'd just flag the relevant email; see the previous section of this chapter).

Examples of Agenda & Admin items would therefore be emails I need to write; phone calls I need to make; a run to the post office to mail a package; a reminder to check something in my online bank account; and so on. This is the closest thing to a regular to-do list within the task manager itself.

Meanwhile, the purpose of only allowing each work project to have a single item in the Priority list should be self-evident. You may be perfectly capable of looking down a list and deciding which project to tackle next, but you can only perform the tasks within that project one at a time. This is a case where it does make sense to carry out the task in the Priority list, then once it's completed drill down into the project, find the next task that should be performed (presumably the one at the top), and promote it to the Priority list. When you next come to look down the list of work projects in your task manager, you'll then see an entirely new task related to that project waiting to be tackled.

EXAMPLES

On the next page are two diagrams illustrating how I use my task manager to track items. As you can see, it's very simple; the project list is in the left sidebar, and selecting the Today view (which I have set as the default) shows me an overview of all the priority tasks in each project, along with the 'floating' Agenda & Admin list.

Clicking on the *Encrypted Bookshelf* project in the sidebar changes the window view to focus on that project, showing all the tasks it contains. The top, starred item is the 'priority' task that appears on the Today list.

The exact appearance of your chosen task manager will vary, naturally. So long as it can handle these very basic requirements, the specific software used doesn't matter.

The Organised Writer

```
> Inbox
> Today                8
> Projects             6
> Someday

Projects:
Agenda & Admin
ENCRYPTED BOOKSHELF (AweNov)
CAPTAIN WONDERFUL (WonCom)
PROJECT GAMEPAD (AweGmz)
Lovely Book Festival
Magazine Article (1,500 wds)
```

★ **Today**

○ **Agenda & Admin**
☐ Write interview answers for Lovely Author interviews
☐ Check frequent flyer miles
☐ Buy ballpoint refills

○ **ENCRYPTED BOOKSHELF (AweNov)**
☐ Turn in first draft — May 1

○ **CAPTAIN WONDERFUL (WonCom)**
☐ Issue #4

○ **PROJECT GAMEPAD (AweGmz)**
☐ Write Act 1 cutscenes

○ **Lovely Book Festival**
☐ Book train for May 29

○ **Magazine Article (1,500 wds)**
☐ Outline article

Figure 2.6 Task manager, 'Today' view.

```
> Inbox
> Today                8
> Projects             6
> Someday

Projects:
Agenda & Admin
[ENCRYPTED BOOKSHELF (AweNov)]
CAPTAIN WONDERFUL (WonCom)
PROJECT GAMEPAD (AweGmz)
Lovely Book Festival
Magazine Article (1,500 wds)
```

○ **ENCRYPTED BOOKSHELF (AweNov)**

☐ ★ Turn in first draft — May 1
☐ Notes due back from editor by July 1
☐ Turn in revised draft — Sep 1
☐ Pitch blog tour and bookstore events

Figure 2.7 Task manager, 'Project' view.

Learn to say 'no'

Nobody likes turning down work.

Writers don't like it, because it feels like an imaginative challenge has slipped through our fingers; the chance to make something new, perhaps even create a new world and new characters.

Freelancers don't like it, because it feels like a revenue opportunity has slipped through our fingers; we never know which gig might turn out to be The One that is surprisingly lucrative, or leads to further opportunities.

So *freelance writers* have it doubly bad, and the strong temptation to say 'yes' to every job we're offered – because it sounds exciting, and because we all need to pay the bills – is too often the seed of our own downfall. Before we know it, we're overcommitted and are drowning in impossible deadlines.

Instead, we must learn to say 'no'.

This seems counterintuitive. After all, my aim is to help you be more productive. How can turning down offers of work help you produce more work?

Well, of course you can't say no to *everything*, or you'll literally have no work to do. What I'm suggesting is that you should turn down more work than you probably do at the moment.

As I've already mentioned, the aim of this system is to help you be more productive by increasing your ability to *focus*. One way to facilitate that focus is by removing things that would otherwise nag at your mind and distract you while you're trying to work. The spectre of looming deadlines, along with the fear you're going to miss them, is one of the most common and persistent stressors of all.

If you're struggling to meet all your deadlines, then you are by definition *overcommitted*, and there are only two ways to solve this problem.

The first is to become more productive. Congratulations! You've already begun your journey along that path.

The second way to not be overcommitted is to have fewer commitments. And that means turning down work.

This isn't as simple or easy as it sounds. In fact, it's a constantly evolving and changing equation for every writer. *How much work do I have on right now? How much am I expecting will come up soon? Do I have the capacity to take on a new job? Can I juggle my existing deadlines to make it fit? Or am I truly booked up?*

The answers to these questions will be different every time you ask them, but there's no time like the present to start. Here's what to do:

1. implement the methods described here in *The Organised Writer*, and thereby increase your productivity/output;
2. after a month, reassess your output speed in light of this productivity increase;
3. now compare that against your current workload.

If at that point you're still struggling to keep up, then the hard truth is you're taking on too much work. I've done it myself many times, and still do on occasion. Creative workloads are notoriously difficult to judge, and their reassessment is an ongoing process, but it becomes easier with time and practice. You'll come to realise that by having less to do you can actually get more done… because the work you *are* doing will come easier, and be of a higher quality.

There is, however, another side to saying 'no' that has nothing to do with productivity and everything to do with value. I'll talk more about this in Chapter 6, *Money matters*, but for now I'll just say that you should never allow your talent to be commodified. Saying 'yes' to every job offer may cause you to be overcommitted, but it can also cause you to be *undervalued*.

The most powerful tool you have in any negotiation is the ability to say 'no' and walk away – if you're unable to do that, then your counterpart on the other side of the table needn't give up any ground. If you're so desperate for work that you'll take on any job, and work to any deadline, for any pittance thrown your way, it won't take long for clients to realise it. And if you think they won't naturally use that knowledge to their advantage, then they've got an offer for you with absolutely no budget, of course they can't afford to pay you, but it'll bring you *amazing* exposure, believe them.

(You shouldn't believe them.)

Saying 'no' gives you enormous power over both your destiny and value, and can even help you become a sought-after talent. Everyone wants what they can't have.

Work to a quantity, not time

Some writers will tell you they write for a certain amount of time every day; three hours, five hours, thirty minutes, whatever. That's certainly a way to keep your time management under control, and also a useful method if writing isn't your full-time job; if you have a day job, children, or other dependants who rely on you being elsewhere at certain times, then you must fit your writing time around those other commitments.

The problem with writing to time is that none of us writes at a consistent speed. Sit a writer in front of a keyboard for two hours every day, and while you'll hopefully get some decent work out of them, the chances of them reliably writing the same amount on each of those days are as close to zero as makes no odds. The chances of them even writing a *good* amount every day are pretty low.

Therefore, I advocate working to a quantity rather than a time period. When I'm working on a novel, I don't write for four hours every day – I write *1,500 words* every day. That might take me four hours; or it might take me just two; or it might take me an entire teeth-gritting day of forcing my fingers to bash away at the keyboard until I drag myself over the word-count line.

With scripts, I don't work to a word count, but I still avoid writing for a set number of hours. Instead I write *five pages* every day, no matter how long it takes me.

Working to a word or page count, rather than for a set period of time, will make you more productive. It's mathematics – unless you're somehow able to guarantee that every day you can sit down for a fixed number of hours and produce enough words to never miss a deadline, then working to a quantity rather than time will by definition increase your rate of output.

It also reduces stress in two ways. First, completing a word count means that every day you know without a shadow of a doubt you've done enough work to meet your deadline, regardless of what the clock says. That may sound like a small thing, but it's a vital piece of knowledge that will lift an enormous weight from any author's shoulders.

Second, once you hit that word count – again, regardless of what the clock says – you can spend the rest of the day doing whatever you like, guilt-free. Of course, if you have admin tasks that need addressing, you should try to clear some of them off your to-do list. But if you then want to read a book, watch a movie, play a videogame, take a long walk in the woods, or just go grocery shopping... you can go right ahead, with no need to apologise or feel guilty for it. You know you've earned it, by hitting your word count for the day, and are on track. That's the point of a quota, after all.

(Not that any writer should ever feel guilty about taking time out to read a book. As the crime writer Mark Billingham puts it, would you trust a chef who doesn't eat?)

This is a fundamental difference between *The Organised Writer* and some other productivity methods; this system isn't designed to punish you, or make you feel guilty, for not achieving goals. Instead it rewards you when you achieve them. And for a writer there is no greater feeling, no bigger swell of contentment and relief, than knowing you've written as much as you need to for the day. 'No writer enjoys writing, but every writer enjoys having written', as the saying goes.

> **WORDS MATTER MOST**
>
> A common question is, 'What happens to my other tasks on days where it takes longer than usual to hit my word count?' While those other tasks are important, they always come second to writing. Put them off till tomorrow, if possible; if that's not possible, put in an extra hour today to get them off your mind. If you think of yourself as a slow writer, this prospect may worry you – but once you begin using this system, days when you truly have no spare time for admin will become rare indeed.

Leisure time isn't just for fun. Allowing your writing brain to relax and take some time off while you engage in other activities is also a great way to generate new ideas and thoughts about your writing. It's the 'shower conundrum'; that strange phenomenon where you wrestle with a thorny writing problem at your desk for hours, but the answer doesn't hit you until you step in the shower – the one place where you can't take notes, naturally. Nobody quite knows why this happens, but it seems sensible to assume it's to do with allowing your subconscious to formulate a solution, rather than trying to sweat one out of your frontal lobes.

Every writer I have ever known – myself included – wishes we could have more time to read, more time with our family/friends/pets, more time that *isn't spent worrying about writing*. While I can't guarantee working to a daily word count will increase your typing speed, knowing you've hit that word count will allow you to enjoy any spare time you have to the fullest.

Productive procrastination

A useful technique to have in your back pocket is *productive procrastination*. It's what's often known as a 'life hack', because you're 'hacking' your normal routine to do things you wouldn't normally do, to make your life more efficient. I just call them 'good ideas', but whatever you call it, productive procrastination is a good one. It's the idea that you should always be doing *something*, even if it's not the thing you planned to do at this very moment.

Procrastination, in and of itself, is a displacement activity. It's what happens when you have a task to do, but for any number of reasons, you can't bring yourself to carry it out. Most of the time, the reason is a self-deception similar to writer's block (which I address, and try to dispel, in Chapter 4). You're perfectly capable of doing the task, but you're afraid you'll screw it up somehow and don't want to face potential failure.

Sometimes, though, there's a more concrete reason: you haven't prepared sufficiently to be able to carry out the task, or you don't feel you have the energy. Issues like these are solvable, but sometimes it's just really, really hard to get started on something. Hence the writer Mikael Awake's wonderful Twitter joke: 'Business idea: a cleaning service staffed entirely by writers on deadline.'

This is where productive procrastination can be useful. Awake's joke is brilliant precisely because it has a ring of truth to it. There's a tendency for creative workers to think we must clear all our minor tasks before starting to write/paint/compose/etc. But the moment you think about it logically, the notion unravels. At its most basic level, which task is earning you money: writing your manuscript, or folding your bath towels?

CLEAN BUT UNHEALTHY

Ironically, the end result of procrastination is a kind of enforced clean mind: when you put something off until the last minute, then rush to get it done at the eleventh hour, you have to clear your mind and isolate yourself from distractions in order to accomplish anything. This 'panic method' can lure you into a repetitive cycle, because while it's effective, it's also enormously stressful, and relies entirely on avoiding catastrophe during that mad last-minute rush. Training yourself to achieve the clean mind on an everyday basis, without the need for a deadline breathing down your neck, will improve all areas of your life and work.

None of us is immune. I loathe making unscheduled phone calls, for example. Even scheduled phone calls aren't my favourite way to pass the time, but unscheduled calls fill me with dread. Perhaps you feel the same way; or perhaps you have no problem with them, but you *do* dread entering your receipts into a spreadsheet. Or doing interviews. Or... whatever. We all have something we hate doing, a task we face with dread.

There are two ways to ensure you're not wasting your time, depending on the situation. They both revolve around the principle of not letting yourself be paralysed, not allowing yourself to sit and stare mindlessly out of the window for hours rather than accomplish something.

If what you're procrastinating about is one of those tasks you dread, and you simply can't bring yourself to do it right now... do something else useful instead. Open up your task manager, find an item you can face carrying out, and get started. Even if it's only entering your receipts, or booking a festival hotel, it's one more thing you can check off your tasks; one more thing you've accomplished and won't need to worry about in the future.

On the other hand, if what you're procrastinating about is your actual work – the writing isn't coming for one reason or another, and you just don't feel you've got it in you – then make yourself *do that thing you dread*. You're going to have to do it at some point anyway, so why not now?

I find this has one of two equally surprising and beneficial effects; either I check off a task that I hate doing (and which inevitably turns out to have been nowhere near as dreadful as I anticipated); or my dread for the task is so great that I miraculously find I've got the energy/will/etc. to start writing today, after all.

Invest the time to set up your system

It will take some time to become used to following these principles. You'll find yourself unconsciously slipping back into bad habits, and have to remind yourself that's not how you do things any more. But you may be surprised by how quickly you also develop *good* habits – because a lot of *The Organised Writer* is about naming and codifying things that, deep down, you already know. Such as how your current methods aren't working very well; that's why you're reading this book in the first place. Many of its principles are just as intuitive and obvious in hindsight, once you start putting them into practice. Of course, that's the kicker: you have to put them into practice, with enough regularity and discipline that they become habits. But that won't take as long as you think.

In Part III, I'll explain the (very few) things you need to own in order to use this system. Once you've bought them – or perhaps while you're waiting for them to arrive – I suggest you re-acquaint yourself with the system's principles, and only begin to rearrange your office when you have everything you need in hand.

When you're ready, you'll need to take a couple of days to set it all up. A weekend is ideal, though any consecutive days will do if that's not possible. Book the time off, clear your schedule, whatever you need to do; but make sure that on those days, you *don't have to work at all*. You must be able to spend them sorting out your entire office, without being interrupted or feeling guilty that you should be working.

Chapter 7 will go into detail of what you'll be doing on those days, and how best to arrange your workspace. Before we get there, let me address the plaintive cries I can already hear from authors reading these words: 'Are you completely insane? I can't afford to take two whole days off! I have deadlines up to here, and mountains of paperwork to deal with, and editors on my back, and, and, and...'

As writers, you should understand I choose my words carefully. That's why the title of this section refers to *investing* your time. Because it's exactly that; an investment in your future productivity. No investment = no pay-off.

I truly understand the reluctance to take time off – whole days, even! – just to rearrange your office. But you're doing a lot more than moving furniture around. You're setting up a system that will pay you back with time, productivity, and mental well-being. If you take a couple of days to implement everything and stick to it diligently, within a month you'll 'earn back' those two days through the increase in your productivity.

Let me emphasise that, because it's not some clap-your-hands-and-make-a-wish notion; it's the whole point of *The Organised Writer*.

It's easy to fall into a trap of thinking you can't possibly take any time off, because your work is going so slowly that any break will only make you fall even further behind. That particular black dog hounds all authors to some extent, and never more so when you're strained from overwork, but it's nonsense; a form of 'sunk cost' fallacy. In fact, if you allow yourself to work in a more organised fashion, the work you do will be more efficient and save you that time you're so desperate to get back.

> **THE SUNK COST FALLACY**
>
> The sunk cost fallacy occurs when you've invested a significant amount into something, then realise it won't ultimately be worth the expense – but convince yourself to continue regardless, because you don't want to 'waste' the investment you've already made. Note that 'investment' here doesn't just mean money; it can be time, effort expended, emotional commitments, any finite resource that you value.

The sunk cost fallacy is so called for a reason. If you feel permanently overwhelmed, the *best* thing you can do is take a break and reassess your working practices, because you're probably not producing your best work anyway. The very act of forcing yourself to step away from the keyboard for a couple of days and set up an *Organised Writer* system will help you relax, so that when you resume writing it'll be with renewed energy and confidence. Once you're working efficiently, regularly hitting your daily writing quota and dealing properly with other tasks, you'll find that taking a day off is no longer the big deal it used to be. As incredible as it sounds, you might even be able to go on vacation with your family for a week and not feel guilty about it.

Think of this time investment as a sort of 'hard reset' in your career; a date on which you'll look back and identify as a *before/after* point. Following these principles means making big changes to your working life – possibly the most significant changes since you became a writer.

For now, though, all you need is a weekend. You won't regret it.

Organise your personal life

The notion of organising your personal time may at first seem paradoxical, even horrible; isn't the point of sorting out your working life to make your personal life more relaxing? Shouldn't you be able to enjoy family time without worrying about schedules, systems, and productivity?

Yes... in theory.

The problem with writers is that we never really stop working. We're always thinking about our work, even if only at a subconscious level. How many times have you been sitting at the dinner table, or watching late night TV, only to suddenly cry out, jump up, and reach for the nearest pen and paper? (Often accompanied by a gentle roll of the eyes from your partner/children/pet.)

This isn't about scheduling, per se – although, if you have a full family life, a shared online calendar where you can all access, make, and keep up to date with family engagements is rarely a bad idea. This is about not insisting work and family life never bleed into one another. I believe that kind of purist attitude is a fool's game for any freelance worker, especially writers. There's also a certain amount of redundancy that goes into keeping work and family separate. If you're disorganised in your writing life, there's a good chance that the chaos of your work already spills over into your personal life. Besides, why maintain two systems? Why have two separate task managers, two sets of filing drawers, two calendars that you must constantly compare against one another before you make plans? Why not just have one system, that you already know how to use, and apply it across your whole life?

While *The Organised Writer* system focuses on your work, the methods can also be applied to your personal life, to help you organise time away from your keyboard. I'm not suggesting you book timed appointments to play with your children, or enter items like 'Shop for groceries' in your task manager (although if I did that, I doubt my own partner would be the least bit surprised...). But there are small, simple things you can do to make the interplay between your work and personal life less stressful, and even more enjoyable.

First, in your calendar application create a category titled *Family*, or perhaps *Leisure/Personal*, according to your circumstances. This can be an import of your online shared family calendar, if you use one; all modern calendar applications allow you to import a 'live' version of such a calendar into your own, so that your work calendar only appears on your computer, but anything you add to the shared *Family* calendar appears to everyone else sharing it. Keeping both calendars visible together in this way ensures you won't accidentally create a work appointment that clashes with family, or vice versa.

Next, use your filing drawers to file both work *and* personal documents. Just as filing by category is often a disaster in waiting (see Chapter 3), so is trying to separate your work and personal files. Combining them means you never have to stop and think where you should look for a file, because they're all in the same place.

Finally, remember to have some kind of note-taking device to hand at all times. Again, this is covered in more depth in the next chapter, but the point is to carry the practice through to your personal time as well. And though I say 'device' – simply because we all have a phone on which we can type notes, if necessary – I include a notebook and pen under that heading. I carry a Moleskine notebook and pen with me everywhere it's practical to do so; in places where it's not practical, I rely on my phone. Whatever you use, your family and friends will be much more amenable and understanding if you quickly whip out a notebook to jot down a sudden thought than if you spend five minutes frantically looking for a scrap of paper while shouting, 'Pen! Pen! Has anyone got a pen?!'

If this sounds like a lot to remember, don't worry. The point is that you *don't* have to remember it; it's all set-up, part of the environment you'll build for yourself as you adopt *The Organised Writer* system. Once that system is in place, it will help you relax more when you're away from your desk, because you'll know nothing on your calendar clashes with family time; you've carried out all the day's tasks; and if you suddenly have a work-related thought, you can jot it down in your notebook.

When you know all those things – when you trust the system enough to remove lingering doubts and memory distraction – you can forget about work and instead relax with your family, spend time with your friends... or even just chill out on your own for a while.

When was the last time you did *that*?

Summary

OVERALL:

- Time management, structure, and routine are key to being organised.

CALENDAR:

- Block out your work schedule four weeks ahead of time; where possible, schedule only one project per day.
    - If you must work on two projects, deal with the most taxing one first.
    - If you have to reschedule, *move* blocks rather than *delete* them, to reinforce commitment.
- Make hard appointments as and when they're arranged.
- Try to avoid appointments of any kind before lunchtime.
- When negotiating deadlines, build +25 per cent 'problem time' into your schedule.
    - Also allow for the 'hindsight effect'.
    - If a deadline is going badly, talk to editors/clients immediately.
- Say 'no' to projects that you can't fit in, or which aren't worth your time.
- Work to a daily quantity, not a set amount of time.

EMAIL:

- Assess every new email for its task contents, then do one of the following:
    - read it, then archive it;
    - deal with it now, then archive it;
    - mark it unread, and deal with it later;
    - delete it.
- Next, do a 'bottom-up' check of unread emails using the same criteria.
- Remember that you don't owe most people an immediate reply, and you don't owe strangers a reply at all.

TASK MANAGER:

- Use a task manager to simply record Project status, and miscellaneous Agenda & Admin items.
- Allow no more than one Priority/Today item per project.
- Make temporary to-do lists for groups of related tasks that must be carried out in a single sweep.
- Use productive procrastination to check off onerous tasks.
- Don't separate your family and personal life into different systems; define them within new categories of the existing system.

CHAPTER 3

Taking notes and making lists

(×) A *disorganised writer* forgets great ideas and loses notes because they have no consistent method to record them, and no easy way to retrieve them.

(✓) *The organised writer* never forgets an idea or thought because they record everything consistently, and store notes in a way that makes them easy to retrieve.

Note-taking, in my view, is one of the simplest and yet most important aspects of being an effective writer. It deserves to be taken seriously.

A vital aspect of any productivity method is its 'systemic memory'; in other words, the notion that the system itself holds everything we need to remember, in an easily searchable form. For writers this means that in addition to our work tasks, the system must also hold our story ideas and thoughts, dialogue snippets that come to us in the middle of dinner, plots that form as we take a shower, and so on.

For this to work, three things must be true:

1. you must be able to easily and quickly record any thought, idea, or task that comes to mind as a note;
2. you must be able to find that note just as easily and quickly at a later time;
3. you must be able to turn that note into something you can act upon, if desired.

You make these things true by adopting habits that allow you to accomplish them with ease. Let's look at each one in turn.

Taking notes

1. You must be able to quickly and easily record any thought, idea, or task that comes to mind as a note.

This is known in the productivity world as *capturing* your thoughts and ideas, before they escape your memory and are lost forever. I'm very fond of the phrase *ubiquitous capture*, a perfect term for the notion that no matter where you are or what you're doing, you should be able to quickly and easily record any thought you have or task you're given. Nobody's quite sure who first coined it. I'm convinced it was Merlin Mann of *43 Folders*, but Merlin himself believes it was David Allen... except the phrase doesn't appear anywhere in Allen's original *Getting Things Done* (GTD) book (see Further reading on page 275). It's possible Allen used it during a live GTD seminar, and the phrase then filtered out into the wider discussion. Regardless of its provenance, the phrase is especially well suited to how writers can and should approach note-taking.

The purpose of ubiquitous capture is twofold. First, it's part of ensuring that you don't forget things, which is a central principle of any good productivity system, and doubly so for writers. Second, being able to capture thoughts quickly and easily means it's not something you need to consciously think about. Making a note becomes a habit you perform it all the time, without effort. You don't run around trying to find a pen; you don't keep rehearsing a thought until you can locate a scrap of paper; you don't block out everything happening around you in case it makes you forget the thing you're trying to remember.

Instead, the process is simple. You have a thought; you immediately record it; then return to what you were doing, secure in the knowledge that you don't have to remember it any more, because you'll see it later when you go over your notes.

> **FORGET TO REMEMBER**
>
> You may think your memory isn't an issue, and there's no chance you'll forget your own great ideas. If you're a young, healthy person, that might be true... for now. But take it from me and everyone else over the age of 30 when I tell you it won't last, and the day will come when you realise your memory just isn't what it used to be. If you hope to make writing your lifelong career – which is surely the aim, right? – it will pay dividends for you to develop and cultivate good habits now, so that as your memory becomes less reliable with age those mitigating procedures are already established.

This is self-evidently helpful if you're with family or friends. While they may be used to your writerly ways, I can confidently say every one of them would prefer you to be relaxed and thinking about work as little as possible while you're together.

But capturing thoughts in this way is also helpful when you're working. How many times have you spent hours wracking your brain to solve a thorny story problem, without much success... then, five minutes after you give up and do something else, the solution suddenly pops into your mind? Sometimes it's not even related to what you're working on; you could be in the thick of a project when a completely new idea gatecrashes its way into your thoughts. It happens all the time, but these thoughts are often fleeting and decay quickly – if you don't capture the thought right away, it becomes ever more elusive to rediscover, rapidly fading from memory. At the same time, you don't want to divert a lot of brainpower to dealing with it, because then you risk losing your focus and train of thought on the project currently underway. Being able to record that thought without much conscious effort, in a way that feels habitual and non-distracting, is invaluable.

The next question most people ask is, 'Which thoughts should I note down?' The short answer is: all of them.

(The longer answer is also *all of them*, but allow me to elaborate.)

How do you know which idea is going to be important? How do you know which thought will still be relevant in six months' time? How do you know which story concept that hits you at two in the morning is the one that will turn out to be a breakthrough?

You don't. You only come to know these things in hindsight – when you look back and see the precarious chain of events, happenstance, and good fortune that led to wherever you are now. Before you reach that point, you have no way of predicting which idea will make a difference and which will die on the vine.

That's why you record them all. No matter how random, how small, how half-baked, how unfinished it may be; if you have a thought, record it right away.

Finally, then, let's look at the logistics of doing so. The simplest way is to carry a notebook and pen with you at all times. It's the simplest, cheapest, and most reliable option for recording your thoughts. Notebooks don't run out of battery, don't light up and disturb people in dark environments, don't beep at inopportune moments, and dropping them on the floor won't induce a coronary. The only real risk is running out of either ink or paper, which is easily solved by carrying spares if you know you're running low.

There's something ineffable about making notes with pen and paper that embeds them more effectively in one's memory, and helps build a deeper conceptual understanding of our thoughts. Studies have shown that taking notes by hand is more effective than doing so on a computer (see Further reading on page 275 for links); handwritten notes are simple, natural, and afford better recall and understanding.

With all of that in mind, what's the best way to actually take such notes? Once again, ten writers will give you eleven opinions, and none of them is technically right or wrong so long as their method works for them.

I use a single notebook at a time, for all notes across all of my projects. I know writers who dedicate one to each project, and keep all relevant notes and brainstorming in each separate notebook, but I find this baffling. Do they never have ideas for more than one project at a time? Or do they carry a dozen notebooks everywhere they go? What happens to ideas that turn out to be unworkable? Do they happily discard a quarter-full notebook? Perhaps I'm the odd one out, but when I have initial conceptual thoughts about a story idea, I rarely know if it'll become a fully fledged project. Many ideas fizzle out before they reach the drafting stage. Even if you restrict yourself to one notebook per project you're actively working on, you still need somewhere else to jot down ideas for new and future stories. For me, that makes a single notebook for *everything* the simplest solution.

To make a note, I turn to the first blank space (not necessarily a new page) and write a title – if it's related to an existing project that will often be an abbreviation of some kind, or for unrelated thoughts I'll simply title it something like *New Idea* (if the new idea in question has a particular hook I might use that for its title, e.g. *Crime Idea* or *Spy Plot*). Next to the title I jot down the date, and dog-ear the page corner.

Then I write, until I've recorded everything I wanted to get down. If I finish my notes less than three-quarters of the way down a page I draw a line underneath, to mark the next blank space to be used. Finally I close the book, put the pen away, and return to whatever I was doing.

USING YOUR PHONE

All of the above works splendidly if I have a notebook, but what else could I use? There are occasions when it's not convenient to pull out my notebook, and for some people handwriting anything is not a realistic option.

A smartphone is a perfectly good way to take notes, so long as you're confident you won't run out of battery, and you're comfortable typing on it (or speaking into it – most smartphones have 'voice memo' functionality, and even those that don't will normally allow you to call your own number and leave yourself a voicemail as a last resort). There are occasions when I will make a note on my phone rather than in my notebook if it's more convenient, such as if I already have my phone in my hand when the thought strikes. I generally only use it for very short entries, as I don't particularly like typing on my phone and prefer writing longer entries in a notebook. You may differ, and if for some reason you simply can't use a notebook, by all means go ahead and use your phone instead.

How do I make notes on my phone? Pretty much in the same way as my paper notes, albeit without the dog-ears and drawn lines. I use the built-in Notes app on my iPhone, because it syncs with all my other devices, auto-dates each note, and it's very quick and simple to open and use. You may prefer a different app, possibly on a different device, and that's fine – though I strongly suggest you use one that syncs your notes back to your computer, or at the very least to somewhere you can access them in the cloud. If your phone is damaged or becomes unworkable for some reason, you don't want to lose all your notes with it.

Whatever app you use, be consistent – use it, and only it, to make notes. Don't jump around between apps, because then when you want to find something you wrote earlier you'll have to search in half a dozen different places. Building familiarity with reliable tools is a key aspect of making *The Organised Writer* system work, and note-taking is no exception, so find one good app and stick to it.

On my phone, each note has a title. The difference between this and the notebook is that I may already have a note relating to the project about which I want to capture a thought. If so, rather than creating a new note I find the existing one, scroll/swipe down to the bottom, and begin typing my new thoughts as an addendum. If no note for this project exists, or it's just a random thought, then I'll create a new note and title it. I don't need to type the date; the phone will automatically record when the note was last modified.

When I've typed out everything I wanted to get down, I close the app and return to what I was doing.

USING YOUR COMPUTER

The notebook and phone methods are used when I'm out and about. If I'm at my desk, however, I simply make the note directly on my computer.

This is why it's important that my notes sync back to my home computer – so that when I open the app on my desktop, any notes I made on my phone are ready and waiting for me. To make a note, the process is much the same as on my phone. I can open the app in a couple of keystrokes or clicks, and then once again I choose a title or locate an existing note to append. Once again, I type out whatever thought I want to get down, to off-load it from my mind. Once again, when I'm finished I close the app and return to what I was doing. If it's a short note, the whole process might take less than fifteen seconds.

I keep emphasising the last part – closing your notes and returning to whatever you were doing – because it clarifies the objective of this system. Have a thought; quickly record it as a note; then put it out of your mind, so that it's no longer a distraction.

Whichever method/s you use, whether you use one notebook or two, do it all on your phone, or a combination of the two, the important thing is to ensure you *have* a method that suits any occasion; one you're comfortable enough using that you can do so quickly, easily, and reliably. Any method that you find difficult, or takes a long time, is almost as bad as no method at all.

2. You must be able to find that note just as easily and quickly at a later time.

You've captured all your random thoughts and ideas. Now what do you do with them? How do you make them easy to find and look up?

You write them all out again, this time on your computer.

Remember those dog-eared corners? Find the first one and read the project title. Now open your working document for that project, make a new notes file (or comment, or page, depending on your software), give it the same date as the handwritten note – and begin typing, verbatim.

This is a bit of an acid test for adoption of the system, but one I hope you won't stumble over too much. The old adage has it that 'writing is re-writing', and every author I know would agree. Perhaps you're the exception, and the first thing you type is always perfect. It's possible, but let's face it, pretty unlikely – which means you're used to writing your manuscripts two or three times, perhaps even more. Doing the same thing with your notes therefore shouldn't be onerous.

There's also a wider point to this part of the process, though. You'll note I said you should *begin* typing verbatim. That wasn't an idle choice of words, because it won't stay verbatim for long. As you type these notes up, you'll inevitably think about their content, with the added perspective of the time passed since you first jotted them down. That perspective will invariably spark new thoughts and insights into these ideas as you rewrite the notes – thoughts which you should go ahead and insert into the transcript. This part of the process is invaluable; you already have the initial note written down, so now you can digress as much as you want, chasing down as many stray thoughts as you can muster, without worrying that you'll lose track of your original thoughts. By the end of this stage I've normally exhausted every idea related to a specific note or concept that I have, and can be confident about moving on to the next topic.

When I've finished typing up the note in question, and everything that was in my notebook is now in the computer (as well as those new thoughts and insights) I straighten the dog-eared corner, take my pen, and draw a big X over the pages. This has two purposes. First, it simply gives a visceral sense of satisfaction – a feeling that something has been accomplished, because now when I flick through my notebook I can see at a glance all the notes that have been transcribed. But it also does so without obliterating the note from view. If disaster strikes and for some reason I need to type something up all over again, the contents of my notebook are still legible enough to do so.

What if the notes aren't specific to an existing project? To be honest, truly project-agnostic notes are rare for me – even if the 'project' is little more than a collection of vague thoughts, I'll nevertheless give it a working title of some kind, whether something evocative or purely descriptive like *Crime Story*, to keep them all together. If that's not the case, and the note really is just a fragment of an idea with no current home, I type it into a simple 'scratch' entry that contains all such random snippets and lives permanently in my Notes application.

SHOEBOX APPLICATIONS

Rather than a 'scratch document', you might prefer to use a specialist 'shoebox' tool such as Yojimbo or Microsoft OneNote to collect these random thoughts. These applications are designed to receive just about anything you throw into them – text snippets, PDFs, Word documents, web pages, images, voice memos, and more – so you can retrieve and review them later. I dislike these applications, but if you're comfortable using one and know you can rely on it, go ahead. The important thing is that you be consistent.

What if you made the notes on your phone, or in a computer document, to begin with? It's already typed up, so you only need to copy and paste it into the relevant work project... right?

I disagree, and recommend you *re-type* those notes into the project notes all over again. If you only copy/paste, you're not engaging with the material, and are denying yourself the chance to reassess those notes properly. Re-typing them makes you actively revisit them, which will spark those new ideas and insights I mentioned.

(The equivalent of the final 'cross out with an X' stage here is to simply delete the original note. Sadly, it's nowhere near as satisfying!)

Finally, what if you don't *want* to think about the notes as you're typing them up? What if you just need to assemble them as fast as possible, so you can get on with writing the draft?

To be honest I can't think of many writing jobs, even front-line journalism, which run to such tight deadlines that you literally can't take ten minutes to think of new ideas as you type up your notes. If that's truly the case, of course you can simply type them out verbatim (or cut and paste from your notes app), then get down to the 'real' writing. However, the point of taking notes this way isn't just to ensure you don't forget anything; it's also about maximising the chances of producing your best work. When you make a note, all you're thinking about is getting it out of your head and down onto paper. When you transcribe it later, your head is in a completely different place, and you might be amazed at the further insights and perspective that brings.

3. You must be able to turn that note into something you can act upon, if desired.

You might still wonder; what's the point of all this? Why do all this writing, and re-typing, and rewriting?

First, as mentioned above, writing out your notes twice (maybe even more) gives you the opportunity to dive deep into your own thought process, and chase down every branch of an idea you can possibly come up with.

Second, having your notes typed up within a work project makes them easily accessible, and viewable by date, when you come to write the draft itself.

Finally, the simplest reason of all: having them typed up on a computer means you can search for and inside them. Most software will index not just a document's file name, but also its contents; so even if you don't remember where to find a note you're seeking, you can simply search your computer for a fragment or turn of phrase which you know the note contains, and find the relevant project in the search results. You simply can't do that with paper notes, and it's one of the biggest benefits digitisation brings to a writer's life.

Making lists

You've learned the art of making notes, and all is well. Every story idea you have is now recorded, never to be forgotten again. Now what about thoughts you have that *aren't* related to stories? What about, well, *everything else?*

That's where the art of making lists comes in, and for that we return to the same notebook in which we record our ideas.

When I say the 'same' notebook, I don't mean a second notebook of the same type. I mean it literally. In my view, notebooks shouldn't be used as reference libraries; rather, they're temporary holding spaces that contain your thoughts only until you can transfer those thoughts to a more permanent and useful location, such as your computer. In the same way you don't need a separate notebook for each project you're working on, you don't need one specifically for non-story notes either.

(Adherents to the 'bullet journal' style of task management do in fact use their notebooks as a kind of reference, as it stores their tasks and schedule for the day. But that's a different issue to making non-work notes which you'll later need to type up.)

Non-story notes and tasks don't always need to be recorded in your notebook. If you're already using your computer or phone when you suddenly think of a task you need to perform, or a calendar appointment you need to make, you should enter it directly in your task manager or calendar as appropriate. This is also true when it's simply easier and less distracting to use your phone, such as walking down the street, or standing in line at the store. In situations like these, jotting something down in your notebook is actually harder than pulling out your phone to make a note.

But the reverse is also true; if you're already writing in your notebook, breaking away to get your phone out will be distracting, and potentially spoil any flow you might be enjoying (yes, it's possible to achieve a state of flow while making notes). In such a case it's easier to stay in the notebook and write the thought or task out there instead, to be dealt with later.

I make non-story notes in the same way as for story ideas – date it, write it, rule off below. They're just (normally) shorter. Then I return to what I was doing beforehand and immediately put it out of my mind, like any other note, secure in the knowledge that what I've captured will be entered somewhere more appropriate when I transcribe these entries.

That process is also simple; when typing up my notes, when I come to a non-story entry I quickly decide if it should go in my task manager or calendar. Hard appointments get a calendar entry; everything else goes in the task manager, either in its appropriate project or the catch-all Agenda & Admin category for 'floating' items. If it's something entirely new and worthy of its own project, I'll create the project there and then (this is another reason to use a simple task manager, where creating new projects is fast and easy).

That's it. Simple, effective, and using the same basic principles as your other note-taking methods – which helps them become habitual.

Remember also that this is only for thoughts which come to you while you're doing something else, and therefore necessitate making a note to aid your memory. Tasks given to you by email, or incoming physical mail that requires some action on your part, should be assigned tasks as part of your daily schedule when you've finished writing for the day, as discussed in Chapter 2.

Job sheets

Before I became a full-time writer, I was a graphic designer. I initially worked in small design agencies, followed by a small magazine publisher, then finally a very large magazine publisher, after which I took up writing full-time.

On my first day at the first agency, I was introduced to the concept of a *job sheet*. They're not unique to the design industry, but many types of work have no concept of them, so I'll briefly explain.

A job sheet is a pre-printed sheet of paper (there are digital equivalents, but we'll stick with paper for reasons that will become apparent) on which you track a piece of work's progress. When commencing a project you fill in general information such as the client, fee, deadline, etc. As work continues, progress is marked on the sheet by a combination of checkboxes and notes, so anyone else can look at the sheet and immediately understand the work's current status.

Job sheets are invaluable in these environments; like medical charts, they enable people working in multi-person organisations to pass a job from one member of staff to another, even from one department to another, without losing critical status information along the way. They also enable supervisors to review progress at a glance.

In that first design agency, job sheets were a blank form taped to the front of a very large envelope. The form was filled in with ballpoint, and all physical notes and assets relating to the design job – photographs, bromides, printouts, etc. – were contained in the envelope.

Later, when I worked at a small publisher, each designer handled several magazines so job sheets were less granular. By then design had also transformed into an almost completely digital discipline, so very few physical assets were required. Each job sheet was still a form we filled in with ballpoint, but now it covered an entire issue of a magazine. We each kept a clipboard with our current stack of magazine job sheets.

Finally, at a very large publisher, I worked on a single magazine of much greater complexity. So it was back to one job sheet per feature/column/editorial, this time taped to the front of a manila folder which contained hard copy of the article's text, outsourced illustrator contracts, design sketches, and related printouts. Still filled in with ballpoint, though. These sheets allowed us to pass design tasks to different members of the art team while retaining at-a-glance status information for whoever worked on the section that day. As the art director, I also had a clipboard with separate job sheets devoted to prepress, to track the overall progress of each issue through its journey to the printers.

How is this relevant to a writer, working alone in their converted garage? The only people you 'pass' work to are your editors or producers, and by that stage the status of each draft is pretty clear to all. You're the only person doing the actual writing. You don't need to worry about whether other people know the in-progress status of your current work, do you?

No, probably not. But unless you occupy that blessed position of only working on one manuscript at a time, there's a good chance *you* need to be reminded of a project's status when you come back to it after a couple of weeks spent working on something else.

This is one of the main reasons I started to lose the plot a few years into going freelance. I foolishly thought I was leaving all that administration behind me, that I'd never need to look at a job sheet again, and all I'd need to worry about from here on out was, well, writing. Everything else would just sort of take care of itself, wouldn't it?

(Stop laughing.)

The slow realisation began after I first recognised that I had to somehow get organised. I was working on half a dozen different comic scripts at once – not at all unusual in that field – and the only way I could discover their status was to open the script document, scroll around, figure out which point I'd written to, and only then decide if working on that particular script was the best thing for me to do that day.

Maybe that doesn't sound so onerous, but I had to do it for every script in progress, to decide which should take priority. I had no way of knowing, at a glance, how far along each script was, which one I should work on next, or what the deadline was. With half a dozen scripts in progress, that wasted a lot of time every morning as I re-read script after script, trying to figure out which would be a better use of my time. When I also began writing novels and short stories, things really started to get out of hand. And for me in particular, this so-called 'method' was made even more difficult because I almost never write in a linear fashion; I jump around from chapter to chapter and scene to scene, going back and forth throughout my manuscript, which makes it hard to know how close I am to completion just by looking at the script itself.

You may assume this was a eureka-like moment whereupon I exclaimed, 'A-ha! Job sheets!', but you give me too much credit. It wasn't until I tried to use other productivity systems that I finally had my breakthrough. Checking off yet another insanely-granular to-do list for a comic script, it struck me that I kept making the same lists, over and over again, each time changing only a few details; the work title, the publisher, the issue number, the page rate. The actual list of tasks (*Script scene 1, Revise scene 1, Polish scene 1, Script scene 2, Revise scene 2, Polish scene 2...*) was the same for every script. Not only that, but the non-writing elements of a project's status – whether I'd received pencilled pages from the artist, whether I'd looked them over and given notes, whether the artist had then followed up with inked pages – didn't fit neatly into a list of writing tasks. Some of them weren't even tasks, but merely things I needed to know.

Surely, I thought, there must be a way to keep track of all the 'draft/revise/polish' writing micro-tasks, *and* see things like whether artwork had been turned in or approved, at a glance without digging through list after list in my task manager? By then I was already using manila folders to keep all the documents related to a script – notes, outline, contract, art printouts – together in a single place. Every time I worked on a project, I would take that folder from my desk tray and keep it in front of me for reference…

Eureka.

I won't deny that I had a certain amount of trepidation about letting job sheets back into my world. I thought I'd left it all behind. Would they even work in such a different environment? Or was I just setting up another administrative tripwire for myself to fall over and unceremoniously discard in a months' time? Could it really be this simple?

Yes, it could. Job sheets, it turns out, are an invaluable tool for *anyone* working on multiple simultaneous projects, especially if you're struggling to stay organised. No matter what kind of work you do, if it involves creating several different things at once, you can benefit from using them. Remember we talked about off-loading tasks from your memory, back in Chapter 1? Job sheets achieve the same thing, but instead of tasks, you're off-loading *project status information.*

DOWNLOADABLE JOB SHEETS

You can download PDF versions of all the job sheets shown here from www.organised-writer.com, though I encourage you to make your own where possible, to better suit the way you work. Don't worry about making them look as 'designed' as mine; you're the only person who needs to see them.

Let me show you how they work. Here's an example of a standard 'short form' job sheet:

GRAPHIC NOVEL JOB SHEET

JOB INFORMATION

TITLE   **PUBLISHER**

FEE: **WFH/CO**   **CONTRACT?** ☐

1. Research …………….. ☐   2. Notes ………………… ☐

3. Plot ……………………. ☐   4. Breakdown ………… ☐

DRAFT

Dialogue ☐   **Panel descriptions** ☐   **Polish** ☐

PUBLICATION

Sent to Publisher ☐   **Invoiced** ☐   **Paid** ☐

DESIGN

Story Art ☐   **Cover Art** ☐   **Cover Design** ☐

Interior Design ☐   **Backmatter** ☐   **Uploaded** ☐

Archived ☐   **DATE PUBLISHED**

Figure 3.1   Example job sheet.

The above is my basic, single-work sheet for graphic novels. I have a pile of blanks already printed out; when I begin a new project I take one and fill in the details with a ballpoint.

Title, *Publisher*, and *Fee* are entered at the start. *WFH/CO* is *Work-for-Hire* or *Creator-owned*, a peculiarity of the comics industry that depends on the job, publisher, and contract. Speaking of which, *Contract?* can also hopefully be checked off right at the start... though not always, and if I'm still waiting for my copy to come through, an un-checked box here is a useful reminder to chase up whoever's responsible for that.

After I've filled in all the information I can, I tape the sheet to the front of the job's manila folder (if it doesn't yet have one, now's the time I take an empty folder and assign it to the project). Here's what a job sheet for a novel might look like when attached to its project folder. The sheet itself is very similar to that for a graphic novel, but you'll notice a few medium-specific changes.

Here we have *Title*, *Publisher*, and *Fee* again, but there's no *WFH/CO* box, and now there *is* a field to show which *Agent* is handling this book. The *Draft* section has different labels (I'll explain the 'zero draft' later), while the *Editorial* and *Payment* sections are specific to the book industry. Nevertheless, you can see the shared principles between the two job sheets, and those principles can be easily adapted to different media and working methods.

You may wonder why I don't tuck the job sheet inside the project folder, rather than taping it to the front. Isn't this all a bit... *analogue?* Well, yes. But attaching the job sheet to the front makes it unavoidable – not only *can* I see it when I pick up the project folder, I *will* see it. I don't need to open the folder, rifle through its contents, or try to remember where I put the job sheet. It's right there, every time, plain to see.

Making the job sheet unavoidable also increases the sense of off-loading. I don't ever panic and think, 'Wait, did I do

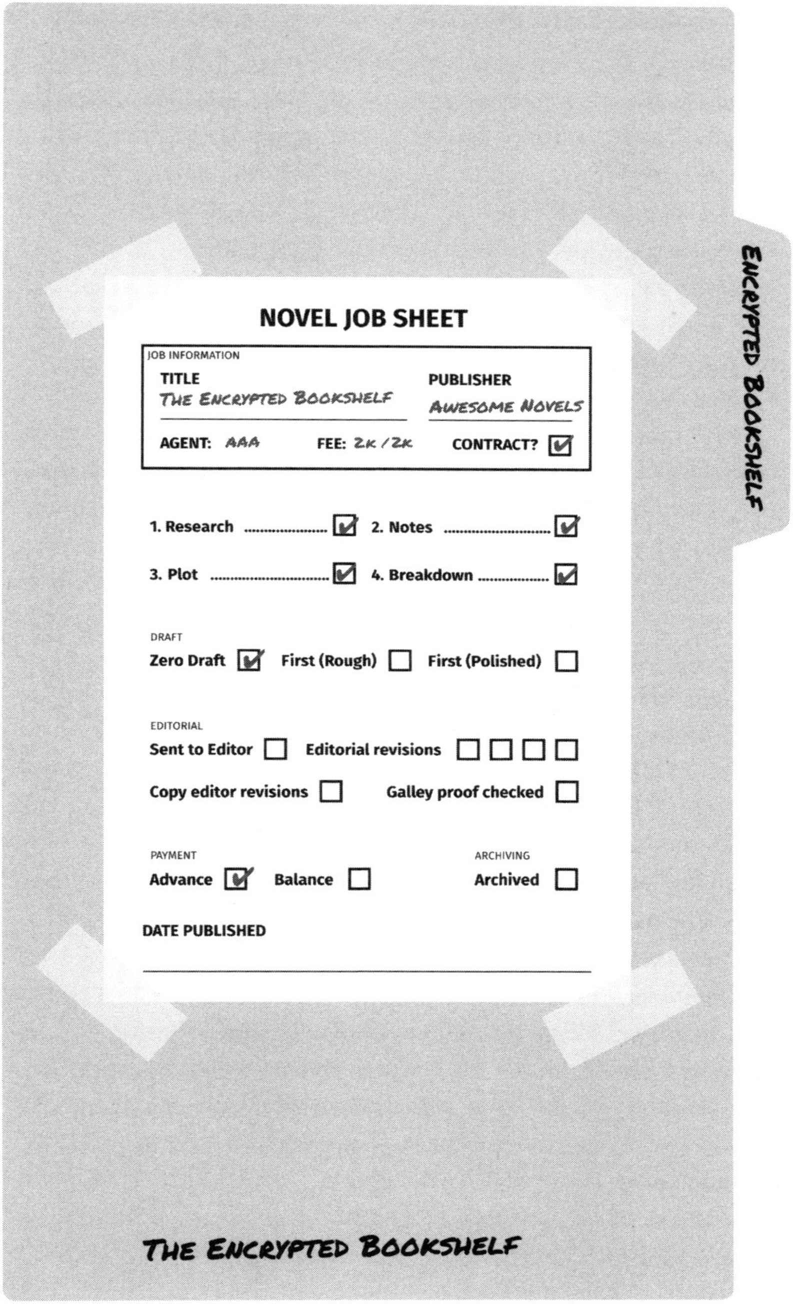

Figure 3.2 Example novel job sheet taped to a manila folder.

X on that job...?', because I only have to pick up the folder to immediately see the answer. I can therefore put a project aside for any length of time, confident that when I resume work I'll immediately know its status without having to memorise that information. It's difficult to understand how liberating this is until you try it for yourself.

How I record the project's status is where the remaining checkboxes come in. *Research*, *Notes*, *Plot*, and *Breakdown* are all stages of work before the 'real' writing begins. In truth, I don't ever really stop researching or making notes throughout a project, and the plot can certainly change as I write the script; the point of checking these off is to say to myself that I've done enough to begin writing. *Breakdown* is most relevant to comics and screenwriting, though other areas might also find it useful. In comics, because the medium is tied to the physical space of its pages, *Breakdown* means boiling down the plot to page-by-page elements until I know what will happen on each page, e.g. a scene may last five pages, but I'll break it down further to outline the beats that will take place on page 1, then on page 2, and so on. For a screenplay, it means breaking down the overall plot/treatment into individual scenes (and in TV it has a very specific meaning, but studio productions also have a much more formal way to track each project's progress than mere job sheets).

Next come checkboxes for each writing stage, which I tick off as I complete them. On the graphic novel sheet this includes things like *Dialogue*, *Panel descriptions*, *Polish* – when writing comics I make multiple passes for each element, in that order. When I check off *Polish*, the script is therefore ready to be turned in.

Thus we near the end, with elements like *Sent to Publisher*, *Invoiced*, and *Paid*. Most of the time I can check off *Sent to Publisher* and *Invoiced* at the same time, though that's not always possible. *Paid* is of course my favourite box to mark as complete.

The specifics of this part of the checklist will vary according to the type of work, and your contract, e.g. in the novel version you can see the single *Paid* box becomes two, *Advance* and *Balance*.

The final checkbox on every sheet is *Archived*. We'll deal with this in detail later, but you should have some form of archival system for everything related to the job (both physical and digital) to ensure the relevant work and documents are safely stored, and easy to retrieve in the future if necessary.

You'll have noticed there's also a *Design* checklist near the bottom of the graphic novel sheet. That's because I design many of my own books – which won't be relevant to most of you, and this is why I encourage you to make your own sheets. Not only is every medium different, but every writer works differently. Even besides things like design and breakdowns, a notable number of writers are also 'pantsers', those freaks of nature who never outline before beginning to write, and thus have no need for the *Plot* checkbox...

> **'THE TIMES THEY ARE A-CHANGIN''**
>
> When I first made these job sheets, the Archiving section had a *Disc burned* checkbox, because upon finishing a project I would burn a CD-ROM of the files and store all the discs on a shelf. Now I store everything on a networked media server. Who knows where they'll be in another ten years?

At the very bottom of the job sheet we have *Date Published*, which is entered only when the book hits shelves (that's also when I archive the files). Don't be tempted to write this out in advance – we all know how easily release dates can shift...!

You may think recording a publication date is frivolous, but I find it both pleasing and useful. Pleasing because, though it's easy to grow blasé about continued publication over time, I believe it's nevertheless always a date to mark. Isn't this why we write in the first place? It's also useful because there'll always be someone – publisher, lawyer, editor – who needs to know when a ten-year-old project was first released. A book will tell you the year, but for other projects (and a more precise answer) writing it here means you'll know exactly where to find it.

Illustrations of job sheets for other media, including screenplays and videogames, can be found in Appendix II. But now let's look at a rather different type of sheet.

COMIC SERIES

Graphic novels are all very well, but anyone who writes monthly comics or other serialised content will wonder how this works with a series. Do we tape a new sheet over the old one every time we write a new instalment?

Nothing so wasteful. Instead, I have a completely different style of job sheet for comic series:

TITLE	CAPTAIN WONDERFUL				PUBLISHER WONDERFUL COMICS			FEE $200/PAGE		WFH/CO	CONTRACT? ✓
ISSUE No.	1	2	3	4	5	6	7	8	9	10	
Research	✓	✓	✓	✓							
Notes	✓	✓	✓	✓							
Plotted	✓	✓	✓								
Page breakdown	✓	✓	✓								
Dialogue	✓	✓	✓								
Panel descriptions	✓	✓	✓								
Polish	✓	✓	✓								
Sent to publisher	✓	✓	✓								
Invoiced	✓	✓	✓								
Paid	✓	✓	✓								
DESIGN											
Story art	✓										
Cover art	✓	✓									
Cover design	✓	✓									
Interior design	✓										
Backmatter	✓	✓									
Uploaded	✓										
Archived	✓										
PUB. DATE	JUN 7										

Figure 3.3 Example job sheet for a comic series.

It may look more complex than the regular sheet, but it works on the same simple principle; I fill in project information when I begin, then check off work progress boxes as I go. It's simply laid out in repeating columns, one for each issue of the series, working from left to right. Think of it like a recording studio's mixing desk, which may seem bewildering until you realise each vertical strip is just an identical set of controls for a single track. This job sheet is even easier, because I simply start at the top and move down each column as I work through the stages of each issue.

In the example above, when I pick up the *Captain Wonderful* folder I can immediately see that all plotting and scripting up to issue #3 is finished (and I've been paid for it), while I've completed the research and notes for issue #4 but haven't yet plotted it (the *Plotted* box is unchecked). Thus, plotting issue #4 is the next action I need to take on this project. In the *Design* section, I can also see that issue #1 has gone to press, while #2 is awaiting the story artwork before the issue can be designed and uploaded to the publisher.

When I've plotted issue #4, I'll check off the *Plotted* box in that column and put the project folder back in my desk tray. Next time I pick up the folder to work some more on this project – no matter how far in the future that may be – I'll see that the next thing I need to do is a *Page Breakdown* for issue #4, i.e. the next unchecked box in that issue's column.

This sheet can track up to fifteen issues of a series, but what happens on a long-running series when I come to issue #16? That's when I remove the sheet, file it in the project folder, and replace it with a new one – starting at issue #16 – taped to the front of the folder. It doesn't happen frequently enough to be an annoyance.

Remember, while all of the job sheets you'll find in this book can be downloaded from *organised-writer.com*, I encourage you to make your own, suited to your projects and workflow. However you use them, I hope you'll find job sheets as useful and productivity-enhancing as I do.

Files and archives

There is only one type of file in the *Organised Writer* system, and there are only three possible locations where a file might reside; your desk trays, your filing drawer, or your archives. Setting up each of these locations is dealt with later in the book, but here I'll explain what they're for, and how to determine where a particular folder should be placed.

Right away, you're probably thinking a folder's location is connected to what's inside it, but it's not. Like I said: *only one type of file*.

That may sound absurd if you've spent your life trying to separate your work from your personal time, or grouping things by category so you know where to look for them.

But, speaking as someone who tried to organise his files along category lines for many years – often with spectacular incidents of failure – I don't believe it's a good approach. For a start, you're giving yourself more mental work to do before you can even file something. There you sit, document in hand, ready to file it away… but now you have to decide which category it belongs in, and where that category is located. Do your bank statements belong in your personal files, or business? Unless you have a separate account for work purposes, they could go in either. How about your credit card statement – never mind personal or business, does that get filed alongside your other banking documents… or is it part of the household budget? What category do receipts from the Post Office come under? How about your air miles? The bill for your broadband connection?

Even if these answers seem obvious now, will they still be obvious when you need to find an item three months down the line? Or will you go searching through all your files until it turns up, inevitably in the last place you look? That's what kept happening to me, until I realised categorisation simply wasn't saving me time, and was in fact increasing my level of stress. By trying to put things in arbitrary categories – and even separating those categories physically, in different filing drawers – I was just giving myself one more task to perform, one more thing to try (and invariably fail) to remember.

There is, however, one thing you'll never forget – something so natural, especially to a writer, that you may as well try and forget how to breathe.

The alphabet.

Every folder in my filing drawer and archives is therefore in alphabetical order. It doesn't matter if the folder is related to work, leisure, personal life, finance, writing jobs, legal matters, family, home... they all go in the same repository, in alphabetical order by contents. This makes filing, and later locating, anything absurdly easy. Want to know where your car documents are? They're under C, in your filing drawer. How about your receipts for work expenses? They're under R for Receipts, *in the same drawer*. Meanwhile, the contract for your decade-old book *Murder, She May Have Written* is with the project folder in your archives, under M. What's right next to it, in the same archive? Your mortgage records, of course.

Does this sound overly simplistic? Good. Its simplicity is why it works so well. Filing becomes completely intuitive when everything is placed in straightforward, permanent alphabetical order.

If the location of a folder has nothing to do with its contents (except its initial letter), how do we know in which of our three locations it belongs? How do we know whether to place, or look for, a folder in the desk trays, filing drawer, or archives?

We do that not by the folder's contents, but by its status.

Your desk trays contain everything that's current, or waiting to be dealt with; work projects in progress, receipts to be filed/recorded, cheques to be sent out, today's incoming mail, and so on. Are you working on a book at the moment? Its folder is in the desk tray, waiting to be worked on. Did your insurance documents just arrive in the mail? Put them in the desk tray until you have time to read and file them. Have you turned in a draft, and you're waiting to hear back from your editor? Pitched a book, but not yet had a response from the publisher? Returned from a trip with receipts you need to enter into expenses? Desk tray, desk tray, desk tray.

(No, they don't all go in the *same* desk tray, but we'll go over that later.)

Things that *have* been dealt with, and/or you need to access on a regular but occasional basis, belong in your filing drawer. The drawer is for files and records that aren't current or ongoing work, but you want to be easily accessible. This year's invoices and receipts (after they've been entered into accounts records), tax correspondence, bank statements, loyalty programs, car insurance documents, manuals and warranties for office equipment... and, in the case of writers, work files for projects to which you want easy access, such as notes and contracts for an ongoing series, or a book that's been published but whose PR cycle isn't complete. If you expect to refer to it more than once in the next year, it should live in the filing drawer.

Finally, the archives contain everything else; anything for which you need to keep records, but don't anticipate accessing more than once a year at most and perhaps even less. Finished work projects, long-term investments, old writing samples, your mortgage documents, the set-up instructions for your computer, your pet's registration records... you may never need to look at some of these things again, but you can't simply discard them. Into the archives they go.

Periodically, it's a good idea to go through your desk trays, and filing drawer, and make sure everything is still where it belongs. You may find a project folder in your desk tray that never went anywhere; take it out and put it in the filing drawer, or maybe even straight into the archives if you think it's truly dead and buried. If there are folders in your filing drawer that you realise you haven't touched in a year or two, take them out and put them in the archives. Ideally, you want as few as possible (but no fewer) files in your desk trays and filing drawer, to make locating what *is* in them easier. Of course, if your desk trays and filing drawer are both full to the brim with project folders in constant use, that's a good problem to have! But leaving folders you have no need to access in those places takes up space and slows you down.

FILING AND ARCHIVING YOUR ACCOUNTS

There is an exception to the 'one place, one alphabet' rule in your archives, and you won't be surprised to learn that it's related to your accounting and tax records.

This is partly for business and legal reasons: if you get audited, your accountant needs to know something, or you need to find a record for your bank... it pays to have your accounts easily at hand, and they're one of the few 'categories' that can be defined and separated easily enough so there's no confusion.

The other reason to make an exception for accounts is simple logistics. Your accounts, as a singular entity, consist of the contents of several filing folders – invoices, receipts, bank records, etc. – which should be combined in a single place for ease of reference. However, it's too much to hold in a single manila folder, and putting a rubber band around a bunch of folders to keep them together is hardly an elegant solution.

Accounts records for the current financial year – bank statements, invoices, receipts, tax correspondence, etc. – are kept in my filing drawer along with everything else, for ease of access. But at the end of each year, rather than place the manila folders in my archives, I transfer the documents from them into clear punched filing pockets, and place those inside a lever arch ring binder. I write the year-end date on the binder's spine label (e.g. *Accounts YE2019*), and store it with my other accounts on a bookshelf.

You may prefer to use a different kind of file binder, or label them in a different way, or store them in the attic. That's fine; the details don't matter. What matters is that *you* know, in an instant, where to find all your accounts and financial records for any given year, past or present.

Packing lists

Writers are not generally 'cool' people. We're bookworms, apt to spend (and probably *have* spent, over the years) more time reading a book than kicking a ball; we're often socially reticent, more likely to be found quietly occupying a corner of a party than busting moves in the centre of the crowd; and many of us are creatures of habit and routine, wanting everything just so in order to get our work done (Exhibit A: you're holding it).

But even writers have their limits, as I've discovered several times when sharing hotel rooms with colleagues. That limit is normally reached at the moment when they realise I'm ticking off boxes on a sheet of paper as I pack my suitcase, and they behold the true depths of nerdery revealed before them. The most common reaction is an audible sigh, a slow roll of the eyes, sometimes a quiet laugh. Then they get home and realise they left their iPhone charger plugged into the hotel's outlet. *Who's laughing now?*

Hello, everyone. My name's Antony, and I use packing lists.

Feels good to say it out loud, you know? Helps me own it. But I'm not here to try and wean myself off them. On the contrary, I'm going to convince you to use them, too.

Travelling can be stressful, and in Chapter 4 I'll explain some tricks and methods to significantly lessen that anxiety. While we're talking about files and lists, though, let's acknowledge that *packing* for travel can potentially make us more anxious than the journey itself. Do I have everything I need? Have I packed enough clothes? Oh, what about a book to read? Don't forget my charging cables from the lounge. And my spare razor. Toothpaste too. Will I need a tie? Oh, and pens. My wallet! Mustn't forget that. What else, what else… (Obviously I'm writing from a male perspective, but I have no doubt readers of other genders are familiar with the same experience as it relates to their own travel necessities.)

Why do we get uptight and forgetful when packing to travel? Because of the imminent and irreversible nature of setting off.

Once you're on that plane/train/boat, you can't easily turn around and come back for something you forgot. Plus, if you're anything like me, you're also paranoid about arriving late and missing that plane/train/boat altogether.

There are two stories I want to tell, here. The first is about why I use a packing list in the first place. Some years ago, my partner and I drove through the night to an old friend's house. At dawn the friend and I were going to meet some more friends, head to the airport, and fly abroad for his bachelor party while the bride-to-be and her friends, including my partner, celebrated at home. Everyone was going to have a great time.

Until, approximately 100 miles from home – and less than 50 from our destination – I suddenly realised I'd forgotten my passport.

Oh, did I mention that my partner was behind the wheel, because at the time I wasn't insured to drive? Let us now pause for a moment, so you may better imagine the subsequent invective to which I was justifiably subjected, and either wince in sympathy or nod in agreement according to your perspective.

Ever since that day I've used a packing list, and since then I've never forgotten my passport or anything else.

You may feel that you'd never forget something so important; that you don't need a packing list to remember what you should put in your suitcase. You may be right, but in my experience writers tend to be what we charitably call 'scatter-brained'. I'm willing to bet you can recall at least one occasion where you've arrived at your destination, only to realise you didn't bring something you should have… or returned home from a trip, only then realising you left something in the hotel. A packing list will ensure neither of those scenarios comes to pass.

But it's not only about ensuring you don't forget things; it's also about peace of mind. If you make a packing list and go through it every time – even for basic items like your wallet, passport, and travel tickets – then you can leave the house with the relaxed confidence of someone who knows they have everything they need. Not only that, but you'll know *as you pack* that this is the case.

A packing list can also allow, even encourage, you to pack light. I've been a 'one bag' advocate for some years, travelling with nothing more than carry-on luggage wherever possible. I regularly spend a week or more abroad with just a single bag. And lest you think I spend the entire time in shorts and sandals, many of those trips are either to work somewhere on-site or to attend a convention, both of which call for a certain level of dress. The longest occasion where I've gone carry-on only was a ten-day trip to the USA, including four days of public appearances at a comic convention. So it can be done… but *why?*

Here's the second story. I was travelling to San Francisco for a comic convention, at the behest of a videogame company for which I'd written a tie-in comic. The comic's artist and I were to spend the weekend undertaking promotional activities for the game publisher, such as signing at their convention booth and appearing at a popular local comic store. I packed everything I'd need, including two suits for appearances, in my checked suitcase. My small carry-on backpack was thus as light as a traveller's dream, containing only essentials like my wallet, boarding pass, and a book to read.

Twelve hours later I touched down in San Francisco… but my luggage did not. I wasn't alone, either; twenty more passengers on that flight were missing baggage, all of us duly informed at the airline desk that it was still in London. To their credit, the airline gave us compensatory toiletry bags, a sleep shirt, and a few dollars.

I should add that this was the fifth instance in two years of my luggage being delayed – five out of ten flights, in fact. But the other delays had all been on the return journey, and while that's still annoying, waiting a day or two for your suitcase to be delivered to your home isn't quite the emergency of landing without luggage in a foreign country where you're expected to make public appearances.

I immediately spent the money the airline gave me on fresh underwear and assumed my luggage would follow me to San Francisco overnight... but it didn't. In fact it didn't arrive until two-and-a-half days later, by which time I'd spent quite a bit of money in order to avoid living, and making those public appearances, in the same clothes for days on end. By the time I finally laid eyes on my suitcase, the convention was half-over.

There had to be a better way. Surely it must be possible to travel without subjecting myself to what were starting to feel like guaranteed delays and frustration whenever I checked baggage?

I returned home and immediately began searching online, where I found Doug Dyment's revelatory website *OneBag.com*. The site is devoted to the art of packing and travelling light, and I won't repeat Dyment's extensive advice here; I urge you to read it for yourself, and give the One Bag method a try. I did, and the results speak for themselves. Now I can check in later; if a flight is cancelled, I don't worry where my luggage is; and after clearing customs I walk straight past everyone waiting at the carousel, always first in line for a cab. I do all this while carrying everything I need for a week abroad in a single bag slung over my shoulder. *Life-changing* is a strong and oft overused phrase, but I wouldn't hesitate to say that learning how to travel carry-on only has changed my life immeasurably.

It all takes some effort and expense, of course. You may need to purchase a new bag, and you'll probably want to buy duplicates of your toiletries, but if you travel a lot it's worth it. When I dedicated myself to travelling light, I spent around £400 on new and improved kit in the first year – but I've hardly had to open my wallet since, as the gear in question has lasted me more than a decade of frequent travelling. Would you be willing to pay £40 per year to guarantee your luggage was never lost or delayed? To me, that's a no-brainer.

Finally – and this is how I'm able to travel with just a carry-on in the first place – a packing list doesn't merely ensure you *do* take everything you should. It also ensures you *don't* take things you shouldn't.

Studies have shown that if you go grocery shopping without making a list beforehand, you're more likely to overspend. You'll buy things on impulse, whether or not you really need them *(Ooh, this item's on special offer! Mmm, that bakery sure smells good!)* and you're also likely to leave without having bought everything you came for in the first place. By contrast, if you make a list beforehand then you're more likely to buy everything you require, stay within your budget, and refrain from unnecessary purchases.

Packing lists can work in the same way. If you only pack what's on your list, you know with absolute certainty that you have everything you need... and not an item more. The purpose is to travel light, not cram everything you own into a single bag.

The first step is to write a 'master packing list' which contains everything you might possibly need for any kind of trip, but no more – so that if necessary you could pack everything on your master list into a single bag. Being able to do that is in itself a great achievement, but here's the twist: before each trip, *remove* any items from the list that you won't need on the specific journey you're about to take.

For example, my master list includes my laptop and its charging cables. But if I'm going on a trip where I know I won't need my computer, I can strike both the laptop and cables from the list, leaving them unpacked – which frees up space and weight in my bag. In another example, I sometimes take a washing line and soap leaves, to launder my underwear in the hotel room. But if I'm only going away for a few days, or I know the hotel has a good laundry service I can use, I won't bother packing the laundry kit.

The crucial thing to remember is that if you take something off the list in this way, *you cannot replace it with something else* just because you now have space! Revel instead in how light, roomy, and easy to carry your bag is.

MASTER PACKING LIST

FOR FLIGHTS:
CLEAR LIQUIDS BAG
☐ Shaving gel
☐ Shower gel
☐ Toothpaste
☐ Cologne

CARRY-ON BAG
☐ ZIP POCKET
 ☐ Passport
 ☐ Travel tickets

☐ UNDERCLOTHES
 ☐ Socks
 ☐ Boxers

☐ CLOTHES
 ☐ Shirts
 ☐ T-shirts
 ☐ Spare jeans

☐ TOILETRIES
 ☐ Toothbrush
 ☐ Shaving razor
 ☐ Deoderant (solid)
 ☐ Tweezers + clippers

☐ MISC (in a packing cube)
 ☐ Ziplocs + carabiners
 ☐ Clothes line + soap leaves
 ☐ Folding hangers
 ☐ Cufflinks + collar points

☐ MISC (loose)
 ☐ Travel tray
 ☐ Laptop
 ☐ Deck shoes

SMALL BACKPACK
☐ Tablet
☐ Notebook + pen
☐ Headphones
☐ Business cards
☐ USB thumb drive
☐ Mobile charging cable
☐ Laptop charging cable
☐ Presentation clicker
  & projector cables

POCKETS
☐ Phone
☐ Travel mints
☐ Wallet
 ☐ Credit cards
 ☐ Driver's licence
 ☐ Cash

Figure 3.4 Master packing list.

(Well, there's one exception: by all means take an extra book to read. Everyone knows books don't count.)

To conclude this section, I present my own master packing list. Yours will be different according to your needs and circumstances, but my example will give you an idea of how to build a list for yourself. To use it, tick each check box with a single line as you pack the item in question; when packing to return from your destination, tick again in the opposite direction, to make an 'X'.

Summary

OVERALL:
- Take a notebook with you everywhere, and use it to record every thought or idea you have, to take advantage of 'systemic memory'.

NOTEBOOK:
- Make notes immediately when a thought comes to you, or as soon as it is safe/convenient; don't rely on your memory.
    - Don't self-censor; no matter how inconsequential, write it down.
    - Title and date all notes where relevant to an existing project.
- Note non-writing thoughts and tasks too.
- Your phone or computer are acceptable substitutes, as long as your notes all sync.

TRANSCRIBE:
- Type up notes as soon as convenient, along with new thoughts as you transcribe.
    - Re-type phone/computer notes, too; don't just copy and paste.

- Transfer non-writing notes to a calendar or task manager as soon as possible.

LISTS:
- Write a master packing list for travel.
  - Strike out items that you don't need on specific trips.
  - Don't replace struck items with new ones, unless it's a book.
  - Make job sheets for your typical work projects.

FILING:
- Everything goes in one of three places:
  1. desk tray, for current matters;
  2. filing cabinet, for matters dealt with but ongoing; file alphabetically;
  3. archive boxes, for permanent storage; file alphabetically.
- The exception is accounts; at the end of each year, the previous year's accounts should be archived together, separate from your other accounts, for easy access.

PART II

Write!

CHAPTER 4

Five pages after breakfast

(×) A *disorganised writer* works when the mood strikes them or they can snatch a few minutes, for however long they feel like it, with no routine or schedule.

(✓) *The organised writer* works every day at the same time, in the same place, and writes to a daily quota no matter how long it takes.

We've all been there; you sit at your computer in the morning, check your email, look at Twitter, open your current writing document, sigh, refresh your Facebook feed and answer some private messages, switch back to the writing document, sigh, make a phone call, check your email again, and when you look up it's suddenly 4pm and you've hardly got any work done. You race to hammer out a few words, which is like pulling teeth, complete a quarter of the work you actually wanted to achieve today, and spend the rest of the evening full of self-directed anger and guilt, beating yourself up for being a lazy arse as a seemingly-impossible deadline looms ever closer.

I've done it, you've done it, we've all done it. There just aren't enough hours in the day.

Actually, there are. Thus far I've talked about organising all the things that *support* your writing; notes, lists, schedule, and so on. Frankly, that's where most writers need help. The act of writing is highly personal, not to mention personalised, and we all work in our own way. Some of us are daydreamers, staring out the window for an hour before we then burst through two hours of solid writing; some of us are grinders, fingers never straying from the keyboard even when it takes five minutes to write one sentence; some of us need to get up and walk around to figure out solutions to problems; some of us even talk to the duck.

> **TALK TO THE DUCK**
>
> This is a term from the world of computer programming which describes figuring out a solution by explaining the problem to someone else. Doing so clarifies the situation in your mind enough that by the time you've finished outlining it, more often than not you've also realised how you can solve it. Because the listener doesn't actually need to talk back, coders who can't easily pull a colleague aside will instead explain the problem to an inanimate object... like a rubber duck.

The point is that many of us have been writing for a long time, and if we had nothing else to do in the world we'd probably be fine. But we *do* have other things to take care of, and so we need to balance the worlds of writing, admin, and personal life without running out of time every day. You may think achieving this will be a complicated juggling act, but the *Organised Writer* method is actually very simple, relying on a single fundamental rule:

> *Every day I write five pages before I do anything else, no matter how long it takes.*

'Before I do anything else' isn't literally true. I've woken up, brushed my teeth, had some breakfast, walked my dogs, and made coffee. What I *haven't* done is read my email, checked Twitter, gone on Facebook, opened the post, looked at my to-do list, or anything else that would require me to think about the world beyond my office walls.

Humans are a social, community-driven species. We have a congenital need and desire to communicate with others, and modern technology makes doing so quicker and easier than ever before. I firmly believe that's a net good for humanity, but it presents real challenges. When we receive an email or text message, when someone posts on our Facebook wall, when we see a conversation about a subject on which we have an opinion, when someone messages us on Twitter... whatever it may be, when faced with these prompts, we experience an overwhelming urge to respond. That urge leaps to the top of our consciousness, occupying a significant part of our mind until it's dealt with. If we *don't* deal with it, it doesn't go away; instead the urge remains, constantly calling to us as our distracted mind begins composing a reply. We can't help it, and it's particularly frustrating for writers because of our need for long periods of focus and a clean mind.

When I first began to analyse my own behaviour, I realised that checking email and social media first thing in the morning wasn't itself an urge – it was a *habit* I'd picked up at some point, and talking to other writers I discovered it's an extremely common one. The received wisdom seems to be that we should 'deal with the internet' before writing, especially if we have friends and colleagues in different locations and time zones. But all too often this approach means we spend all day answering emails, leaving almost no time to actually write.

After some thought, I determined that changing a habit would be easier than resisting an urge, and that if I could somehow change this particular habit it might help me achieve a clean mind. The question was how I should go about it.

When I realised the answer, its simplicity seemed almost too good to be true: *we already have a clean mind when we wake up every morning*. There's a reason we say 'Sleep on it', after all. When we wake it's easier to push yesterday's concerns aside, into the mental file marked 'History', and look at them in a new light. Each day we start afresh, able to approach today's concerns uninhibited by yesterday's anxieties.

So what if we *don't* approach today's concerns? What if we don't even think about them until we've finished writing for the day?

Words, not time

If you already have a clean mind every morning when you wake, the aim is then surely to keep it that way for as long as possible. This means isolating yourself from the real world, allowing your imagination to roam free and write without being 'polluted' by concerns about all the real-world things you'll have to deal with today.

(I'm talking of course about work-related concerns such as phone calls, emails, and social media presence. If you have dependants or other commitments, of course you must deal with them before you can begin work – get the children to school, feed the cat, drive your partner to the train station. But those tasks aren't the kind that will nag at you throughout the day. Once completed, you can forget about them and begin writing.)

With a clean mind, staying focused is easy while your fingers are flying across the keyboard. But what happens when you pause? Very few writers sit down, start typing, and don't stop even for a moment. Daydreaming, pausing while you construct the perfect (or maybe just *good enough*, nothing wrong with that) line in your mind, scribbling down a note about a later section of your story that just came to you… these are all essential parts of the writing process. There's also physical wellness to consider; in recent years studies all over the world have shown that sitting in a chair and staring at a brightly lit LCD screen for hours at a time without interruption isn't the healthiest thing for your body or eyesight. You need to get up, stretch, walk around a little. Even if you're someone who works at a standing desk, you should still take screen breaks every so often. Fix yourself a coffee, brew yourself a tea, fuss your dog for a moment.

But whatever you do when you pause, *do not* succumb to the temptation of your phone; when you notice a plot hole and gaze out of the window to come up with a fix, *do not* 'quickly check your email'; when your fingers lift from the keyboard because you're unhappy with the sentence you just wrote, *do not* 'hop on Facebook for a minute'. This is even the one time of your day when you shouldn't read a book. Don't do *anything* else that would occupy the part of your mind devoted to writing. Instead, stay in the zone and let your mind relax. You might be surprised at what two minutes away from the computer to make coffee can achieve for your story – but only if you don't let yourself be distracted by the real world.

There's a probably-apocryphal tale in Hollywood about a well-known screenwriter who takes a shower every time he feels stuck on a script. Whatever the problem, the solution inevitably comes to him while standing under the shower head, at which point he dresses and returns to writing. As a result (and this is the probably apocryphal part) he takes up to a dozen showers every day.

It's almost certainly not true, but the principle is sound. We really do relax when we're not staring at the page. Taking a shower, playing with the kids, cooking dinner... when we do these things, story problems tick over quietly at the back of our minds, unfettered by stress. Is it so surprising that an answer will then suddenly form, jolting us into action as we instinctively lunge for a notebook?

In fact, there's nothing 'sudden' about it. It's a process that takes time, like any other. The difference is that much of that time passes in the background, while we're consciously occupied with other things.

Some writers avoid distraction during breaks by shutting off their internet access completely – there are system plug-ins that will suspend your wi-fi connection according to a schedule, and others that prevent you from opening certain apps at certain times. For example, you could program one of these apps to completely shut off your internet access between 10am and 2pm.

Or you might set one to allow you web access, but prevent your email program from opening. I know one writer who employs a very low-tech solution; he sets a timer for his work hours, and simply guilt-trips himself into not going online until the timer runs out. That requires a very high level of self-control, but if you can achieve it there's no simpler method.

There are ways to get around all of these solutions. The only way to truly prevent yourself from all temptation is to shut yourself in a room with no computer (or, at least, a computer that isn't online) and refuse to leave until you've finished work for the day. Believe it or not, I know several writers who effectively do this – they each rent a small, cheap office with no internet access, containing little more than a chair, desk, landline phone, and filing cabinet. Every morning they enter with their laptop, sit down, shut the door, and begin writing. They pause for lunch, then return to work for the afternoon, and finally leave at the end of the day. That these people are also some of the most prolific writers I know is surely no coincidence, but simply shutting yourself away from the world isn't desirable or even possible for everyone.

Not all of us can or want to forego internet access completely. Many of my stories feature technology, scientific concepts, and global (sometimes even extraplanetary) locations, and I therefore do a lot of online reference checking. How do I avoid the temptation to check my email, or go on social media? Well, for a start I don't leave those things open in web browser tabs, or in their own applications. Sure, I could open my email with a couple of clicks or keystrokes – but the very act of doing so is deliberate, and enough to remind me that I shouldn't. So even if you open your email without really thinking, the appearance of the inbox in front of your eyes is enough to make you realise what you've done. At that point it's up to you to have the discipline, and be devoted enough to improving your working practices, to immediately close it again. It's easier said than done, I know, but if you do it enough times you'll eventually stop clicking the icon in the first place.

Finally, while it's impractical not to have a phone nearby in case of emergency, try to avoid using it. Don't schedule calls before lunch where possible, and if someone calls you unexpectedly, unless you *know* it's an urgent call, let it go to voicemail. You're a writer, not a heart surgeon – how many phone calls and emails do you get that can't wait a few hours?

> ### 'DO NOT DISTURB'
>
> Most modern smartphones come with a 'do not disturb' feature that suppresses calls and message notifications according to a definable schedule. Many people naturally set this up to activate during the night while they sleep, but you can just as easily have it set during the daytime, too. My phone's DND schedule runs every day from late evening all through the night, then continues in the morning until lunchtime.

Writing with a clean mind and distraction avoidance should become part of your daily routine, as commonplace as brushing your teeth. Working this way will allow you to finish your daily writing quota, however long it takes.

LET'S TALK ABOUT TIME

'However long it takes' is an essential part of this system. Not only should you start work immediately after breakfast, and refuse to be distracted, but you must keep working until you've achieved your daily writing quota. On a good day, that could take as little as ninety minutes. I've done that before now – not often, to be sure! But when you're on a roll, feeling good, and the words come easy, it's definitely achievable. By contrast, I've also had days where it takes eight hours of agony and sweating blood just to crank out a bunch of words that I'd rather throw in the bin. I expect you have, too.

Most days are somewhere in between. This isn't a nine-to-five gig, and it's a rare writer who can predict how long their working day will be with any accuracy. But however long it takes, you must keep writing until you've reached that daily quota; the page or word count you agreed with yourself before you began. Renege on that agreement at your peril, because achieving your quota is what allows the remainder of the system to fall into place. If you take nothing else from these pages, I promise you, focus on finishing your daily writing quota before you do anything else and you will see a benefit.

Now we come to the big question: what *is* your daily quota?

THAT'S WHAT 'MINIMUM' MEANS

The 'five pages' quota works best when writing scripts; graphic novels, screenplays, stage plays, etc. Those script types are formalised enough that five pages is a quantifiable metric of work. That used to be the case for novelists too, back in the days of typewritten manuscripts. But these days, unless you're writing directly into a word-processing document in double-spaced 12pt Courier, 'five pages' is meaningless when it comes to prose. Five pages of single-spaced 10pt Times New Roman in an A4 Word document will look and feel very different to the same amount of work set as 1.5×-spaced 16pt Georgia in a scrolling Scrivener window. (No prizes for guessing which of those your humble author is faced with at this moment.)

Even with these caveats, you must find the quota that suits you. While five pages per day is almost a standard in scriptwriting, you might realistically only be able to manage four… or, in order to meet a deadline, perhaps you *have* to produce at least eight. On the other hand, with novels my quota is 1,500 *words* per day – lower than some authors, to be sure, but enough to write a novel in two to three months so long as I meet the quota minimum every day.

Wait, back up a second. 'Minimum'?

Ah, yes. That's the little secret I haven't mentioned before now; that whatever daily writing quota you set yourself – five pages, 1,500 words, whatever – is your *minimum*. Every day, you have to write five pages. And if you *only* write five pages every day, that's great! The point of a quota is that, so long as you meet it, everything is going well. But what if you're on a roll? What if you hit five pages inside ninety minutes, but you're still in the zone and you want to keep going?

Simple: you keep going. When you're flowing, don't try to stop it. There's no better feeling than when you're *into it* and you enter that fugue state of pounding out words, until you look up and realise you've been sat at your desk for four hours and written a dozen pages. It doesn't happen often, as most of us know all too well, so relish it when it does. Let the flow carry you along, and allow yourself to be delighted at your productivity.

But tomorrow, you still have to write another five pages.

That's the catch – exceeding your quota today doesn't change how much you work tomorrow. Your word count doesn't magically roll over. Every day, you start with a clean mind... *and* a clean page count. Note also that continuing to write because you're on a roll is not the same thing as *re*-starting work after you've already stopped to go through the day's email, admin, etc. Restarting in this way is rarely a good idea.

Something you'll need to address is whether your five pages will be all new work, or revisions of an existing draft. This depends on your working speed, deadlines, and the requirements of each project.

When scriptwriting, I work in a very iterative manner; I throw down the skeleton of a whole script, then go over it to put some flesh on the bones, then I go over it *again* for a final spit and polish (for a more detailed explanation of this process, see Chapter 5). However, I also know I can fairly reliably get my five pages done before lunchtime; so I tend to focus entirely on making my daily five pages new work, then use some of my 'afternoon time' to revise, flesh out, and polish previous rough drafts. If you work more slowly, and regularly have little or no time remaining in the day after writing your five pages, it makes more sense to arrange your schedule to spend some of your primary writing time on those revisions.

That's what I do when I'm revising a novel – even though I use the same iterative process, it takes me most of a day to hit my quota in the first place. So I block out a week or more of primary writing time, after the draft is finished, to carry out manuscript revisions. That said, I have novelist friends who happily work on the new draft of book #1 in the morning, break for lunch, then revise book #2 in the afternoon. If you're capable of that and it's comfortable, go ahead.

No matter how you approach this issue, one important thing you should do – and which will help you make this decision, once you begin practising it – is increase your daily writing quota for revisions. By how much is another decision only you can make. When I'm fleshing out/polishing a script, I expect to get at least ten pages completed per day. With prose revision, it's a minimum of 4,000 words. That may sound like a lot, but remember, this is all *re*writing; the hardest part, initial creation, is done. There's no reason your rewriting shouldn't go at twice the speed, or even faster on a good day.

Like your quota, the question of what counts as revision, rewriting, or proofreading is one that can only be answered with time and experience of your own working habits. As you continue your journey toward becoming an *Organised Writer*, that answer – and thus, where such tasks fall in your schedule – will become easier to determine.

WHAT DO YOU DO AFTER YOUR DAILY WRITING?

You've written your five pages, maybe six or seven because you were in the zone, and it's only 1pm. That's a great day's work – but what now?

First, take a short break. You've earned it, and you can feel pretty good about yourself – something that, let's be honest, doesn't happen every day. Let yourself bask in that warm glow while you get refreshments, maybe eat some lunch. Then return to your desk and commence work on other tasks, secure in the knowledge that you've done all the writing you needed to complete today. That knowledge is vitally important, because it's what helps you relax throughout the rest of the day. If you're trying to do revisions, or proofread a manuscript, or file your receipts, or call a client – and all the time, at the back of your mind, you know you haven't written enough today – you'll be constantly distracted. You'll feel bad for not having done the work, you won't be able to concentrate as fully on those other tasks as you should, and at the end of the day you'll feel like a failure. On the other hand, if you *have* done all your day's work you'll feel light as a cloud, because you know you don't need to write any more until tomorrow. The feeling of accomplishment and confidence this imbues in a writer is (ironically) impossible to describe unless you've experienced it. But if you have, you know what I'm talking about. Feels great, doesn't it? Now imagine feeling like that every day.

Some of the work you do after finishing your daily quota will inevitably also be writing, or 'writing-adjacent'; revising, polishing, proofreading, copy editing, outlining, reading for research. Other tasks will be non-adjacent administration; reading and answering emails, making phone calls, invoicing, and so on. Yet others will be more nebulous, such as checking social media, doing a little online PR, writing blog posts, being interviewed. These tasks are all important, but none of them should take priority over achieving that daily writing quota. That's your raison d'être.

On an ideal day, this is the order in which I structure things:

1. Daily writing quota
2. Emails and phone calls
3. Writing-adjacent revisions/outlining/research/etc.
4. Filing, invoicing, office admin
5. Social media, PR

You may prefer to order the non-writing work differently, but this is how I like to tackle it. If I have revisions or proofreading to do, the email and phone calls give me a break between that work and my daily writing quota; and leaving social media until last means that if I lose track of time, sucked into the daily vortex of Twitter, Facebook, et al., it's okay, because I'm not using up time that should be spent on other tasks awaiting completion.

Finally, after all that's been done, you may find yourself with free time left in the day – even if you don't complete your daily writing quota in a couple of hours, you might still be surprised at how quickly you *can* get it done. The point of attacking the day's writing before anything else is to help you achieve focus, and by doing that you'll write more efficiently, which in turn means you'll finish the work more quickly. This isn't theoretical; it's how the system is designed to work. By the time your office-working friends are just getting their second coffee of the day, you might have finished your day's writing and be ready to deal with emails and phone calls instead. Even on a slow day, it's not often I need to continue past mid-afternoon to make my quota – though *not often* is very different to *never…!*

So then what? You've done your five pages. You've answered emails, made some calls, filed your documents, checked Twitter, and it's still only 3pm. What now?

A RADICAL IDEA: TAKE SOME TIME OFF

If you find yourself with truly 'spare time' at the end of the day, go and enjoy yourself. Read a book; watch a movie; take a walk in the park; play a videogame; join your spouse for the school run. Go and do *something that isn't your job* for a while. You might be tempted to spend any spare time after finishing admin diving back into your manuscript, but outside of exceptional circumstances I advise against it. Your mind is now in a different, and likely non-creative, place compared to this morning and if you try to get back into the draft you're more likely to spin your wheels than be productive. That's a waste of time, and will just make you feel down again. Instead, recharge your batteries with some guilt-free leisure time, secure in the knowledge that you had a productive day. When you return to your desk in the morning you'll have already built up some mental momentum overnight, and will be itching to start typing all over again.

In the meantime, get a good night's sleep – and you may find that comes easier, too. Something that separates (most) creatives from (most) other people is what keeps us awake at night. Most people worry about redecorating the kitchen, or a sudden strange clunking noise in the car, or why their boss gave them *that look* earlier. While creative people aren't immune to those worries, more often what keeps us up at night is a feeling of guilt that we either didn't get enough work done today, or the work we did was no good. I can't help you with the latter (except to say that, as any experienced writer knows, chances are when you read it back you'll find it's much better than you remember) but I can help with the former.

The beauty of having a writing quota you complete every day is that, by definition, you *know* you've done enough. You made that calculation before you even began the project – worked out what daily minimum you needed to achieve, in order to complete the work on time – and now you're in the thick of it, you must trust your past self. Trust that when you made that calculation you did so with clear eyes, and if you stick to the plan you made, no matter how dissatisfied you may currently be with the work, you'll eventually reach the other side and everything will be okay. Because if you hit your daily writing quota every day, you'll also hit your deadlines.

Doubtless you have questions about this method. Let's address some of them.

Q: What if I'm not actually writing a draft right now? What if I'm outlining, or doing intensive research?

There are two possible ways to handle this. One is to write five pages of one project in the morning, then spend your afternoon working on the outline or plot of a second project. If you have the energy and impetus to do this, it's a good way of using your clean mind to focus on the heavy lifting of a draft while still spending some of your additional time preparing for a different project. Try to keep some time at the end of your day for non-writing tasks, though; much as you might love to spend all day doing nothing but writing, too many days like that risks letting everything else pile up. That's exactly what you want to avoid.

The preferred option, if you have the time, is to follow the same practice as writing your manuscript – get up, go straight to work with a clean mind – but work on your outline *instead* of a manuscript, with a similar quota. Measuring quotas for outlines is difficult, especially if you're working longhand rather than on a computer, so you just have to use and trust your own judgement. If you're honest with yourself, you'll know when you've made good progress on an outline and have run out of steam for the day. That's when you can down tools and take a break, before turning to other tasks. In any case, a good rule of thumb is to stop working on your outline/research/etc. at least an hour before you'd normally finish for the day. That should be enough time to quickly deal with your email and a small amount of admin.

Q: You talk about writing first thing in the morning, but I'm not a morning person. I'm not even awake til noon.

It doesn't actually matter what time you get up. Some people think you have to be an early riser to adopt this method, but I disagree. It *is* true that if you wake up at noon, then by the time you've rolled out of the bathroom and pulled on some clothes your inbox will be even more full than it was earlier, and you may have missed some phone calls to boot. But if you implement the system in full you won't be answering emails or phone calls until you've written your daily minimum anyway, so that doesn't matter. The main advantage to being an early riser is that you can write for several hours before everyone who works in an office gets to their desk and starts hassling you.

(I've long believed this is a big part of why so many British comic book writers are successful in the US. Cultural factors aside, the time zone difference means we don't have to get up at the crack of dawn to carve out valuable hours of uninterrupted work time.) You should also consider your age, however. You're most alert in the hours immediately after waking, and as you grow older you'll find it increasingly difficult to maintain that alertness into the evening (everyone over 40, raise your hand. Now do it without yawning). The later in the day you begin work, the harder you may find it to sustain focus and momentum.

Q: I have a day job, and the only time I can find to write is in the evenings.

First, you need to ask yourself – is that true? Or do you just not relish the thought of waking up at 5am to write for a couple of hours before heading out to the day job? Many successful writers wrote their early works doing just that, and while success is never guaranteed, I don't think it's any coincidence that the practice is so common.

But if that's definitely not you – if there's an insurmountable reason you can't make time to write until after you've finished a day job – my advice is to unwind somehow on the way home from work, then establish a writing routine at home that you stick to like clockwork.

Unwinding can mean a number of things. It might be as simple as reading a novel on the train or bus; listening to music or a podcast in your car; even a quick gym or sports session on the way home. Do something completely unconnected to your day job, to mark a transition from that part of your day and put those concerns aside. If you write after work, achieving a truly clean mind will be almost impossible, but mentally separating yourself from the day job can be a big step towards it. It's then vital to establish a routine; like your writing environment, it's part of shifting yourself into 'work mode'. If you sit down at your desk at the same time every day and write, your body and mind will come to associate writing with that time and place, making it easier to adopt the right mindset each time you do so.

This isn't so different from the routine a full-time writer should also try to establish, excepting the need to carry it out at the end of a day rather than at the start. The main difference for anyone with a day job is time, and how to handle the lack of it. When there are other factors relying on you getting a good night's sleep (such as performing well at your day job so you can continue to earn a living) it probably isn't feasible for you to work to a word count, rather than for a set amount of time. That's not ideal, but remember the mathematics we did in Chapter 2; even if you only write 500 words a day, so long as you do it every day, you'll finish a novel inside a year. Writers write; I'm confident you'll find a way.

Q: My agent/publisher/client set a call for 10am and I can't get out of it.

Then don't. Always try to schedule calls for the afternoon if you can – giving yourself time to work uninterrupted and finish your daily writing quota before you need concern yourself with the outside world – but when that's simply not possible, don't beat yourself up. Sometimes these things are out of our control.

Very occasionally, when non-writing tasks are piling up or I know I have a dozen lengthy emails and calls to make, I'll forego my daily writing altogether and instead block out an 'admin day' to deal with as many non-writing tasks as possible. I group all the phone calls I can into that day, and any time not spent on the phone is devoted to answering overdue emails, replying to correspondence, filing records that should have been dealt with a few days ago, and so on.

If you're not in a position to make a call part of an 'admin day' like this, don't worry. Take the call, make your notes, add any necessary items to your calendar and task manager, then put them out of your mind and return to writing. Remember, your notebook, calendar, and task manager are where you offload things so your mind can be clear while you write. Trust the system, and get back to work.

Just write

What happens if the words simply aren't coming? What if you get up first thing in the morning, avoid all distractions, sit at your desk with a clean mind, commit to the work... but nothing comes out? What happens when you get *writer's block*?

Many years ago, as an enthusiastic user of the then-new writing software Scrivener, I participated in the developer's online forum where people could report bugs in the early versions, troubleshoot for each other, discuss our writing, and so on. At first the forum was sparsely populated, but as Scrivener became increasingly popular more and more people joined. Perhaps inevitably, some were very keen to tell everyone else how to go about their work – whether or not anyone had bothered to ask them.

One such user began a discussion insisting the only work worthy of consideration was that which came flowing unbidden from the muse, and anything else was mere hackery. If you weren't *inspired* to write, this person said, there was no point even sitting at your desk. Better to wait until you received a visit from Calliope, lest you produce something unworthy.

It will no doubt amaze you to learn this person had never written a book of their own. But when they did, well, it would surely be... *inspired*. It will probably amaze you less to hear that the published writers on the forum debated this point with some vigour. Everyone's response was naturally different, but centred around a single piece of hard-won knowledge: that true inspiration is rare, and to be a writer – especially one who makes their living from it – you must learn to write even on the days when you feel no inspiration whatsoever. Which will be most of them.

The original poster argued back and even 'doubled down' on their argument. How could anything written *without* inspiration possibly be called Art? What was the point of writing anything inspired more by deadlines than the pure desire to simply create?

What they overlooked – what they couldn't see, in their perhaps well-meaning naivety – was the importance of revision and experience in the writing process. Rare indeed is the classic work that didn't go through several drafts before it attained the form in which we now call it Art, and aspiring writers who think works of genius spring fully formed from the author's head are in for a rude awakening when they begin their own masterpiece. Sadly, before any of us could articulate this properly the discussion had devolved into a shouting match. I made one last post, summarising my own feelings:

> File under 'hard truths': the creative muse is a fiction. If you sit around waiting for the right moment to create, you will die waiting.

A touch melodramatic, perhaps, but true all the same. I retired from the discussion and thought nothing more of it... until I began seeing those words quoted online by people whom I didn't know, and who certainly had no idea who I was beyond the quote's attribution. I soon realised my words had somehow found their way into the strange realm of *online inspirational quotes*, and they now follow me (or rather my vanity searches on Google and Twitter; don't judge me, we all do it) around the internet like a dogged hound. When all is said and done, I suspect this quotation may be the sole thing I'm remembered for, which is a bizarre feeling. Nevertheless, it's a sentiment I continue to stand behind – in fact, time has only hardened my conviction.

The 'muse', at least our modern conception of it, remains one of the most pernicious and destructive concepts in art (yes, and Art). The idea that artists are somehow struck by inspiration from an external source over which they have no control is madness, absolving creators from responsibility to their own work and methods, and I won't have it. Not only because it goes against the methods of *The Organised Writer* – but more importantly because it leads to the common belief that a lack of such inspiration is what leads to writer's block.

Poppycock.

I'm not saying writer's block doesn't exist. It absolutely does… but it has nothing to do with inspiration, and everything to do with fear. Creating any kind of art requires opening oneself up to criticism by those who consume it. The only way to avoid judgement is to never show your work to anyone, but for most of us that's not an option, or even desirable. Writers are inherently storytellers, and what is a storyteller without an audience? Hence the drive to be published, to have people read our work, to hope they enjoy it because then they'll ask us to tell them another story.

We all know this – and it scares the living daylights out of us.

Unlike the audience, we spend every day not just peering behind the curtain, but living there; staring at its patched-up, messy reverse which the crowd never sees. We know how often we 'make do' because we can't quite reach the pinnacle of perfection we're striving for. We know what our first drafts look like, and how terrible they seem compared to the last thing we published. We know how many times we must rewrite something to make it bearable (which is why 'the last thing we published' now seems much better than our current, unrevised blather).

It seems absurd that we could ever forget something so fundamental, but as writers we're very, very adept at removing ourselves from reality to believe a fiction. It's kind of in the job description. The truth is that our first drafts are always terrible; they always need revision; and revision always makes them better. We know this. We experience it all the time. Yet, faced with a blank page, we somehow forget it all over again. When we begin to type and what comes out is that first draft of unfinished thoughts, half-baked ideas, and terrible prose, we convince ourselves the last good thing we remember writing must have been a fluke, and thus we stop.

We're afraid that what we write will be terrible, and nobody will like it. That, my scribbling friend, is the root of writer's block.

> **THE SOPHOMORE SLUMP**
>
> I believe this same fear is behind the dreaded 'sophomore slump', especially after an acclaimed debut; suddenly an author has a reputation to live up to and an audience waiting for another work as good, if not better, than the first. It's why authors who are blocked often turn in a new direction – a different genre, a new character, even a new format – and feel their creative juices flowing again. With no existing work for the new effort to be compared against, their reputation is no longer at stake and thus they can be fearless.

How do we get past it? We *just write*.

To explain, let's turn to another reason why so many writers feel disorganised in the first place. Yes, we have an inherent dislike of admin tasks – *I'm a creator, dammit, just let me create* – but we also have a tendency to beat ourselves up because we think we're working too slowly, and if there's writing that needs to be done, well, isn't that more important than filing receipts?

As is often the case, the answer is *'Yes, but'*. Of course writing is the most important thing we do. A writer who doesn't write is, well, something else. But we do hundreds of things that aren't 'the most important' in our lives, because they're nevertheless necessary for us to live and thrive. The real problem, as writers throughout history have discovered and keep re-discovering time after time, is that the pressure of knowing we must write can lead to us placing such high expectations on ourselves, we can't face staring at a blank page. Instead we find a thousand and one other things to do, none of them particularly important, and use them to procrastinate. It's a short hop from there to convincing ourselves we have writer's block.

You might say, 'So what? I've managed perfectly fine up till now. One way or another I muddle through, and I always scrape under the deadline by the skin of my teeth'.

But if it really was fine, you wouldn't be reading this book. Deep down, you know it's a house of cards just waiting to collapse under the weight of its own hastily assembled, close-enough, that'll-do construction. So let's address the central problem: how do you make sure your writing is on schedule and going to plan? You already know the answer: by sitting your backside down and writing, without procrastinating. How do you do *that*?

By writing any old rubbish, no matter how terrible.

No, you didn't misread that. Allow me to digress for a moment to talk about *discipline*. We're writers; creative people who like to think of ourselves as free spirits with a general healthy dislike of authority, and an appreciation for a certain amount of hedonism. *Discipline*, therefore, can be almost as foul a word to creatives as *gymnasium* – though I strongly advocate that if you're physically able to do so, you should reconsider that as well. Regular gym-goers will know that it's a rare day when we wake up and think, 'I can't *wait* to go and work out!' But we drag ourselves out of bed anyway... and then, post-workout, we regret nothing because we feel so much better. In fact, we're glad we forced ourselves to go.

Writing can be the same. Think of the last time you stared at a blank page, dreading even beginning to type, but gritted your teeth and began anyway. Chances are that several hours later you finally finished, exhausted, and were glad you forced yourself to begin, hard as it may have initially been. You can call that whatever you like if it makes you feel more artistic, but I call it discipline. One born of experience, because you *know* it'll be worth it in the end, and you *know* you can go back in and fix the draft later, no matter how bad it is at the moment.

That discipline is central to *The Organised Writer*. It's what leads to a productive output, and efficient use of your time. It's why I emphasise the importance of making a schedule and sticking to it; why I advocate for making writing the first thing you do every day. Those things actually make being disciplined easier, by turning it into a habit – and keeping up that habit will allow you to write better and more effectively. With your writing completed for the day, you'll be more relaxed when you come to deal with your non-creative to-do list, which makes carrying out those tasks easier, which means you'll be more relaxed when you come back to your desk tomorrow morning, and so on. It's a virtuous cycle.

Efficiency isn't the only benefit, though. There's also an artistic reason for letting go of the notion you must be inspired. It's a reason veteran writers know instinctively, but is sometimes hard to articulate. It's what our naive forum poster didn't understand when they were banging on about 'inspiration':

Writing more will make you a better writer.

To literary purists, that may sound controversial. But why? Nobody doubts that playing more tennis makes you a better tennis player, welding more makes you a better welder, or singing more makes you a better singer. How many times have you begun writing something, then abandoned it after a few pages when you realised it's not going to work? We've all done it, it's part of the creative process. But how many of those aborted projects *taught* you anything? Not many. Probably none at all. How could they? The only thing they taught you was that your initial idea wasn't good enough to hold up an entire story. That's nothing to be ashamed of. Exploring ideas is the best way to discover if they're worthwhile, and inevitably some won't be. But imagine if that's all you ever did: start project after project, never completing anything, never finishing a story. How much would you learn? How much would your writing improve?

Finishing projects is hard. A novel, a screenplay, a comic book, a play; whatever it is, sooner or later the work becomes a grind, and your writer's mind starts to rebel. Your 'inner editor', that horrible self-assessing voice that lives inside us all, says this isn't as good as you thought it would be when you started. It doesn't live up to the version that sparked your imagination in the first place. Nobody's going to want to read this tripe. What on earth do you think you're doing?

Experienced writers learn to put this inner voice aside and soldier on regardless. Backside in seat, fingers on keyboard, just keep writing. Because you know – you *know*, from your own hard-won experience – that when you reach the end of that first draft, two things will happen. First you'll read it back and think, 'Huh, this is better than I thought'. Then your very next thought will be, 'Oh, these parts aren't working, and I think I know why'.

This second realisation – that now, without the pressure of writing the draft, you can not only see flaws but also how to fix them – is the key. *You can't have that realisation until you've finished the draft*, because you can't see flaws in the shape of a story until you observe the whole thing. While you're still thick in the weeds of a draft, it's too easy to convince yourself that everything done so far is immutable, and any fix you need to make will somehow have to be done in however many pages you have remaining – which is almost impossible. Thus we're tempted to give up and abandon the project entirely.

Here's another hard truth: your work, especially early drafts, inevitably comes up wanting. It's never as good as what you imagined in your head when you started. Every writer experiences this, and so we make a bargain with ourselves to improve it during revision. But trying to revise before the draft is finished is flying blind. Sure, you can fix sentences here and there, rewrite the same paragraph a dozen times, insert some foreshadowing for that character who didn't exist until you were a third of the way into the book, and so on. But you can't see the whole story, because it's not finished. And you can only finish by sitting down in that chair and putting one word after another.

Of course, even when our manuscript has been through a dozen drafts, copyedits, and proofreads, we're still not happy. That's normal. My feeling is that if I look at something I've written, no matter how polished, and don't think, 'Oh, that could be better', then I might as well hang up my keyboard and do something else. Because to reach that point would mean either I've written the perfect story, or I've stopped caring (and I know which of those my money's on). To finish a story is to say, even if only to ourselves, that it's the best we can do even though we know it's not perfect. And *because* it's not perfect, that's really hard. But we do it anyway, because there's always next time… and now that we've learned from this project, next time will be better.

So don't sit around waiting for inspiration. Just write.

Writing on the move

The need to travel can throw a real spanner in the works, depending on your temperament and ability to write in unfamiliar environments. I regularly work on-site at videogame studios; spend hours on trains to attend meetings with publishers, producers, and agents; attend conventions and conferences, at home and abroad; travel to deliver lectures; visit stores for book readings and signings… there are some months I spend more time away from my desk than working at it.

You might think all this travel would play havoc with my deadlines, and I'd be lying if I said it doesn't sometimes have a domino effect that leads to occasional 'crunch time'. But by and large, travelling isn't a problem for me – and it doesn't have to be for you.

> **'CRUNCH TIME'**
>
> This term was seemingly first used during the administration of US President Lyndon B. Johnson, but is now most commonly associated with software programming and development. It describes the practice where, as deadline rapidly approaches, everyone works twelve-hour days and all time off is cancelled in order to finish the project. Crunch time is to be avoided wherever possible… but sometimes it's not possible.

Not all writers want or need to travel as much as I do, but it's a rare specimen indeed who never has to leave the house for a meeting, travel to a conference, or go on a research trip. What can you do to mitigate the effects of travel on your schedule and workload? How much work can you really get done on the road, and how do you go about doing it when you're away from your desk – the one place where most of us feel completely comfortable?

OPTION 1: DON'T WRITE!

Believe it or not, this is the solution I most often employ. I don't write while I'm travelling.

Oh, believe me, I've tried. Seduced by a thousand masochistically romantic tales of writers locked in hotel rooms, hammering out One More Draft; burning the midnight oil in an anonymous motel until they collapse, exhausted, over the keyboard; skipping the fancy publisher's dinner at a conference because they just *have* to get this script finished for tomorrow's deadline. Lured by these and other siren songs, I used to dutifully take my laptop with me to conventions, or whip it out on the train, or hunch over the keyboard in an airplane seat.

But it was miserable, and I couldn't do it. There's something about being on the move that buries the drafting part of my brain under a layer of mush, and after several years of packing my laptop, swearing that *this time* I'd get some writing done – before inevitably reaching the end of the trip and realising I hadn't written a word – I had to admit it wasn't working. Worse, I was wasting valuable time agonising over not writing instead of doing something useful.

As a result, I now do whatever I can to ensure I don't *need* to write while I'm travelling. I block out my schedule to work around any trips, and try to clear deadlines before I leave my desk.

What *do* I do, then? Stare out the window, slack-jawed? Sure, from time to time. Mostly I take the opportunity to plot story outlines, note down ideas, and brainstorm. That's a kind of writing I *can* do while I'm travelling; in fact, I can fill notebook after notebook with the stream of consciousness that comes pouring out when I'm not at my desk, and it's very productive for me. I've outlined novels while sitting in the corner of a loud, raucous party; made notes on a screenplay with one hand while chomping away at a flaccid train-issue sandwich in the other; plotted comic books 36,000 feet in the air.

You may be the exact opposite. You might have great difficulty brainstorming while on the move, but conversely find it easy to draft manuscript pages. If so, more power (and a large dose of envy from my direction) to you – by all means carry on. My point is that you should find whatever *you* can do in those environments, and arrange your working schedule around it.

An important caveat is that I'm only talking about what you do in the 'free time' periods of any necessary travel; while you're on the move, sitting in your hotel room, and so on. If you're actually working on location, then of course you have to write, but that will be an environment set up for you to work in. In the case of screenwriting or videogames it will also occupy you 24/7 in any case, leaving very little time for anything else.

(If you genuinely can't write even in those circumstances, you may have stumbled into the wrong line of work.)

There's one other option for what to do with your travelling time, one that I regularly pull out of the bag, so to speak: *read a book*.

Writers must read. That's a truism so tried and tested it needs no elaboration. Every writer I have ever known, myself included, has a to-read pile that is not only as long as their arm, but never seems to get any shorter. Hardbacks, paperbacks, ebooks, magazines, bookmarked articles, you name it; we acquire reading material like a magpie acquires tin foil.

But when are you going to read it all? You've got writing to do, and much as you may love reading and understand its necessity, nobody's actually paying you to crack the spine on a book. They're paying you to write. As most of us work at home, we can't even use commuting time to catch up. When your 'commute' consists of walking from the kitchen to the spare bedroom, there's not much time to stick your nose in a paperback. I don't miss having a day job at all, but I do miss the 'free reading time' afforded by my daily train journey! So why not read while travelling? Put that time to good use, and make a dent in that to-read pile.

Whatever you decide to do when you travel, remember that it's essentially free time. Don't spend it sweating over a blank page if you can at all help it. Make notes, daydream, brainstorm – or simply read a book – and you'll arrive at your destination more relaxed, less hassled, and with a fresh mind. Everybody wins.

OPTION 2: DO ADMIN (BUT STILL DON'T WRITE!)

Option 1 assumes you can leave work behind at your desk while you're travelling. That's not as absurd as it may sound. Unless you're travelling four days out of every five for weeks at a time, there's no reason you shouldn't be able to get all your work done at your desk, on schedule, before you leave; thereby allowing you to relax while you're away from it.

But sometimes you just can't.

Maybe you *have* been travelling four days out of every five for weeks at a time; or you returned from vacation intending to clear up a bunch of tasks, but have been suddenly called away again; or perhaps you've simply been lax and allowed stuff to pile up.

It happens. In those circumstances I still try to avoid doing actual, creative writing work on the road if I can – and instead I focus on *everything else* that needs doing, but doesn't require a whole lot of creative focus or imagination.

Answer emails. Schedule your calendar for the next few weeks. Make (and take) calls. Do some invoicing. Pay some bills. Read over a contract. Proofread your latest manuscript. All these things have to be done at some point, and your task manager doesn't care *where* they get done. Completing admin like this not only allows you to once again arrive in a more relaxed state, knowing you've checked off a bunch of tasks that needed doing. It also means that when you return to your desk those same tasks, which otherwise would be sitting there waiting for you, have been taken care of so you can stop worrying about them. It's like a gift from your past self.

> ## OVERHEARD ON A TRAIN
>
> I've already mentioned how much I try to avoid phone calls in general; you can imagine that I like making phone calls in public even less. But sometimes, you just have to bite that bullet. I once had a ninety-minute call with a film producer while on a train in England, using my smartphone connection to reach him in LA via Skype. The call dropped out and had to be reconnected every single time we passed through a tunnel or switched from one cell tower to another, and even with my best sotto voce everyone seated within five feet could hear my side of the conversation – to varying degrees of amusement. I spent the entire call wishing the earth would swallow me up, but the conversation was important to us both so, ridiculous circumstances aside, we coped. Doing so meant I could begin work on our notes immediately upon returning home, rather than having to wait another day to take the call in the first place.

To do this sort of thing you need tools ready at your disposal, and, while tablets continue to become ever more useful, realistically you probably want a laptop, which, in my case, is the very thing I try not to travel with. But again, sometimes you just can't avoid it. If your reason for travel – on-site work, conference lecture, whatever – requires you to bring your laptop anyway, then you might as well put it to good use and deal with some outstanding admin.

If your main computer is a laptop, it will be ready to use in this scenario. On the other hand, if like me you use a desktop computer at home and have a separate laptop for travel, you'll need to make a viable away-from-desk machine for these administrative, non-creative tasks. I'll describe how to set it up accordingly in Chapter 7.

OPTION 3: IF YOU MUST WRITE, SIMULATE YOUR DESK

Not every writer uses or needs a desk. Some writers – an increasing number, in fact – are perfectly happy to take their laptop to a coffee shop for the day, or go to a library, or work at their kitchen table, or even sit on their couch in front of daytime TV (that one baffles the hell out of me, but I know people who do it). If you're one such writer, you might have an easier time of travelling than the dinosaurs among us who still cling to our home offices and fixed desks.

Regardless of whether you use a permanent desk, or flit from coffee shop to library to couch, one thing that can help you get work done on the move – if you absolutely, positively, have to work and there's no way around it – is to create an environment as close to your normal writing situation as possible. For many of us, that means effectively simulating our desk. Of course I'm not talking literally. Don't take your pen tidy and rubber-band ball with you everywhere you go, and always make sure you're fully dressed. But there are many other things you can do.

First, try to recreate the noise environment from your normal working space. I already talked about different writers preferring different levels and types of noise as they work, but unless you're someone who can write creatively in the middle of a bustling cafe at happy hour, recreating your normal environment usually means cutting out as much extraneous noise as possible – which means buying headphones. Even if you *are* that rare creature who can blank out noise, you might still consider getting a pair for when the environment is less a bustling cafe and more a humming, pressurised metal tube flying 36,000 feet above sea level.

I always recommend buying the most comfortable pair of noise-cancelling headphones you can afford. Comfort is paramount simply because you may find yourself wearing them for hours at a time, while noise cancellation is essential to cutting out environmental noise, allowing you to focus on your work.

The next step is to make your laptop resemble your at-home working environment as closely as possible. As mentioned above, if your laptop is your main work computer, that's already the case. But if you normally work on a different computer, you should take some time to set up your laptop. First, make sure to install copies of any application you use on a regular basis. Second, arrange the desktop screen's folders and icons to match your home computer. Finally, replicate whatever directory structure, hierarchy, and file taxonomy you use at home.

A travel-only laptop doesn't have to contain *all* the same files as your home computer. Cloud services like Dropbox, iCloud, Google Drive, OneDrive, etc., are your friends. You shouldn't rely on them exclusively (and should always back up regardless) but they're useful to ensure you have access to all your necessary work files, without cluttering up a travel machine with your family photos or music library.

I'm always surprised by people whose travel laptops contain entirely different apps, with completely different file structures, to their home machines. It makes finding and doing anything on them twice as difficult as it should be, and increases the cognitive load on your brain every time you need to search around for a work file. That's a waste of energy, and an opportunity for severe frustration; two of the last things you need while trying to work in what may already be a challenging situation.

TRAVELLING DOS AND DON'TS

The following advice is mostly applicable when you simply have to write on the move, but it can also apply to those times when you've adopted Option 2 and are doing a spot of admin. Some of it may seem prosaic, but it's all taken from my own experience (and pitfalls) over the years.

Backing up while travelling

I previously mentioned cloud services and backing up, and of course you're already running regular backups on your main machine at home (*aren't* you?!). You should also strive to back up while you're on the road.

First, if you keep your files on a cloud service, always download the latest versions of those files to your laptop before you begin work. Travelling network connections are flaky at the best of times, even in nice hotels, and especially so in certain far-flung regions. There's little more dispiriting than making changes to a document that lives in the cloud, only to suddenly see the dreaded eternal spinner of death and realise everything you've done for the last half hour (or more!) is about to vanish forever in the digital ether.

If you're working on local copies of those files, short of a system-wide crash that's not going to happen. Instead, you only need a connection to upload changes when you're finished... and if that connection chokes halfway through, you can just try again, because the 'real' document is still there on your laptop drive.

Cloud services have been a real boon to working on the move, and I wouldn't be without them, but they're no substitute for an actual backup.

I also previously said you should keep the contents of your laptop drive light – to paraphrase Einstein, it should be as full as necessary for you to work, and no fuller. Facilitating backups is another reason why this is a good idea. The less you have on your laptop's drive, the easier it will be to back everything up to a portable hard drive every day.

At time of writing, solid-state drives (SSDs) are still orders of magnitude more expensive than traditional spinning hard-disc drives (HDDs). While the trade-off with the latter is their excruciatingly slow speed compared to SSDs, you're only using them to make a backup, not edit hi-res video. Speed is thus a tertiary concern, after reliability and capacity.

Take your portable drive with you whenever you travel, and every night back up your laptop to that drive. Some people like to run a full cloning program; some simply copy their entire 'work' folder to the drive, overwriting the previous copy. Whatever your method, develop a habit of doing it every night without fail. Then you can rest easy knowing your files are on two separate drives – and hopefully also in the cloud.

> **HOW MUCH IS TOO MUCH?**
>
> IT professionals, and backup aficionados, will tell you that even a disc-cloning backup isn't enough, because hard drives are inherently unreliable; their mantra is, 'Two backups equals one, and one backup equals none.' If you're somehow able to make an additional backup to another separate drive, and store that drive in a different physical location to yourself every night while you travel, go ahead. But for the majority of us that's not only impractical; it's overkill. Three copies – the original, the backup, and one in the cloud – is enough to prevent against all but the most catastrophic disasters. If all three of those somehow fail simultaneously, I'd venture to suggest you have bigger problems than retrieving your latest manuscript.

TRY TO WORK BEFORE EVENING MEALS

Our body naturally wants to rest after eating, especially a large meal. It's a natural instinct, and not one easily overridden. I often find focusing on mentally taxing tasks like creative thinking much more difficult after an evening meal. So when I have to get some work done late in the day, I try to restrict myself to a light snack rather than a large meal until I'm finished.

(LEGAL DISCLAIMER: I am neither a doctor nor nutritionist, and I'm positively *not* advocating you skip meals altogether! Please don't do anything silly, and take good care of your body. It's the only one you have.)

IF TIME IS MONEY, USE ROOM SERVICE

If you find yourself working into the evening at a hotel, don't forget that room service exists. It's normally not much more expensive than what you'd pay at a nearby restaurant anyway, and will save you all the time you'd otherwise spend going to that restaurant. If you're on a serious deadline and need to get work done, those hours are valuable.

NO ALCOHOL UNTIL YOU'VE MET YOUR QUOTA

This may seem obvious, but when away from home it can be tempting to have a drink at your side, because why not? I'm no puritan, and enjoy a good whisky as much as the next author, but my opinion is that you should never drink while writing. Quite apart from the issue of dulling and slowing down your thought process, there's also the question of situational association. If you drink every time you sit down to write, pretty soon you may not be able to write *without* taking a drink. That way lies trouble.

Summary

OVERALL:

- Begin writing as soon as possible after waking, and continue until you make your daily writing quota.

MY DAILY STRUCTURE:

- Achieve my daily writing quota.
- Deal with emails and phone calls.
- Do writing-adjacent revisions/outlining/research/etc.
- Finish work time with filing, invoicing, and office admin.
- Save social media and PR for the end of the day when I have time to spare.

DAILY WRITING QUOTA:

- Try to write with a clean mind.
    - Don't check email or social media until you've hit your quota.
    - If you must go online for research, stay focused.
- It's easier to revise a bad draft than to write it in the first place.

- If you're in the zone, keep writing beyond your quota… but tomorrow you have to hit your quota again, it doesn't roll over.
- Set your phone to 'do not disturb' during your normal writing hours.

AFTER WRITING:
- Take a break, then return to deal with non-writing tasks.
  - If you have proofing, outlining, revisions, etc., deal with them after email, but before social media.
- Don't feel guilty about enjoying leisure activities so long as you hit your quota.
  - And try to make time to read, regardless.

TRAVEL:
- If you can avoid writing while travelling, do so.
- If you can't avoid it, try to simulate your desk environment.

CHAPTER 5

From scribbles to script

Let's take a break from admin and organisation for a moment. In this chapter I'll show you how I put *The Organised Writer*'s principles into practice, by taking you through my process for turning an idea into a fully fledged story.

Every writer is different, of course. We all have our own ways of building a story, our own methods to draw strands and ideas together, and my process certainly isn't for everyone. But it's the one I've used and refined over many years. Because of its overarching nature, it's media-neutral; the same basic steps apply whether I'm writing a novel, screenplay, graphic novel, short story, or even a non-fiction book like *The Organised Writer*.

1. Initial notes

The first stage is simply taking notes as ideas come to me – often while I'm doing something else, much to my continued annoyance. This is done in the manner described in Chapter 3. First, I write down any and all thoughts in my notebook. Then, at a later time, I transcribe them onto my computer along with additional ideas and connections that come to me as I type and re-read them.

2. Initial plot

At some point I've had enough thoughts and ideas about a project to feel ready to begin working on the plot, to figure out what might happen in the story concerned. Exactly when I reach that point can't be quantified; I either feel ready or I don't, and only experience and instinct can really tell the difference.

The first thing I do is re-read all those notes I previously typed up, because this plotting stage can occur weeks or even months after I first began making notes, and by then I've inevitably forgotten most of what I wrote early on. I also often find I have a new perspective thanks to the time passed, and a residual memory of other notes I've made since. So as I re-read the notes more thoughts and ideas will come to mind, just like during transcription, growing out of what I'm reading. Sometimes the new thoughts will themselves spawn new ideas, and then it becomes a race to get everything down, to take note of every branch and leaf of an idea that comes to mind, until finally there's simply nothing more I can think of. I do this on a desk pad, and as with my initial note taking I don't self-censor; any idea, no matter how bland or outrageous, is noted down.

The main difference between this and earlier stages is the intent; whereas before I was feeling my way around the seed of an idea, now my thoughts are aimed directly at the plot and/or characters in the story that's beginning to form. I focus on every story branch, plot development, progression, character arc, and resolution I can think of. Once again, nothing is rejected outright; sometimes entirely new characters and plot ideas will come to mind, and they're not discarded – but I do assess them in terms of how useful they are to the story's core concept, and they're built on or left fallow accordingly. (Though I've also had occasions where a new idea is a terrible fit for the current project… but could easily become its *own* project. Those are fun.)

Taking new notes on paper means I'm not distracted from the notes I'm reading on-screen, and also allows me to scribble lines, arrows, and dividers on the page. I can literally draw connections, make superscript notes in the margins, and box out related thoughts. There isn't a computer program in the world which can do that as easily as pen and paper, and when I'm focusing on story the ability to easily make those scribbled connections is invaluable. Once I'm done, though, I'll type up those notes as if they were from my notebook – and if I'm lucky, doing that will spark another round of ideas and thoughts as I go, until I really am spent.

You can imagine that this is sometimes a long process. It often takes days, and the only real way to 'know' it's finished is to have something approaching a full plot formed from these notes. Not necessarily in close detail, or written out as prose; it's more about having the 'shape' of a story, where I can clearly envision the major points along the way. Bringing this stage to a close therefore draws again on instinct and experience, with a feeling that either I have nothing more in the tank for this particular idea, or I now have a solid enough base plot that I'm ready to begin writing an outline.

3. Bullet-point outline

I now move on to drafting the plot in bullet-point form. These are often laughably vague, e.g.

- *Mole delivers intel*
- *Intro sting*
- *IRC chat re. puzzle*
- *Doorkicker flashback*
- *Argue w/ therapist*

That's how the bullet-point outline for my novel *The Exphoria Code* starts, but even if you've read the book I'd forgive you for not recognising it – and the first dozen versions were even less decipherable. At this point I'm not trying to write anything readable by someone else. It's all shorthand, abbreviations, references to working titles, and so on that nobody but me needs to understand. I'm trying to get a mostly-complete story down in order, so I can figure out if it might work.

(Note I said 'might', because let's face it, we never actually know if it will work until we write the finished piece.)

If I'm still trying to solve fundamental structure issues I'll do this longhand on paper, as if I were still making notes. If I'm more confident about the story, and I think it's closer to locking down, I'll write these bullet points directly into the project document on the computer.

It's important to emphasise that the first version of a bullet-point outline is often no good. That's fine. Returning to the 'just write' principle, it's easier to see the problems by looking at a whole entity, even if it's poor. When I've identified those problems I write another bullet-point outline, trying to solve as many issues as possible. Naturally, this will often give rise to new problems, or highlight ones I missed the first time. And around and around we go.

For me writing is a progressive, iterative process where I look for new directions and find my way to the solution by trying out lots of different things. If I discover plot holes that are simply irredeemable, I can completely eliminate the paths leading to them – or if I think they can be saved with a little more thought, I'll backtrack until I find a better branch to follow.

It won't have escaped your notice that there's a lot of *re*writing going on. I've already written out the same things, or variants of them, several times and I'm still only at the outline stage. But this isn't redundant work. Each successive generation of notes and outline brings the story into sharper focus, and sorts the good ideas from the bad. If something survives all the way from the initial notes through several iterations of the bullet-point outline, it must have some merit. Likewise, if an idea dies on the vine during the first outline, it probably wasn't strong enough to begin with. This is all part of the editing process.

From scribbles to script

> **RIP IT UP AND START AGAIN**
>
> After dozens of revisions and adjustments, outlines can too easily become bloated and unnecessarily convoluted. If you worry you're starting to lose the main thread of the story, try this: re-write a new outline entirely from memory, without consulting any existing notes.
>
> This exercise helps you focus on the essential core of the story, as only the strongest elements from previous versions will come to mind, giving you a clear picture of what stands out. Only when this from-memory version is finished should you look at your old notes, to see if anything else from your previous outline can now be re-incorporated into this new, cleaner version.

Once again, my finish line here is somewhat vague. The target is to have a solid, workable story progression in bullet-point form, with only a few minor plot holes or problems remaining.

Why not keep going until it's perfect, with no plot holes or problems at all? Because that's basically impossible. There will always be problems, no matter how carefully I plan ahead – and even if the outline seems bullet-proof, something will inevitably happen while writing the draft that makes me realise it isn't. There's no point in letting such problems prevent me moving ahead, but it takes experience to judge which problems are minor enough that they can be resolved later without too much grief.

4. Treatment/Pitch

I have my outline, so now it's time to write a treatment and/or pitch. This step is optional, depending on the circumstances of the project. I normally don't pitch novels, because many editors nowadays only want to see full manuscripts for a new series; and if it's an existing series, the 'pitch' will more often simply be a chat with the editor. Short stories and single comic issues are much more concise, but their brevity is why I also wouldn't bother pitching them; they're almost impossible to judge from a pitch, so editors will again want to see the whole work.

On the other hand, many major projects will need to be pitched. Movies, TV, videogames, long-running comic series, and even work-for-hire franchise novels; it's rare indeed for anyone to commission such a work without an extensive pitch or treatment.

To clarify terms: a *treatment* is an overview of the entire story, generally written in a brief narrative style, as if I were describing the story to a friend over lunch. A *pitch* is more or less the same thing, though often in a more perfunctory style, and additionally contains more detailed elements like backstory and character biographies. Pitches will even sometimes have a section explaining why the project is a good fit for whomever I'm pitching to; a film producer, a comics publisher, a videogame studio.

To write a treatment, I take my final bullet-point outline and write it out as prose, expanding on it with more plot detail, discussion of character motivations, maybe even lines of dialogue sprinkled throughout. There will inevitably still be gaps and holes in the close details, but that's part of why this stage is useful; writing the story out like this often gives me a better idea of where such problems may arise.

The end result here is easy to define; a full narrative treatment, from start to finish, of the entire story. Once I have that, and I'm happy with it, I'm done.

5. Breakdown

Next comes the breakdown, which differs greatly according to project and medium. If I'm writing a screenplay, I need to decide what happens in each scene – and then further, how those scenes should be paced, who the point-of-view (POV) character is in each, and where the act breaks and turning points should optimally fall.

For a comic series I must decide what happens in each issue, and even what happens on each *page* of that issue. If it's a novel, I want to figure out the scenes contained in each chapter; and, if there are multiple points of view, whether I need to move any chapters around to balance the distribution of those viewpoints.

How you do a breakdown largely depends on the writing software you use, or whether you use software at all. Some novelists and screenwriters continue to do this longhand using index cards pinned to a cork board, or sticky notes on a wall, rather than trusting it to software at all. Regardless of medium, the principle is the same; I take the treatment (or bullet-point outline, if I skipped the treatment stage) and break the story down into scenes.

6. Manuscript

Now, *finally*, I write the damn thing.

(I shake my fist in jest, because without those earlier stages I wouldn't have the confidence to begin writing at all.)

The first stage of this is what I call a 'Zero Draft' – some call it a 'rough draft' (though that can mean very different things to different writers), screenwriters often refer to it as the 'vomit draft', and Anne Lamott famously calls it the 'shitty first draft'. I say Zero Draft because for me, it's what comes before the true First Draft – and, like zero itself, whether it can be said to truly exist is a question worth pondering.

That's because the Zero Draft will never, ever, be seen by anyone except me. It's a quick run-through of the manuscript, completely unpolished and in places even unwritten, that I write as quickly as I can; unconcerned by trifling matters like consistency, plot holes, or good writing. It's filled with notes like *[[xxxxName]]* and *[[Check!]]*, reminders to look up a name or place, and things like *[[this is where they argue – Refer Back Later]]*.

> **NOTE TO SELF**
>
> I use double square brackets to enclose notes to myself because they're easy to type – I don't even need to hold down the Shift key – and they never appear in the final format of any kind of manuscript. At the revision stage, I can quickly search for '[[' and be immediately taken to any remaining notes in the draft. It's the same principle as the note (TK) in journalism, to indicate information yet to be supplied; that letter combination occurs so rarely in regular English that it can't be mistaken for part of the story, and thus will be flagged up by any good copy editor.
>
> (I used to use triple square brackets until I discovered that the screenwriting app Highland, created by screenwriter John August, uses double square brackets to denote its own in-line comments. Sometimes, conformity is no bad thing.)

The Zero Draft is fast and dirty, and the result is borderline unreadable, which is why it will never be seen by anyone else. But it's *finished*, and that's the important thing, because – hewing again to the 'just write' mantra – now it can be rewritten. Here's another mantra for you, and I want you to really etch this one in your mind:

It's easier to rewrite anything, even the worst writing ever, than to write something for the first time.

The Zero Draft is a manifestation of that belief. It's a headlong dash to get the bare bones of a story down as quickly as possible, without pausing to focus on quality control, because writing on the blank page is always the hardest part of the process. Anything I can do to remove obstacles and barriers will speed up that process, which in turn allows me to progress to the more enjoyable part (i.e. revision) as quickly as possible.

The other reason I recommend Zero Drafts is simply that, by the time I write the end, I'll inevitably have veered from my outline in places (sometimes by a little, sometimes by a lot) and will have also had ideas and revelations along the way that mean I need to go back and change things about the start... and the middle... and everywhere else.

Aspiring writers never believe this part will apply to them. Experienced writers nod their heads in sad recognition.

It's much easier, not to mention better for my mental well-being, to make those changes if I didn't spend an hour trying to craft a perfect line in the first place. If I don't feel attached to the prose, to turns of phrase or clever wordplay, I'm more capable of being ruthless with it, revising and excising whole paragraphs, scenes, or chapters with gleeful abandon. *Kill your darlings*, they say. Well, that's a whole lot easier if I never really fell in love with them in the first place.

Remember: the Zero Draft's sole purpose is to be rewritten and forever replaced by a better version.

This is another stage where the ending is obvious; I know I've finished the Zero Draft when I write THE END.

7. Rewriting

But it's not really the end.

Now I go back and make all those changes to the Zero Draft; I flesh out descriptions, rewrite dialogue, check dates and facts, lay down foreshadowing for later events, decide which of the three different eye colours I've given a character they should actually possess, and so on.

For me, this is the most fun stage of the whole writing process. Writing a Zero Draft is an arduous journey through peaks and valleys of emotion, with my mood swinging wildly between elation and despondency, alternately convinced I'm writing a work for the ages or the worst dreck I've ever committed to paper. That's normal, and a roller coaster every writer knows only too well. When I'm rewriting, though, that part is over. Now I have a draft, and all I'm doing is *making it better*. Polishing, tweaking, laughing at my own jokes, enjoying a half-decent passage that I don't fully remember writing, making unrelated things fit together properly... I'm taking concrete steps toward making it more like the thing I had in my head when I first began writing.

> **REPETITION AND REPETITION AND REPETITION**
>
> One last thing I always do is just check for word repetition and overuse; there are certain words I know I literally overuse if I'm not careful, and I'll often just spend some time just literally going through the document with the find/replace tool, literally just searching for those words so I can remove or even just replace them in places where I've literally repeated them several times in the space of just a few paragraphs.
> (Side glance to camera two.)

After finishing the final draft, I put it aside and out of mind. I make sure it's backed up, put the project folder back in my desk tray, and work on something else for a while – at least a week, if possible. That's normally long enough for my memory of a story to evaporate sufficiently that when I return to it, it's like reading someone else's work. Thus, I can go over the manuscript one final time with an almost-fresh pair of eyes. It's amazing what some time away from my own work does to my observational skills; now, with the greatest of ease I notice repetition, awkward phrasing, continuity errors, and more – things I simply didn't see before, no matter how closely I looked.

In a way, this is a quintessential *Organised Writer* principle in action. Putting the manuscript aside for a while offloads it from my mind, because I know there's no point in constantly thinking and fretting about it; instead I'm trusting my 'future self' will read it with fresh eyes, and thereby improve it.

That's how I go from idea to story. Hopefully you can see how the principles of *The Organised Writer* pervade my method, and help me ensure I'm always producing the best work I can.

Summary

OVERALL:

- Make notes, outline the plot, power through the rough draft, then revise.

STAGES:

- Make initial notes.
- Figure out the plot.
- Bullet-point outline.
  - Look for big problems, re-bullet as necessary (but don't worry about small problems).
- Write a treatment or pitch, if desired.
- Break down the story into chapters/scenes/pages as necessary.
- Write the Zero Draft, following the 'just write' mantra to keep going until it's finished.
- Rewrite, checking for word repetition and overuse.
- Put the manuscript aside for at least a week, then proofread it again.

PART III

Non-writing stuff

CHAPTER 6

Money matters

(✗) A *disorganised writer* doesn't keep track of their finances, has no consistent method of quoting prices or invoicing, and flounders in chaos while trying to do their own taxes.

(✓) *The organised writer* regularly updates their financial records, delivers quotes and invoices with confidence, and hires an accountant to deal with tax matters.

When I became a full-time writer I foolishly thought all I'd have to do was write, turn in an invoice every now and then, and not worry about 'corporate business type stuff'. There's a good chance you once thought that, too.

But the truth is that being a freelancer means you *are* a business, and the product you're selling is you, your time, and your writing. You are the CEO, the CFO, the VP of marketing, the sales manager, the pitch person, the account manager, the line supervisor, the secretary, the engineer, the quality assurance division, the logistics and shipping department.

For creative freelancers, this can be a culture shock. It certainly was for me – even though I was fortunate enough to have taken business classes while studying graphic design, and subsequently spent nearly a decade working at a variety of creative companies, from two-person design agencies to one of the biggest magazine publishers in Europe. Despite all that I struggled at times to get a handle on the business side of things, so I have enormous sympathy for anyone who jumped straight into freelancing with no business background.

Even if you're not a full-time writer you should approach the non-creative side of writing like a business, and ensure you're doing all of the following:

- make sure you get paid on time;
- pay what you owe others promptly;
- file your taxes by the due date;
- store paperwork where you can easily locate it.

Is all this office work less important than your creative output? Yes, of course; without the writing there's no business to start with. But conversely, without the business there would pretty quickly be no writing, so start thinking of yourself as a businessperson and entrepreneur. It may seem odd to use such language in this context. After all, you don't have to wear a suit; you're not dealing with venture capitalists; you don't employ a fleet of sales representatives, have two hundred staff, or run a factory.

But when you appear at a conference, you're not going for fun, you're making a business trip to represent yourself and your work. When you sell a piece of writing, you're not just 'doing a bit of freelance', you've sold a product for which you must raise an invoice. Thinking of yourself as a businessperson will help you make decisions in a dispassionate manner, and approach the financial and administrative side of your work with open eyes.

Don't panic. It's not as hard as you think, and I'm not here to bamboozle you with legalese about tax returns, business management 101, and so on. Let me explain how you can spend less time worrying about that stuff, and more time writing.

> **DISCLAIMER**
>
> For legal purposes, I'm bound to state that nothing in these pages should be taken as financial or legal advice, or replace the advice of a qualified and certified professional in such matters. As always, I'm just speaking from my own experience.

Hire an accountant

You: Should I hire an accountant?
Me: Yes.

Well, that was easy.
Oh, what's that? You have a rebuttal?

You: I don't want to hire an accountant. It will cost me money.
Me: Are you an accountant yourself?
You: ... No.
Me: Then stop dithering and hire one.

This is rule #1, the most important advice concerning your finances I can give. So many of my fellow writers spend time and energy struggling through their own accounts and taxes, and there's no need for it. Yes, accountants cost money. But any good accountant will *save* you money in the long run, because they understand tax codes and deductible expenses and all that jazz better than you ever will. By contrast, most writers – myself included – are not only bad with numbers, but break out in a rash at the sight of a twenty-page tax code instruction leaflet. An accountant will save you time and stress.

Your next task is to find one. Probably the best option is to ask fellow writers for recommendations; or, if you're a member of a writer's guild or society, many such groups maintain a list of recommended accountants and lawyers who are familiar with the writer's life and the vagaries of our business. Finally, you can of course look for yourself. Make sure to check which services prospective vendors offer, and where possible try to find someone who already has creative freelancers among their clients. You may also want to ask if they require you to use particular software packages.

There's one final, rare possibility: what if you *are* an accountant? It's not a crazy idea – my own first accountant was a financial director who also wrote fiction and comedy on the side. If you're in a similar position, and assuming there are no legal conflicts of interest, go ahead and do your own accounts... if you really want to. But do you? I'd advise you to hire someone else regardless, to ensure there's a fresh set of eyes looking over everything.

Hiring an accountant isn't just about saving money, it's also about reducing stress in our working lives. For most of us, trying to do our own accounts is a significant source of that stress.

How I learned to stop worrying and love the spreadsheet

You've got an accountant. Well done! But you still need to keep track of your income, expenses, receipts, and so on, in order to give your accountant accurate records when they come to sort out your finances and tax returns.

Keeping accurate, timely records is good business, as it allows you to see your own budgetary status and prevent nasty surprises. But it can also save you money. While your time is undoubtedly valuable, let's be honest – it's probably not as valuable (or rather, as *expensive*) as your accountant's. It costs almost nothing for you to spend an hour or two each week maintaining accurate financial records. By contrast, that same time spent by your accountant every week would cost you dearly.

My accountant deals with a lot of creative workers; writers, actors, musicians, and so on. After first engaging them, I asked if the records I was supplying were sufficient; did they have everything they needed, was there anything more I could do? They laughed and recounted how a certain actor, at the end of each year, would visit their offices carrying a cardboard box. Stuffed inside the box were receipts, bills, remittances, bank records, and more, all loose and completely unsorted. He would hand over the box and (I imagine somewhat sheepishly) say, 'There you go, sort that lot out for me'.

Knowing this actor's body of work, however, I imagine he could easily afford the many hours of extra time for which my accountant would subsequently bill him to sort through such a mess.

Record-keeping needn't be intimidating. Simply drop paper receipts, bills, etc. in your desk tray inbox as you accumulate them – whether that's through the mail, upon returning home from a business trip, or even generating them yourself if you print out documents received electronically. When you receive digital records, you can drop those in a finances inbox on your computer (see Chapter 7 for how to set that up). At time of writing physical records are slowly beginning to disappear, as we all instead move to PDFs, PayPal invoices, digital bank records, and so on. But the transition isn't complete, and will take some years yet. In the meantime, most of us have a combination of physical and digital records to track and file – which is one more reason why keeping your own records of financial activity is so important.

With those records in the appropriate inboxes, you must then deal with them by blocking out 'admin time' to enter everything you've gathered into your accounts spreadsheet.

How often is 'every so often'? By now you surely won't be surprised when I say, *'It depends'*. I rarely need to schedule more than a couple of hours per week; over time I've developed a habit of doing record entry upon returning from the gym on

Saturday mornings, when I always have an hour or two spare. If I'm away from home that day, I'll instead make a single calendar appointment to deal with it late afternoon on the following Monday.

You may find your own admin runs don't even need this much time. A writing career doesn't tend to generate huge amounts of paperwork, and many authors' records probably won't require more than an hour of attention per week. The only way to be sure, then, is to try it and see. Begin by scheduling two hours every week for admin – either in a single afternoon block, or two one-hour sessions, whichever suits you best – then reassess how it's going after a month. If you find you always seem to need more or less time, alter the scheduled appointments appropriately, and try that for another month. Or, if you find two hours per week is just right, carry on as you were. Becoming an *Organised Writer* is a process of evolution, not a one-time solution. You don't have to get everything right first time, and making adjustments is not only normal but recommended.

Most of the time this sort of financial record-keeping isn't time-sensitive, but there are exceptions. The first is making records for regular accounting periods. These will vary according to your circumstances: your accountant may require you to supply quarterly records, or even monthly (though that's rare for a writer). At the end of each financial year you'll also have to ensure your records are up-to-date before turning them in. Whatever the requirements, you should set up reminders for any such regular periods. I use repeating calendar appointments, usually set to alert me a couple of days beforehand so I have time to collate the records and turn them in.

If you're incorporated, and conduct your business through a company, there will be additional requirements. Your accountant will make you aware of them, though you should never be afraid to ask just in case. You may have sales tax/VAT to sort out, payroll admin and taxes to track if you do indeed employ an assistant, company expenses to reimburse, and so on. These must all be dealt with – mostly by assembling records and passing them to your accountant – at certain regular periods, and you should again set up repeating alerts to remind you when they're due. For good measure, ask your accountant to also give you a nudge as the time approaches.

The second kind of time-sensitive accounting is any bills you have due. Some writers, such as novelists, may have very few bills and expenses as part of their work. Others, such as graphic novelists or screenwriters, may have bills coming in from suppliers, collaborators, other writers, and who knows what. You may also have to pay for a website, your mobile phone, union or guild dues, cloud storage, and various other expenses that can't be dealt with easily through an automatic bank payment.

I have a calendar reminder that repeats once per month to remind me to pay any bills still outstanding. I say 'still' because sometimes, as part of the weekly record-entering process, a bill crosses my desk and if I have the time and funds I'll pay it there and then, before filing it. If I come across a bill and *don't* decide to pay it right away, it remains in the inbox until my monthly alarm reminds me to pay it instead.

Let's go through a typical occasion when you've decided you're going to enter outstanding files into your records – imagine this is your late Friday afternoon admin, the last task you need to accomplish before you can start the weekend. Hold on to your hats, because what follows is detailed and granular. I've tried to answer questions you may have – such as 'I have both paper and digital files, what order do I handle them in?' – so that you don't simply throw up your hands and return to your previous bad habits.

Keep *The Organised Writer* to hand when you first go through this process. Bookmark pages, or photocopy the chapter summaries and appendix checklists. It may take a while for you to break your old habits, but as you practise these methods they'll become second nature and you'll reap the benefits.

1. EXPENSES – DIGITAL

First, deal with digital files. Go through the records inbox on your computer and open any payment receipt documents you find, be they PDFs, Word docs, whatever. Enter the amounts from each one into the *Expenses* portion of your spreadsheet, along with a record of where and when the expense was incurred. Then move those documents to your financial records folder.

If, due to your business arrangements, you have payment receipts that aren't reimbursable personal expenses, deal with those first. Then go through your inbox a second time, opening all the documents for reimbursable personal expenses you've made. Once again, enter them with details of where and when you incurred them, but this time into the *Reimbursable Expenses* portion of your spreadsheet. Then move the documents to the relevant filing folder.

2. BILLS DUE – DIGITAL

If you've reached that time of the month to make payments, look over the inbox again, this time opening documents for bills yet to be paid. The order of work here is slightly different. For each one, first enter the amounts, vendor, invoice numbers, and references into the *Expenses* portion of your spreadsheet as before. But before you can file these documents they require a further action – which is of course that you must pay them.

Fire up your online banking, PayPal account, or whatever method you intend to use to pay the bill in front of you. Pay it, and download a receipt if you're able to. Then file the bill and receipt together in the appropriate financial records folder. Repeat this for each bill in your inbox.

If the payment site won't allow you to download a receipt, you can make one yourself. A simple screen grab of the payment confirmation page is better than nothing; or if you're on a Mac, you can *Print* the web page as a PDF document, a method I use all the time.

> **PHYSICAL PAYMENTS**
>
> You may have some bills that can't be paid electronically. In those cases I suggest you draw up and make the payment (e.g. a cheque sent by mail), but wait to file the bill document until the payment has been confirmed by your bank. Such payments are becoming vanishingly rare, though.

3. RINSE AND REPEAT – PAPER

Finally, all that should remain in your digital inbox are your own *unpaid* invoices. We'll return to those later; for now we're going to go through the whole process again, but this time with our paper documents.

…Wait, *what*?

It may seem counter-intuitive, but this is a good example of how and when to examine your usual habits, and the 'normal' way of doing things, to determine if there's a better and simpler way to achieve the same result. When we hit a problem in a story we often look back to the start and figure out where it began to manifest, because most of the time a problem at the end is caused by an error of judgement we made at the beginning that has since spiralled out of control. Why not do the same with habits, routines, and methods that aren't working? Instead of thinking, 'How can I tweak this method to improve it a little?', consider what fundamental aim you're trying to achieve, forget the received wisdom you've absorbed over the years, and try to imagine a better way to accomplish the same result – something completely new and different, even.

Many of *The Organised Writer* principles such as five pages after breakfast, filing cabinets within arm's reach, and the 'just write' philosophy are the result of such thinking. This approach to financial records is another. What are we trying to achieve? To enter all our records into a spreadsheet with the least amount of effort, and the least chance of error. Is there a better way of doing that?

Most people will naturally assume that dealing with each *type* of document – say, all your receipts – at once is the most efficient way to handle them. If all your receipts are entirely physical *or* entirely digital, then that's true. But here in the twenty-first century, most people's lives are both physical *and* digital. We receive and generate a mixture of paper and digital records, and the cognitive load – the literal amount of thinking you must do – when moving back and forth between the two is significant. By contrast, moving from digital receipts to digital bills keeps you in the same mental workspace of 'digital files on your computer', requiring just a couple of clicks to bring up new documents and switch tabs on your spreadsheet.

In my experience, moving your attention from one *medium* to another – physical to digital, and vice versa – is more disruptive than moving from one *type* of document to another within the same medium. Restricting the cross-medium move to a single occasion lowers the cognitive load required to deal with it. Thus: *all your digital files first, then all your physical files.*

So once you've finished with your digital files, gather up your paper receipts and bills, and enter their details into your spreadsheet in the same manner. When you're finished with each document, place it in your filing drawer.

Don't put off your paper files. You may feel a temptation to finish dealing with your digital files, then think, 'Oh, I'll get round to the paper next time…', and send them back to the bottom of the pile. But repeat this a few times, and before you know it you're drowning in that sea of unprocessed paper again. Allow enough time in your 'filing sessions' to deal with both digital and paper, and follow through on both.

4. INVOICES

Now you can move on to your own invoices (for the fine art of invoicing itself, see later in this chapter). For simplicity's sake let's assume they're all of a kind, i.e. either all digital or all physical.

As with other documents, open them all up (or gather them in a stack, if they're on paper) along with any corresponding remittance advices you've received from clients since the last time you carried out this task. Assuming you use online banking, simply log in to your account, then check each outstanding invoice against your statement to see if it's been paid. If you don't bank online, you can check manually against your latest bank statement.

You may already be confident certain invoices have been settled; if you were paid by cheque, or received a remittance advice from the client, the money's almost certainly already in your account. But... cheques bounce, mistakes happen, and documents get sent in error. Until you see it on your balance report, assume nothing.

If an invoice has been settled, check off the *Paid* column on the *Income* portion of your spreadsheet, file the invoice along with any remittance document, and move on to the next. If it hasn't been paid, check the invoice date. Is it overdue? If not, close the document and leave it until the next time you run this task, by which time it might have been paid. If it's overdue now, don't close the document; leave it open while you move on to the next.

By the end of this process, in an ideal world you'll have filed several invoices as paid, and the others will be closed because they're not yet due. Sadly, we don't live in an ideal world and some clients pay late. If, after going through your invoices, some remain open because they're unpaid and overdue, it's time to send reminder emails (or make reminder calls, or however you prefer to deal with it).

This is why you should leave invoices till last, and particularly why admin tasks like this should be undertaken only after you've finished writing; you can't be certain how long it will take. If all goes well, you might be done with this whole task – receipts, bills, invoices, the lot – in fifteen minutes. But if it gets complex, and especially if you need to chase payments, it could take an hour or more. So write that email, or make that call, with the overdue invoice open and in front of you, only closing it when you're done.

Those open documents are effectively a temporary to-do list of People Who Owe You Money.

FILING DRAWERS FINISH LAST

I've referenced the 'finance folders' in your filing drawer several times. It's important to emphasise where they come in the process of a document moving through your system, and that is *dead last*.

The very act of placing a document in your filing drawer marks it as dealt with, so you know everything in that location has been received/paid/entered/etc. as necessary. Once financial documents are filed, therefore, the only time you should need to look at them again is when your accountant asks to see them.

If a bill is still due, if you're still waiting for a client to pay an invoice, if you haven't yet entered a receipt into your spreadsheet... then it stays in your desk trays. The filing drawer is to hold documents you've already dealt with. It's not a directory of things waiting to be done.

(NB: You'll probably also have digital equivalents of your filing folders, and the same principle holds: nothing goes in them until it's been dealt with.)

THE SPREADSHEET

We now have a handle on how to go about entering our records. But enter them into what, exactly? Here's where the fabled spreadsheet rears its head.

> **REGIONAL DIFFERENCES**
>
> The expected caveat: I'm writing this from the perspective of a British author whose accountant handles all interactions with the tax collector. Readers in other countries may be compelled to use certain software or government-compliant templates for their records, and I can't speak to that specifically. I hope that showing you my approach can help you improve yours.

My annual spreadsheet (see Figure 6.1 overleaf) has four tabs – *Income*, *Expenses*, *Reimbursable Expenses*, and *Balance*.

Income is a record of every invoice I send, as well as all un-invoiced revenue such as royalties or profit share. I divide the year up into quarters, separated by blank horizontal rows so I can easily pull out individual quarters for my accountant.

The information columns are self-evident. With the number columns I enter relevant figures into *Gross* and *Bank Charges*; the *Net Total* cell has a formula which automatically subtracts the latter from the former to show a final amount.

The bottom rows of each quarter, and the table as a whole, use formulae to show the sum total of each column.

Next is *Expenses* for recording bills received, money paid to collaborators and subcontractors, etc. This is also divided into quarters, and the information columns are again self-explanatory. *Invoice Number* here is for the client's number, on any bill I receive; *My Reference* is for my own purchase order number or reference relating to that order, if I have one.

Reimbursable Expenses records all non-invoiced expenses such as train tickets and hotel rooms for conventions, food and drink while working somewhere on-site, stationery store purchases, and so on. As with previous tabs, the year is broken up into quarters.

(You may wonder why this tab is separate to the other *Expenses* tab, and it's simply a matter of convenience for accounting purposes. If you run your work through a corporation, it also makes calculating reimbursement payments from the company simpler.)

Finally we come to *Balance*, containing a single big table that retrieves the *Income* and *Expenses* totals from earlier sheets, and subtracts the latter from the former to show a running total of the year's profit before taxes.

It really is that simple. This spreadsheet, along with any supporting documents, tells my accountant everything they need to know while also allowing me to easily keep track of my finances. All it takes is an hour or two each week to keep it completely up to date.

TOW Ltd Accounts

Income			Expenses	Reimbursable Expenses				Balance		
Date	Job	Client	Invoiced?	Invoice Number	Gross	Bank Charges	Net Total	Paid?		
Q1 (Apr-Jun)										
10 Apr	ENCRYPTED BOOKSHELF advance	Awesome Novels	☐		£2,000.00		£2,000.00	☑		
27 Apr	PROJECT GAMEPAD on-site work	Awesome Gamez	☑	AG-2020-2	£2,500.00		£2,500.00	☑		
15 May	Short story	Awesome Mags (US)	☑	AM-2020-1	£350.00	£8.00	£342.00	☑		
1 June	Book royalties	Awesome Novels	☐		£1,200.00		£1,200.00	☑		
10 June	Conference appearance fee	Splendid Con	☐		£400.00	£10.00	£390.00	☑		
20 June	PROJECT GAMEPAD narrative design	Awesome Gamez	☑	AG-2020-3	£3,000.00		£3,000.00	☑		
				Q1 TOTALS:	**£9,450.00**	**£18.00**	**£9,432.00**			
Q2 (Jul-Sep)										
4 July	CAPTAIN WONDERFUL #1 sales	Wonderful Comics (US)	☑	WC-2020-4	£4,000.00	£16.00	£3,984.00	☑		
12 July	PROJECT GAMEPAD scriptwriting	Awesome Gamez	☑	AG-2020-5	£1,500.00		£1,500.00	☐		
3 August	Conference workshop fee	Delightful Con	☑	DC-2020-6	£700.00	£4.50	£695.50	☑		
15 August	ENCRYPTED BOOKSHELF balance	Awesome Novels	☐		£2,000.00		£2,000.00	☑		
20 September	PROJECT GAMEPAD scriptwriting	Awesome Gamez	☑	AG-2020-7	£2,500.00		£2,500.00	☐		
				Q1 TOTALS:	**£10,700.00**	**£20.50**	**£10,679.50**			
Q3 (Oct-Dec)										
XXXDate	XXX	XXX	☐		£0.00		£0.00	☐		
				Q3 TOTALS:	**£0.00**	**£0.00**	**£0.00**			
Q4 (Jan-Mar)										
XXXDate	XXX	XXX	☐		£0.00		£0.00	☐		
				Q4 TOTALS:	**£0.00**	**£0.00**	**£0.00**			
				TOTALS:	**£20,150.00**	**£38.50**	**£20,111.50**			

Figure 6.1 Annual spreadsheet, Income tab.

TOW Ltd Accounts

	Income	Expenses	Reimbursable Expenses		Balance	
Date	Expense Type	Where	Invoice Number	My Reference	Amount	Receipt?
Q1 (Apr–Jun)						
3 April	Mobile phone bill	AAA Phones	MAR798123	MOB2020-1	£25.00	☑
10 April	Monthly bank charge	My Bank Ltd	987654-321	MB2020-1	£10.00	☑
15 April	Accounting services	A. Caunt & Ant, Inc.	654321	ACC2020-1	£500.00	☑
3 May	Mobile phone bill	AAA Phones	APR798123	MOB2020-2	£25.00	☑
10 May	Monthly bank charge	My Bank Ltd	987654-322	MB2020-2	£10.00	☑
3 June	Mobile phone bill	AAA Phones	MAY798123	MOB2020-3	£25.00	☑
10 June	Monthly bank charge	My Bank Ltd	987654-323	MB2020-3	£10.00	☑
			Q1 TOTALS:		**£605.00**	
Q2 (Jul–Sep)						
1 July	Captain Wonderful artist payment	Joe Artist	2020-Art-5	CW001-ART	£2,000.00	☑
3 July	Mobile phone bill	AAA Phones	JUN798123	MOB2020-4	£25.00	☑
10 July	Monthly bank charge	My Bank Ltd	987654-324	MB2020-4	£10.00	☑
3 August	Mobile phone bill	AAA Phones	JUL798123	MOB2020-5	£25.00	☑
4 August	Translation services	Hans Gruber	—	TEB2020-1	£150.00	☑
10 August	Monthly bank charge	My Bank Ltd	987654-325	MB2020-5	£10.00	☑
3 September	Mobile phone bill	AAA Phones	AUG798123	MOB2020-6	£25.00	☑
10 September	Monthly bank charge	My Bank Ltd	987654-326	MB2020-6	£10.00	☑
			Q1 TOTALS:		**£2,255.00**	
				TOTAL:	**£2,860.00**	

Figure 6.2 Annual spreadsheet, Expenses tab.

TOW Ltd Accounts

	Income	Expenses	Reimbursable Expenses	Balance	
Date	Expense Type		Where	Amount	Receipt?
Q1 (Apr–Jun)					
15 April	Train tickets (PG on-site)		British Rail	£100.00	☑
15 May	Hotel room (PG on-site)		Lovely Hotel, London	£700.00	☑
20 May	Train tickets (Splendid Con)		British Rail	£80.00	☑
10 June	Hotel room (Splendid Con)		Splendid Hotel, Brighton	£400.00	☑
					☐
				£1,280.00	☐
Q2 (Jul–Sep)					
4 July	Printer paper		AAA Stationery	£5.00	☑
20 July	Train tickets (Delightful Con)		British Rail	£65.00	☑
3 August	Lunch (Delightful Con)		Delightful Café	£13.00	☑
4 August	Hotel room (Delightful Con)		Delightful Hotel, Manchester	£325.00	☑
XXXDate	XXX		XXX	£0.00	☐
				£408.00	
Q3 (Oct–Dec)					
XXXDate	XXX		XXX	£0.00	☐
				£0.00	
Q4 (Jan–Mar)					
XXXDate	XXX		XXX	£0.00	☐
				£0.00	
			TOTAL:	**£1,688.00**	

Figure 6.3 Annual spreadsheet, Reimbursable Expenses tab.

TOW Ltd Accounts

Income	Expenses	Reimbursable Expenses	Balance
Yearly Balance			
TOTAL INCOME (Gross)	£20,150.00		
TOTAL EXPENSES	£2,860.00		
TOTAL BANK CHARGES	£38.50		
TOTAL REIMBURSABLE EXPENSES	£1,688.00		
YEARLY PROFIT:	£15,563.50		

Figure 6.4 Annual spreadsheet, Balance tab.

If you're at all familiar with spreadsheet software, you'll have no trouble building a document like this. If on the other hand spreadsheets are alien to you, download a template from *organised-writer.com* and modify it to suit your circumstances.

Invoicing

Exactly *how* you go about raising an invoice is up to you. Some writers use an online work-tracking and invoicing service, some invoice through a payment system like PayPal... and then there are dinosaurs like me who fill in a form on our computer, create a PDF, and send it as an email attachment. It doesn't really matter, but how you apply that method does.

Invoice as soon as you finish the relevant work. If you're turning in a document over email, where practical you should send the invoice alongside it; or, if the invoice needs to go to a different recipient, raise and send it immediately after turning in the work itself. If you're working in batches, and can't invoice until the whole thing is done, send it along with the final batch of work. If you're expecting revisions, and can't invoice until they've been dealt with, send it along with those final revisions.

Whatever the situation, there will come a point when you're eligible to invoice, and you should then do it as soon as you're able. Don't wait; don't batch all your invoicing for different jobs together with the intention of doing it all in a single afternoon; don't delay. Things inevitably fall through the cracks, and this is one thing you can't afford to lose track of. It's how you make a living.

Once you've sent the invoice, immediately enter its details in your accounts spreadsheet, and file the document itself – either in your *Pending* desk tray if it's paper, or a digital equivalent if it's on your computer. When you get paid, mark it as such on your accounts spreadsheet (this is why my spreadsheet has a *Paid* checkbox for every line item) and file the invoice away. If you receive a remittance advice from the client, file that alongside it – digital remittances get renamed to match the invoice, paper remittances get stapled to the invoice and filed away.

If you have many different clients and some are, shall we say, less than speedy about processing invoices, schedule a regular block of time each week to review your spreadsheet for outstanding payments and chase up overdue clients. We all wish this wasn't necessary, but 'You should have paid me last week' is a tale as old as time itself, and sometimes you just have to demand your money. Again, this is your livelihood. Don't apologise for expecting to be paid on time.

Find your price, and stick to it

Let's finish by moving from how you invoice to how *much* you invoice for.

You may be a pure novelist or playwright; a journalist who works for a standard per-word or per-article rate; a subcontracted editor doing piecework; or any number of other positions where your rate is fixed. But if you do negotiable/creative work-for-hire – as a feature writer, columnist, copywriter, speaker, scriptwriter, journalist, maybe even a ghostwriter – you'll have a rate. That rate will differ between writers, and even between media; my rates for screenwriting, graphic novels, and videogames are all different. So I'm not going to dictate what you should charge, but I will remind you that all good writers' guilds and unions make their minimum pay rate figures public, so even if you're not a member they can help guide you towards a reasonable rate.

There are, however, two things I will happily tell you.

The first is that you're probably not charging *enough*. Writers are terrible – gobsmackingly, head-slappingly awful – at figuring out how much we should be paid for something. Meanwhile, clients are equally bad at understanding how much work goes into a given piece of writing. A 500-word press release may only take twenty minutes to type, but if typing was all it took a machine could do it. The writer must first decide *which* 500 words to type, spending time to come up with just the right phrasing. That composition time also draws on the learning and experience the writer has built up over the years, which is valuable – if it wasn't, the client wouldn't need to hire a writer in the first place.

I know some writers baulk at demanding high rates. You feel like you're asking too much; multiply it by every working day in the year, and you'd be earning twice as much as the client's full-time staff! While that may be true, the important difference is that you're *not* full-time staff, and you *won't* be working every day of the year. The nature of a freelancer's life is 'feast and famine', sometimes going weeks at a time without a gig – before inevitably landing five at once with the same deadline. What's more, those full-time staff receive all manner of benefits freelancers don't: paid sick leave, paid vacations, paid maternity leave, paid bereavement time, employer's pension contributions, handling payroll and taxes... it's easy to forget about the often-invisible perks of full-time employment, but freelancers receive none of them. To afford to live, you must cover those costs yourself – so you need to be paid well. In return, you make a promise to the client that when they *are* paying you, you'll give them 100% of your time and attention. But first comes that rate.

And if you find yourself in a position where your rate is non-negotiable, there's still something very simple you can do to ensure it's worthwhile: figure out how much *time* the offered rate is worth. A one-off gig that pays less than a day of your living budget is not something you should spend half a week writing.

On the other hand, recurring gigs are freelancer's gold; while a weekly web column that pays, say, £200 won't make you rich by itself, over a year it represents £10,000 of income. That's enough to justify spending a little extra time and effort where necessary.

The second thing I'll tell you is that once you've found your rate, you should stick to it. Don't give discounts.

Hang on, though; what about good, regular work? Clients themselves will often ask this question: 'We'll give you lots of work, so can we get a rate discount?' Generally, your answer should be no. But occasionally – very occasionally – you might want to do it for one of two reasons.

Reason one: the client is a charity, academic organisation, or small concern to which you actively want to donate your skills. I doubt there's a writer out there who wouldn't happily give up some time and expense for their local library, for example. Those cases are a value judgement, and if you feel strongly about it, go ahead.

Reason two: the client is willing to offer a *contractually guaranteed* 'kill fee' in return for a significant amount of work. This kill fee is a minimum payment made even if they cancel the job halfway through, or suddenly decide to use another writer, or whatever. And it shouldn't be a token amount, but the equivalent of at least 50% of the total fee, or several weeks of your rate, whichever is higher. Why is it so high? Because that work represents an opportunity cost, and taking it on will prevent you from taking on other jobs of a similar size while you're engaged with this client. In exchange for a discount, the minimum amount has to cover that opportunity cost.

KILL-FEE EXAMPLE

Let's say a client and I have agreed a job will take thirty working days, and in return they want a 20 per cent discount. I agree – so long as the client guarantees a minimum fee for half of that time, i.e. fifteen days. If the job goes off without a hitch, everyone's happy. Even if the job ends after twenty days, no harm, no foul. But if work is cancelled for some reason ten days into the job, the client will owe me a further five days of the discounted rate payment, to make up that fifteen-day minimum.

To some of you this may sound crazy, and crazily entitled. It's at this point in the conversation where someone will often say, 'That's all very well for you, Mr Bigshot, but none of my clients would ever agree to that'. To which my usual response is: have you asked them?

Kill fees are common in journalism, paid by editorial departments in lieu of final payment if they spike a piece of commissioned work before publication. In film, 'pay or play' agreements for actors and directors guarantee payment even if a studio cancels the project or decides to employ someone else. Almost all high-paying sports contracts are guaranteed in case of injury or being benched, while high-flying businessmen commonly negotiate 'golden parachutes'. And these examples don't even involve discounts. So it's hardly unreasonable for contract writers to ask for guarantees in return for dropping our rates.

If you think I'm being paranoid about work suddenly being cancelled – if you've never been in a position where you've been hired to write something, only for it to be shut down before completion – then I envy you, because I've seen it happen many times to myself and others. Some years ago a videogame developer hired me for a job that was scheduled to last several months, and in return asked for a 25 per cent (!) discount. I agreed, figuring the sheer amount of work would make up for the reduced rate, but after just ten days the project was cancelled. I'd lost out twice – not only had I performed ten days of work for only three-quarters of my usual rate, I'd also turned down other work offers in the meantime because I thought I'd be occupied... by a project that had now collapsed around my ears. A guaranteed minimum would have lessened that blow, or made the client think twice about asking for a discount in the first place.

The final argument made in favour of discounted rates is that you'll get more work from the client, or referrals to other potential clients. And sure, you might... but you can bet your bottom and heavily discounted dollar they'll want future work to be done at that same reduced rate. How many more days will you now have to work, to make up for the income lost by discounting? How many more jobs must you juggle, and how much more stress must you endure, as a result of not earning enough on the jobs you've already agreed to?

I previously mentioned the importance of learning to say 'No' in the context of figuring out your schedule. Turning down discounted work is also in your financial interest, because you risk devaluing yourself. If you discount for everyone, is it really still a discount? Or have you effectively just reduced your standard rate?

RACE TO THE BOTTOM

Discounting doesn't just hurt your own bottom line, it also hurts others in your industry. If enough do it, clients will come to expect low rates from everyone. This can deteriorate into a race to the bottom, and you may find yourself having to lower your rate again just to keep pace with everyone else. This is why writers' guilds strive to enforce minimums.

I also advise against working on too many small 'bitty' jobs, even for people willing to pay your full rate, if you can avoid it. Such jobs require a large amount of schedule-juggling, and increase the danger that when a big, lucrative job finally comes along you'll find yourself unable to take it on – because you've already made too many time commitments to a dozen tiny jobs. *Quelle horreur.*

There's one huge and obvious caveat to all of the above: it assumes you're an established freelancer with skills in demand. If you're just starting out, or are struggling for work, then by all means be more flexible. When I was a novice freelancer I'd do just about anything that paid, no matter how small or time consuming, simply to establish myself and pay the bills.

But there will be times, even early in your career, when some people are simply not willing to pay enough for your talent and skill, and the quality of work those provide. If you can hold your nerve and say 'No', you'll be glad of it in the long term.

Summary

OVERALL:
- Hire an accountant, and keep track of your income and expenses with a simple spreadsheet.

KEEPING RECORDS:
- Invoice as soon as the work is done.
- Place all expense receipts in your inbox (physical or digital).
- Block an hour or two each week to enter and check invoices, expenses, and bills due.
  - Deal with all digital records first, then paper.
  - Don't file invoices or bills due until they're paid.
  - File receipts as soon as they're entered.

YOUR ACCOUNTANT:
- To submit regular filings, remind yourself with recurring calendar appointments.

YOUR RATE:
- Find your price and stick to it.
  - That rate is probably more than you currently charge.
- Only give discounts in rare or exceptional circumstances; where appropriate, require a guaranteed minimum in return for a discount.

CHAPTER 7

It's a set-up

(✗) A *disorganised writer* works in an environment of disorder, with no design or structure to their office, files, and desk, and a sense of frustration with their tools.

(✓) *The organised writer* works in an environment they control, knows where to find anything they need at a moment's notice, and keeps to hand a selection of trusted tools they can rely on.

Many writers are obsessed by equipment and environment. If only we had the 'right' gear, and the 'right' place to work, everything would be so much easier; we could be more productive; all would be right with the world.

It's nonsense, of course. I know successful authors who began their careers working in the small hours at a kitchen table, or in between dealing with kids and housework, or locked in a cramped and cluttered spare bedroom. Jane Austen famously wrote at a tiny table near the front door of her house; Roald Dahl worked in his shed, on a piece of wood laid across his lap; Nabokov drafted *Lolita* on index cards while travelling. One old friend of mine wrote his first novel on a beat-up laptop in a one-room fleapit, finishing the manuscript the day before he was evicted.

That doesn't make the desire for everything to be *just so* before we start work any less real. It's another form of procrastination, like the feather duster that magically appears in a writer's hand when they're on deadline.

Nevertheless, it draws us in because there's a grain of truth to it. If you set up your working space in the right way you *will* be more productive, and you *will* develop good habits that enable you to work more efficiently. The key is that word 'habits' – the way in which this will help is over the long term, not as a sudden panacea. If you struggle to write for more than a few minutes every day, buying a new keyboard or tidying your study won't magically enable you to write for six hours straight tomorrow. But if you set up your working space in an organised way and continue to practise the right methods, over time you'll find those few minutes become a few hours – and the more you do it, the easier it becomes.

There are no floor plans here, no branded must-buy shopping lists. I won't tell you which computer to buy, or how to arrange your desk. I'll tell you what I use, but in my experience such things are far from universal because my ideal computer, chair, notebook, or bookshelves won't be yours. Yes, you need a desk; but it doesn't have to be the same as my desk.

(I almost wrote, 'Yes, you need a chair', but stopped myself because that's a perfect example of what I mean; I may need a chair, but perhaps *you* prefer to work at a standing desk.)

I'll explain the principles of what you should strive for in office space layout, to make your working life easier and reduce cognitive load; and I'll discuss what types of equipment, both hardware and software, will enable you to write in a more organised fashion.

You may wonder why this chapter isn't right at the start of the book. After all, setting up your work environment will be your first concrete step along the path to becoming an *Organised Writer*. But knowing how the system works will help you understand the reasons behind the advice that follows. Otherwise you might blindly follow instructions with little understanding of *why* a file drawer of manila folders is useful, *why* you need four inbox trays, or *why* you should invest in task manager software. Having read the previous chapters, you now know the answers to those questions.

Take a weekend

To sort out your office space you should take a weekend, and do nothing else. Clear everything – your deadlines, social calendar, even family commitments if possible – so you can spend the entire weekend setting up your work environment, ready to begin as a newly anointed *Organised Writer* on the following Monday.

You may think it won't take two days to rearrange your office, but this isn't just about moving furniture around. This is about sorting and arranging the contents of your entire working life… and then perhaps moving furniture around.

YOU WILL NEED:

- A filing cabinet (or at least one drawer) and hanging files
- Archive filing boxes
- Manila folders
- Four stackable desk trays + labels
- Job sheet printouts
- Sticky tape
- A permanent marker
- A ballpoint pen

I'm assuming you already have a computer, printer, phone, etc. The above items are what you need specifically for an *Organised Writer* setup. If you don't already have all of the above, buy them at a stationery supplies store. Yes, you'll have to spend a little money, but it really is only a little. A filing cabinet will undoubtedly be your most expensive purchase, but a second-hand one will suffice if you can find it. Using quality tools is important, and if you can afford to buy a new, high-quality filing cabinet, you should; but the important thing is getting one that works reliably, regardless of how old or shabby-looking it might be.

Everything else – files, folders, desk trays – is a minimal cost. If you're struggling, I know that can be difficult to hear; when your cupboard is bare, being told you 'only' need to spend £50 on equipment is painful, and may even sound elitist. I promise that's not the intent, and the outlay will be worth it.

How many files and boxes you should buy will vary according to how long you've been working, how many previous jobs you'll need to file, how many current jobs you're working on, what kind of work you do... I recommend starting with fifty hanging files, fifty manila folders, and five archive boxes. If it turns out you didn't need that many, well, now you have some spares. On the other hand, if you know before you even start that won't be enough, double those amounts.

For job sheets, either print out templates from the *organisedwriter.com* website, or design and print your own. Remember, don't fret over their design if that's not your forte. The *information* on them is what matters, not how fancy they look. Take another look at the *Job Sheets* section in Chapter 3 and decide what you need to track.

DAY ONE

On the first day, clear everything out of your workspace except your desk, computer, and chair. I'm not joking. Move everything else off your desk, remove everything from your drawers, take every work-related item off your bookshelves... pens, tools, files both old and current, everything. Place the whole shebang in a corner of the room – making sure you can still get in and out, of course.

You may be tempted to sort through items as you take them out of your drawers and off your shelves, but don't. That part comes later. If you try to sort items now, before you know it the sun will have set and you'll have barely shifted half the stuff you need to. Besides, you aren't yet in a position to decide what to keep and what to discard. Resist the temptation, and concentrate on just clearing everything out.

When your space is clear, take a few minutes to make sure it's also clean. This isn't about writing, per se, but untidy workspaces are likely to be dust traps, and your health is no less important than your work. No need to go crazy; just run a duster and vacuum cleaner around the place.

Once everything is both clear and clean, begin to...

Set up your filing cabinet

Your filing cabinet should be within easy reach of your desk. If it's possible within your office space, being able to open and place/retrieve items from it without even leaving your chair is ideal – if you're using a drawer built in to your desk rather than a whole cabinet, that may be the case anyway. If placing the cabinet so close to your chair isn't feasible, it should be no more than a few steps away. This is crucial; if your files are on the other side of the room, or in another room altogether, it just won't work.

Why is it so important that your files are close to you?

You're going to use that filing cabinet a lot – much more than you think, and certainly more than you currently are. As I've mentioned before, the less convenient something is, the less likely it is to become a habit.

When you have a document that must be filed, or when you need to retrieve something from those files, you should be able to do so without effort. The 'pure alphabetical' system is part of this principle, as it reduces the frustration of wondering where something might be filed, and so is having those documents easily to hand. Being able to simply turn in your chair, open a drawer, and immediately locate what you're looking for sounds like a small thing, but in practice it makes a big difference.

With your filing cabinet in place, populate the drawer/s with hanging files. These will hold your manila document folders when you file them. As we're using an alphabetical system, you may feel labelled tabs on the hanging files aren't necessary, but it's your choice. I have twenty-six lettered tabs to make locating those tricky L/M/N/O files around the middle easier.

That's all for now. Close the drawers and turn to the desk trays.

Set up your desk trays

Take your four desk trays, stack them into a single tower, and with the labels and permanent marker title them as follows, from top to bottom:

1. *Inbox*
2. *Current*
3. *Pending*
4. *Future*

Place the trays somewhere on your desk within easy reach. This is *even more important* than the filing cabinet placement; you *must* be able to reach your desk trays without moving from your keyboard (rotating your chair is fine, but if you need to move the chair, your trays are too far away).

Again, this is about convenience and creating new habits; if you have to get up from your chair to look in your desk trays, the chances of it ever becoming a habit are close to zero.

Find a home for your archive boxes

There's no need to label your archive boxes yet; we'll get to that tomorrow. For now, decide where you're going to store them and place them there.

Unlike your filing cabinet, the archive boxes are for files that you won't need to refer to very often; no more than once a year, perhaps even less. They can therefore be stored pretty much anywhere, and don't have to be within easy reach. They should still be in your office space, and not inconvenient to get to – again, the more difficult it is to reach them, the less likely you are to do so – but if a high shelf at the back of the room is the most sensible place to store them, that's fine.

Sort and replace your souvenirs and tools

Now use the remainder of day one to sort through your existing equipment, discarding what you no longer need or want.

It can be hard to throw away things you've owned for a long time, even if you don't use them. I understand, and I won't dictate what you should or shouldn't keep. But you should distinguish between *souvenirs* and *tools*, and divide the items in your office space into those two groups.

Some souvenirs are obvious. Your first royalty cheque, an award trophy, a formal invitation to a book launch, etc. Mine include that first cheque in a picture frame, a model of the typewriter on which I first wrote stories as a child, my *Atomic Blonde* premiere tickets, and so on. Such souvenirs probably already have a place on your shelves or in a cabinet, because they're obviously ornamental. Replace them accordingly.

There are other souvenirs, though, which we fool ourselves into thinking of as tools. The old fountain pen you haven't used in a decade; the half-filled notepad you don't write in any more because it's too big to carry around; the desk jotter you used for two days and then shoved in a drawer; promotional ballpoints that have never been used and whose ink is now dry in any case. Some of these may have real sentimental value, and if so they should be put on display with your other souvenirs. But many such items are frankly a load of old tat that you don't use, don't care about, never look at, and are keeping only because 'It might be useful some day'.

Discard those items. Don't hesitate, don't procrastinate. Get rid of them right now. I promise you won't regret it; in a month's time you'll wonder why you ever hung on to them.

UNUSED NOTEBOOKS

If you're anything like me, cleaning out your workspace will reveal a host of empty writing pads and notebooks that you're loathe to discard because, well, who doesn't always need blank paper? But if you've had them for years and never used them, ask yourself why that is. Are they a type you don't like using? Are they the wrong size for your desk/purse/pocket? Is the binding awkward? Does the paper not hold your pen's ink well? These aren't trivial reasons – comfort with your tools is important. Whatever the reason, there must be one, or you would have used those notepads by now. So make peace with yourself and either give them to someone else or recycle them. Don't keep them on a wistful hope they'll magically become useful one day. Instead, find the pads or notebooks you do like, buy half a dozen, and stick to using them.

With your souvenirs now on display, and all 'fake tools' discarded, you should be left with only the tools you want and need to work with. Your favourite coffee mug, your good ballpoints, your best pair of scissors, paper clips, sticky notes, and so on. When you put them back, you'll be amazed at how much less space your tools now require.

Don't just blindly replace things where they were before. With each item, take a moment to consider, 'How often do I need to use this? Does its location and ease of retrieval match that need?' Keep items you use all the time – your notebook, pen, phone charger – within arm's length of your desk chair, either on your desk or in a top drawer. Less frequently-required items can go in a bottom drawer, a cupboard, or even on a shelf.

I can't decide what your essential tools are; that's a very personal matter. Perhaps you already had all of your tools positioned in their optimal place. Regardless, it's worth taking a moment with each item to check if that's the case. Don't be afraid of changing things around if it will make your life easier.

DAY ONE: OPTIONAL

The above tasks will probably take all of the first day. Well done! You've made great progress. Now go and relax, have dinner, watch TV, and get some rest before tomorrow.

However, some of you may find that clearing out your things, setting up your filing, and sorting/discarding/replacing your souvenirs and tools doesn't take that long. Maybe you've done all that, and it's still mid-afternoon. Now what?

Well, you can go ahead and take the rest of the day off anyway. You're perfectly justified in doing so. Chill out, eat, sleep.

But…

You may feel good, and want to keep going. That's fine too. If you want to make a head start on tomorrow, by all means begin to sort through your files as outlined below. Just don't feel you *have* to; it's okay to take some time off.

DAY TWO

Good morning! Sleep well? Had a good breakfast? Excellent.

On day one, you created a space in which you could start anew. You set up a working environment that will enable you to be more organised, more productive, and more relaxed.

Now it's time to fill that space with your work.

'Is this still relevant?'
Take your stack of manila folders and a permanent marker. Now pick up one of the documents you cleared out of your desk/shelves/etc. yesterday – it might be a contract, a stack of notes, a manuscript printout, your telephone bill, whatever – and decide whether you still need it.

If it relates to a current project, or is a record you want/need to keep, then naturally the answer is yes. If so, skip to the next section.

But you probably have a lot of documents – notes, ideas, sketches, and so on – that, like fake tools, you keep around 'just in case'. Projects you've been casually thinking about for years, but never get round to; expired insurance documents; a half-finished concept you'd forgotten about till you saw it in this pile; personal bank statements from a decade ago.

It's time to ask a tough question: *is this still a going concern?*

For things like the aged bank statement or expired insurance policy, that's an easy question. With creative documents, it's a little more tricky.

A good way to answer is with a thought experiment. Imagine that tomorrow, someone will offer you an outlandish dream gig; something you're excited to do that will take care of all your current monetary concerns, and consume all your working time for the next year. Perhaps it's a million-dollar book deal, or a three-picture screenplay contract, or funding to design a huge videogame from scratch.

Now look at the document in your hand, and ask yourself; if that happened, would I be okay forgetting about this idea? Would I be happy to just let it go, forever?

If the answer is *yes*, then the truth is it doesn't mean that much to you. Get rid of it now, and make space in your life (and mind) for new ideas and projects that you're excited about instead. This isn't judgemental; there's no shame in looking at a five-year-old idea you once thought might be cool to tackle, and realising the only enthusiasm you can now summon is a desire to not let it go to waste. But ideas go to waste all the time. Focus instead on making new ones about which you're enthusiastic.

On the other hand, perhaps you *are* still enthusiastic about this project. Maybe, even if that dream gig came along, you'd still want to do this one at a later time because it calls to you. If so, go ahead and keep it. That's just as valid. The important thing is that you're honest, not least with yourself, in your assessment.

Give a manila folder an appropriate title
You've decided you're going to keep this document, so take a manila folder, place the document inside, and write the name of the project to which it belongs (if it's not a work project, write its description, e.g. *Phone bill*) on the folder *twice* – once at the base of the folder, and once on the tab – so it will be visible no matter where the folder is located. This is because most folders will reside in two places during their lifetime; first they'll live in your desk trays, where the base of each folder will be visible to you when stacked. Then, after the project is done, they'll move to either your filing cabinet or archive boxes, where the tab of each folder will be visible.

If the document isn't part of a work project, you can skip straight to the next step of filing. But assuming it is related to work, take a blank job sheet and fill in the project details and current status. Then tape the job sheet to the front of the manila folder, and you should have something that looks like this:

NOVEL JOB SHEET

JOB INFORMATION

TITLE: THE ENCRYPTED BOOKSHELF
PUBLISHER: AWESOME NOVELS
AGENT: AAA   FEE: 2K/2K   CONTRACT? ☑

1. Research ☑   2. Notes ☑
3. Plot ☑   4. Breakdown ☑

DRAFT
Zero Draft ☑   First (Rough) ☐   First (Polished) ☐

EDITORIAL
Sent to Editor ☐   Editorial revisions ☐ ☐ ☐ ☐
Copy editor revisions ☐   Galley proof checked ☐

PAYMENT
Advance ☑   Balance ☐

ARCHIVING
Archived ☐

DATE PUBLISHED
_____

THE ENCRYPTED BOOKSHELF

Figure 7.1 Active job sheet taped to a manila folder.

File the manila folder

Finally, whether or not it's a work project, place the folder wherever it belongs according to its status; ongoing concerns in your desk trays, recent records in your filing cabinet, old records in your archive boxes. Let's deal with each in turn.

Desk trays

It's time to talk about how these work. You have four trays, in this order from top to bottom:

1. Inbox
2. Current
3. Pending
4. Future

Your *Inbox* is for everything yet to be dealt with. Incoming mail that's just arrived, receipts from a trip that haven't yet been entered, newly arrived bills for payment, etc. The Inbox is mostly loose pieces of paper, hence it goes on top so that it's easy to put things in or take them out.

Current is where the action is. Any work project in progress resides here, in its manila folder. This is why you write project names at the bottom of the folder, as well as on the tab; so you can identify them when stacked up in a desk tray.

Pending holds projects that are either finished on your end and awaiting publication, or for which your work is done but now you're waiting on someone else to perform a task. Books due to be published, screenplays awaiting notes, graphic novels waiting to be drawn, and so on.

Future is where you put projects for which you've made notes, and intend to write, but haven't yet begun in earnest; maybe they're not ready to pitch, or perhaps you're still working on the outline. These project folders have a desk tray in case you have a sudden idea, and want to review the existing notes or add new thoughts. Periodically, maybe once every couple of months, you should go through this tray and see if there's something on which you can or want to begin work – or, conversely, if you no longer care and can discard it.

Filing cabinet
If a folder belongs here, just open the drawer and drop it into a hanging file in alphabetical order.

Archives
For now, anything destined for the archive boxes should simply be placed *near* them (maybe even on top) rather than *in* the boxes. Otherwise, you risk wasting lots of time going in and out of those boxes as you complete today's filing process. Only when you've completed the entire task of sorting and filing your documents should you put all the folders from this stack in their relevant archive boxes, and label the boxes (see below).

You may think filing any folder at this stage is missing a step; after all, isn't the folder potentially incomplete? What if there are other documents relevant to the same project still in that big pile of stuff in the corner, waiting to be filed? Shouldn't you keep every folder out on the floor, until you know there are no more documents to go inside it?

No. This is how the system works, and working through this routine today will demonstrate how easy it is to file documents that you come across – because you know exactly where they belong. This is your first step to creating a new habit that will serve you well in the future.

Now return to the very start of this loop. Take another document, and another manila folder; give the folder a title; attach and complete a job sheet if appropriate; then file it. And again, and again.

Only two things should make you pause this loop. The first is when you pick up a document that belongs to a project for which you've already created a folder. In such a case, simply locate the folder (in your desk trays, filing cabinet, or archives) and place the document inside it. Now pick up another document, and begin again.

The other potential reason to pause is when you pick up a document and simply aren't sure if it's still a going concern. You should ask this of every document you file, and it's inevitable that for some of them, the answer will be 'No'. Don't confuse *a going concern* with *still required* – unlike tools, some old papers must be kept for legitimate (sometimes legal) reasons long past their term of usefulness. But, as with your tools, it's worth taking a moment to consider the question and make an informed decision. If you do want to keep the document, in your archives or elsewhere, continue as normal by placing it inside a labelled manila folder. Otherwise, simply discard it, pick up another document, and begin the loop again.

Sorting your documents will almost certainly take up a big portion of day two, but at the end of it you'll have filed or discarded every piece of paper in your office. Congratulations! You're almost done… but not quite.

Paperless projects

At your computer, check your work files to see if you have any current projects with *no* paper documentation at all. It's increasingly likely, as so many of us now work entirely on computers, and even use digital contracts.

The Organised Writer system is designed to not let such projects fall through the cracks. For each paperless project you have, take an empty manila folder; title it; attach and complete a job sheet; and put the folder in the relevant place. You may not have any paper documents to go inside the folder, but now you have a job sheet to track the project's status.

Digital notes

Notes on paper are dealt with by the 'loop' described above, of filing or discarding. Any digital notes, though, will need to be consolidated. If they relate to an existing project, they should be moved/transcribed into the relevant digital project folder, just like how paper notes go in a project's manila folder. Ideas for future projects, which don't yet have a home, may require a little more work to ensure they're all located in whatever application you use to make and store digital notes. If you have notes scattered across many different applications, I advise you to decide on one and consolidate them there. The *Software* section later in this chapter can help you with that decision.

> **CULLING NOTES**
>
> Every so often, it's worth conducting a clean-up of your digital notes. If I find myself with half an hour to spare, and haven't done it for a while, I like to go through my entire Notes application to clear out old notes and ideas that are no longer relevant, consolidate related notes together, and so on. Remember, this is just for 'idea notes'; if a note is relevant to a current project then it should already have been moved or retyped into the appropriate digital project folder.

Standard folders

There's no universal list of folders for every writer. However, these are some non-project folders almost everyone will need, and are thus worth making in advance:

- Credit card statements
- Bank statements
- Invoices sent
- Bills received
- Receipts for expenses
- Tax correspondence

Again, use your discretion; all your bank statements may be online, for example, or you might only invoice digitally. But if any of the above items are things you have on paper, make and label the folders now, and put them in your filing drawer. When a relevant document arrives you can simply open the drawer, find the folder, and drop it inside. I remake these folders at the start of every financial year.

This is a good time to set up your 'digital inboxes', for any of those files which *are* going to be digital. For each such file type, create a folder on your computer where they can reside. It's a good idea to label these by financial year, and keep them all together; see *Taxonomy* later in this chapter for suggestions on how to organise your computer folders.

Spare folders

Hopefully you have some manila folders left over. This is good; so good, in fact, that if you *don't* have any spare, you should buy some to keep in stock. Then put your spares within relatively easy reach, similar to your filing cabinet. Why within reach? Because every time you begin a new project, or a new type of document arrives that you need to file, you're going to grab a manila folder; title it; attach and complete a job sheet if necessary; then file it where it belongs.

I can't emphasise enough that you should do this for *every new job or document type* you have. Don't hesitate, don't try to double up different types of documents, don't worry about 'wasting' a folder on a single piece of paper. Create a new folder and file it.

Yes, this means you'll get through manila folders at quite a rate. No, that's not a problem – in fact, it's how the system works. You should be able to locate anything, at any time, without having to think where you put it. If you need to find your car insurance, where are you going to look? In your filing drawer, because it's current but not an ongoing concern. In the drawer, where will it be? Under *C* for *Car Insurance*. Not under *I* for *Insurance*, or *H* for *Home Insurance* because you put all your insurance together to save money on manila folders, or *F* for *Financial Documents*. Sure, those might all make sense – but which one is it? In which category did you decide, months ago, to file your car insurance? Just asking yourself this question slows you down, causes stress, and can even potentially lead to lost paperwork. Remove uncertainty: *C* for *Car Insurance*, every time.

It's a set-up

Fill and label your archives

At the end of the filing process you'll know which folders can be safely archived, meaning you don't expect to need to refer to them more than once a year. The majority of these files will be finished projects from years past, but it can also include things such as closed bank accounts, correspondence with former agents, legal documents no longer active but that can't be discarded, and so on.

Like all your documents, they should now be in manila folders. Old, finished projects should have a completed job sheet attached; you don't need to track their status any more, but it's still handy to have information like the publisher, fee, and publication date to hand at a glance.

Before you go any further, look at those finished projects and ask yourself; are all their related digital documents archived and/or backed up? That's the final task on every job sheet, after all. If any projects haven't yet been archived digitally, put their folders in a separate pile, which we'll return to in a moment. The remaining folders – those with no digital component – can now be distributed among the archive boxes, filed alphabetically like your filing cabinet. To begin with, if you have five boxes I recommend labelling them as follows:

A–E

F–J

K–O

P–T

U–Z

But this is another case where you must judge for yourself the best distribution. These days I have seven file boxes, with *A–E* replaced by *A–B* and *C–E* (I did so much work on the *Dead Space* franchise that I have a plethora of folders under 'D'), while *K–O* is now further divided into *K–M* and *N–O* (thanks to my less exciting but no less paperwork-laden mortgage). The standard five served me well for many years, though.

If you run out of space and need to buy a new box at some point, don't worry. Just re-label the boxes as necessary with a permanent marker, covering up the old labels with new ones if you have to. Nobody will judge you on the beauty of your archive box spines.

When you've finished filing that first batch of folders in their appropriate boxes, return to the pile of jobs which have digital aspects. If there are only a small number of such jobs, deal with their digital archiving now (see *Software* later in this chapter for suggestions of how to do so), then file the manila folders away in the archive boxes. If on the other hand you have many ready-to-archive projects with digital aspects, leave the manila folders aside for now. In the next stage, schedule some time in your calendar over the coming week – say, an hour or two each afternoon – to deal with them, and place each manila folder in its archive box only when its related digital files have also been dealt with.

TOO MANY FILES!

You may have a lot of documents; too many to sort and file in the space of a single day. If so, spend day two dealing with only your current work and business files (work in progress, current bank statements, etc.) so you can at least begin work again tomorrow. Then take another full day at some point to deal with the remainder; if you've done your sorting well enough, most will go straight into the archives.

Don't delay this task, though! It's tempting to leave those files sitting in a big pile on the floor of your office, and expect you'll get round to them eventually. But isn't that attitude what got you in trouble to begin with? Instead, schedule a day on your calendar to deal with them as soon as you're able to – perhaps next weekend, or maybe even during this coming week. Don't let them sit on your study floor for weeks that become months that become years.

To-do list and calendar

Your files and folders are now sorted, and your office space is the tidiest and most organised it's ever been. There's just one more thing to do. Sit down at your computer, open your calendar and task manager, and populate them with your appointments, projects, and tasks just like we discussed in Chapter 2.

Unless you already have a big list of tasks to draw from, you'll simply have to wrack your brains and enter these as they come to you. You almost certainly won't remember everything in one go. As with the document folders, the aim of this system is to make entering an appointment or task quick and easy enough that you can do it on the spur of the moment, as the thought strikes you, without it being a hassle. So try to remember everything you can… but tomorrow, or the day after, when you suddenly remember something else, don't panic. Fire up the calendar and/or task manager, make an entry, then return to what you were doing. That's going to happen a lot over the next few weeks as you begin using the system, so don't worry. It'll become less frequent as time goes on, and you develop the habit of entering new appointments and items as they occur.

Start now with your current projects. Go through your desk trays, from *Current* through *Pending*, and create related projects and tasks in your task manager as appropriate. If you already know a certain project needs to be worked on over a particular span of dates, go ahead and block out that time in your calendar. If you have existing deadlines for projects, note those in the calendar as well.

When you've finished entering your current and future projects, move on to those you'd *like* to do at some future date; the projects you've been thinking about, but haven't yet set in stone or begun to write. Give them project entries in your task manager, maybe even create a *'Brainstorm Project X'* task within each project, but don't promote it to your *Priority* list. It's in your task manager to remind you, as you look down the project list in future, that this is something you want to work on – but until you *are* working on it, it stays off the *Priority* list.

This goes for personal 'projects' as much as work; if you'd really like to learn Spanish, but haven't yet enrolled in a class, go ahead and make a *'Learn Spanish'* project in your task manager, with a task labelled something like *'Research classes in my area'*. That alone is a small step towards actually doing it. Remember, the separation of work and personal life in this system is done by time, not lists. If you need to plan a family holiday, make a project for it in your task manager (and *do* promote its first task to your *Priority* list, or your family won't thank you). One task manager, one calendar, one filing cabinet; whether it's work or personal, you always look in the same place.

Finally, open your calendar and enter any outstanding or regular appointments you can think of, such as a monthly reminder to pay your credit card bill, a quarterly reminder to send your records to your accountant, a weekly reminder to write your email newsletter, and so on. Anything that must be carried out on or by a certain regular date should be a recurring item on your calendar. This is also a good time to enter birthdays and anniversaries as yearly-repeating events – I set these with alerts to remind me a full week before the date, so I have enough time to buy and send a card, book a restaurant, order flowers, or whatever is called for.

... and relax

That's it – you're done!

Oh, there's plenty more you *can* do. The following sections will go into more detail on using the right hardware and software, backing up and archiving digital files, organising your computer's work folders, and more. But you can work through these in your own time.

You've done everything you need to begin your journey as an *Organised Writer*. Relax, have something to eat, and sleep well tonight – knowing that tomorrow morning you'll get cracking on those five pages.

Hardware

Hardware is a catch-all term encompassing many different things a writer might use. In this section I'll look at the essentials, as well as items I consider not essential, but good to have. I'll also tell you what I use myself – but remember, what works for me may not be exactly right for you.

WORKING ENVIRONMENT

Your office space itself is hardware, in a sense. What constitutes the right space is a question only you can discover for yourself; we all work best in different places and environments, and sometimes it takes a while to figure out. No matter where you are, there are some good practices you can follow.

First, assuming you sit down to work, *don't skimp on your chair*. You're going to spend hours and hours – in fact, most of your waking life – in that chair. When I'm in my home office, I spend something like seven to eight hours a day sitting at my desk. Over the course of an average year, that equates to a little over 2,000 hours spent in the same chair – a figure which already takes into account how much time I spend travelling. Remove those trips from the equation and you can easily add another 300 hours to my desk-sitting time. Every single year.

So don't skimp. Make sure you're comfortable, that your posture is good, that it's at (or can be set to) the right height. That might mean spending a chunk of money, but it's worth every penny. There's a natural resistance to overspending on furniture – 'Oh, it's just a chair' – but quite apart from how much time you'll spend in it, think also how long it will last compared to, say, your computer. You'd expect a good chair to last at least ten years, right? In that same time span you'll probably refresh your computer twice (maybe more), each time spending at least several hundred pounds, and you won't think twice about it because you know it's essential to your work. Your chair deserves the same investment.

Again, I'm not telling you what to buy. You may actually be perfectly comfortable, and ergonomically correct, on that kitchen chair you hauled up to the spare bedroom. But if not, buy yourself a better one.

> **STANDING DESKS**
>
> If you prefer to stand while working, a chair won't be as important to you; but you should give the same attention to whatever floor mat you stand on while at your desk. And if you don't use a floor mat, give one a try. I don't stand myself, but I have friends who do, and they all swear by a high-quality mat for their long-term comfort.

The second most important piece of furniture in the room is your desk. In fact, theoretically you could work in a room containing nothing more than a chair and a desk, though I wouldn't advise it.

Again, don't skimp – make sure your desk is the right shape and height for you, and if it has drawers or pedestals check they can hold what you need. I work at a desktop computer, and my desk has a keyboard-holding tray that slides out from underneath the main surface at exactly the right height for me. Depending on your seat and desk height, you may want to look at something with the same feature, although in recent times they're becoming less common – possibly because many people now do all their work on a laptop, even at their home desk. If you're one such person, you may instead want to find a stand that raises the laptop screen to eye level, and buy a separate wireless keyboard to place on the desk itself to avoid working hunched over for hours at a time.

Desks are a case where I can speak from personal experience about prioritising the right desk for you, no matter how much or little it costs. Mine is a cheap, clunky thing I bought from a high-street retailer more than a decade ago, because it was one of the only models that would fit my relatively small study. I fully intended to replace it with a better, higher-quality desk as soon as I could afford to... but then it turned out to be exactly the right height and size for my purposes. My current desk and chair combination is without question the most comfortable I've ever used, and allows me to work for long periods without fatigue. Frankly, the desk is on its last legs (the filing pedestal fell to pieces, and I had to replace it with a cabinet!) but I'm loathe to replace it with anything other than an exact copy. I keep meaning to hire a carpenter to make me a better-quality duplicate. One of these days...

How big should your desk be? At a minimum it should have enough space for your computer, a notepad, and your filing trays, but beyond that it's a matter of taste. Mine also contains a desk phone; stationery items I like to keep handy such as pens, scissors, and a stapler; a charging stand for my phone; a small desktop scanner; and enough space for a beverage. Being a podcaster, I also have a digital audio interface and microphone boom crammed on there.

Whatever items may be on your desk, you should strive to keep the important ones within easy reach. Your notebook and filing trays, especially, should be immediately to hand without much thought or effort. The more you have to think about retrieving them, the less likely you are to use them. My notebook sits right in front of me on my desk, alongside a desk notepad I use to jot notes and thoughts during phone calls, Skype meetings, and podcast recordings. My filing trays are within arm's reach on one side of my desk, and my filing cabinet is on the other side, where the filing drawer pedestal used to be. I can take phone calls, make notes, check my trays, file projects – and write, of course – while barely turning in my chair, let alone getting out of it. The end result of this arrangement is that I *do* take notes without effort, I *do* regularly clear my trays, and I *do* access and use my filing cabinet – because it's actually more effort to let things pile up, to find somewhere to place things 'for later filing', than to just file them right away.

STATIONERY

Every writer I know has a certain fondness for stationery. I suspect it's an unconscious nostalgia; pens and pencils are often the first tools we use to tell stories as children by drawing stick figures, writing stories longhand, or drawing comic strips. But a love of stationery can be a double-edged sword. On the one hand you relish the thought of trying out a dozen different ballpoints to find your favourite, on the other hand you're likely to keep trying dozens more, never settling just because you love pens.

(I may be projecting somewhat. *Je ne regrette rien*.)

Nevertheless, I suggest you take some time to find the best everyday pen for you. A good pen, one you're comfortable using, that writes effortlessly and doesn't break, spill, or clot, is a wonderful thing. When you find the one that suits you I recommend buying at least a dozen of that exact model. Again, this is an area where you don't need to spend a fortune – my favourite disposable ballpoints cost under £2 each. That's less than a single high-street coffee, and in return it gives me weeks or even months of worry-free writing in my notebook. If you think I'm being melodramatic to suggest a bad pen can be a cause of worry, you've evidently never bought a pen just because it was cheap, or the first thing to hand, and then hated using it every time you try to write. That distaste gets in the way of your thought process, and in the way of writing. By contrast, if you find the pen that's right for you and make sure it's always at hand, you won't give it a second thought when you come to make a note or scribble out an idea. That's how all your tools should be.

Why buy a dozen of the same pen? So that you're never without a replacement when ink runs out, yes; but also because you're going to seed them around the place, to ensure there's always one to hand. Leave one on your desk at all times – never take it with you, never remove it from your desk. Put another in your handbag/backpack/daybag, whatever you take when you leave the house. Again, don't remove it from the bag. If you use it

It's a set-up

while out of the house, replace it in the bag and leave it there, even when you return home. If your notebook has a loop for holding pens, put one in there too. Put one in the glovebox of your car, by the front door key holder, in your travel suitcase's miscellaneous items pocket... wherever you go there should always be a pen within easy reach.

Note that I'm talking here about your everyday notes pen. You may have a 'best' pen, something more expensive, that you prefer to use for signings or official documents. A nice fountain, perhaps, or a premium ballpoint. Obviously I'm not suggesting you buy a dozen of those.

If you use non-disposable pens – i.e. with ballpoint refill cartridges – you should ensure you also have a healthy supply of refills, and keep at least one in your handbag/backpack, in case you run out of ink while away from your desk.

You may think it odd to spend more than 500 words discussing ballpoint pens, but I disagree. This isn't something you pull out of a kitchen drawer to write a shopping list; it's a professional tool, fundamental to your work. It's worth taking the time, and spending a little money, to find the one that's right for you.

There are a dozen more little things to stock up on – stationery items you won't need often, but will be grateful for when you do, and come to use without giving it much thought. Being able to pick up a stapler within arm's reach, open the drawer next to me to immediately find a paperclip, or take a pair of scissors straight from my desk tidy all reduce friction in my working day.

The following items are what I regard as essential for a small office. They needn't all be in your desk (though they can be, if you have space) but they should be no more than a few steps away:

- stapler;
- staple-remover;
- paper clips, and folding binder clips;
- address labels, both pre-printed with your address, and blank for mailing (I keep mine filed in my cabinet, under *A* of course);

- pair of scissors;
- ruler;
- clear sticky tape;
- parcel tape;
- padded envelopes big enough to mail a book;
- permanent markers;
- pushpins, if you use a cork board.

You should also have spares/refills of appropriate items like your notepad, paper and toner cartridge for your printer, staples, etc.

COMPUTER AND PERIPHERALS

Your computer should be the best you can afford. People will argue (and argue, and argue) over which operating system you should use, the best manufacturer to buy, which 'digital ecosystem' you should join, and more. When it comes to computers, personal taste really does matter. On this overall point, however, I won't equivocate; *buy the best computer you can afford.*

This device, this metal or plastic case of silicon and circuits, is the primary tool of your working life. If you're a full-time writer, it's how you earn a living; if you're a part-time writer, it may not be how you earn a living yet... but it's probably how you'd like to. A good computer is one that lasts for years, works reliably, and doesn't cause anxiety because of low-quality parts or manufacturing. These are all aspects worth paying for.

I'm not suggesting you spend beyond your means. Don't shell out thousands of pounds on a high-end computer if you're strapped for cash. But as with your chair and desk, frugality for its own sake is a false economy.

While we're here, let's also talk peripherals. You're almost certainly going to want a printer, for example. My advice to any writer is to buy a *laser printer*, not an inkjet model. Laser printers are cheaper, more reliable, and can print multiple pages of text faster than any inkjet. Unless you're a photographer, you don't need a printer to produce glossy pictures taken with your phone. What you do need is a machine that can print all 400 pages of your manuscript in half an hour without needing an ink change, and for that a laser printer is ideal. It will cost more initially, but toner refills are relatively cheap, and each of them will print twenty times as many pages of text as a poor, overworked black inkjet cartridge before it needs replacing.

You may also need a *scanner*. Since faxes have finally gone the way of the dodo, many publishers and clients will now send you a contract via email; ask you to print it, sign it, and scan it; then email the scans back to them. The sooner we all move on to digital signatures the better, in my opinion, but until then a scanner is often necessary. You can now buy printer/scanner combination machines, but again, if the printer in question is an inkjet, I recommend avoiding it and buying a separate cheap scanner instead.

Finally, an *external hard drive* for backup is essential. Modern hard-drive storage is absurdly cheap, and the price only goes down with each passing year. Buy a hard drive at least as big as the one in your main computer, and use it to make regular, full backups at home. Note that this is different to backups you may make while travelling, as discussed in Chapter 4 – for those you should have a separate external drive. Don't take your 'home' backup with you on the road!

Software

Strictly speaking, of course, you don't need software at all. You could write longhand, or on a manual typewriter, and insist on all contact being via post and telephone. I wouldn't necessarily advise it, but it's possible, and I do know writers whose only concession to the modern era is a non-internet-connected word processor.

If you use a computer and/or smartphone, though, you can't avoid software – and while the default applications can often be fine, they're not always the best for a particular problem. Always consider what you really need them for, and if you can replace them with something more suitable.

I write on a Mac, as I've mentioned already. In fact, I've used Macs continually since 1988 so I'm extremely familiar and comfortable with them. By contrast, while I've occasionally used a Windows PC for work purposes, and managed to muddle through, I wouldn't pretend to be au fait with them or their software ecosystem. Combine that with software's potential to have a short lifespan, plus the fact that you might be reading this years after publication, and it would be folly of me to insist you use specific software applications.

Instead, in this section I'll make general recommendations of *types* of software that you'll find useful in your quest to be an *Organised Writer*, and what sort of features are useful for our purposes. Any software that meets these criteria will then suffice.

That said, you may want or need recommendations to get started. I'll tell you what applications I use on Mac and iPhone; fortunately, many also have Windows and/or Android phone versions. For those that don't I'll suggest equivalents on those platforms, but remember to take the suggestions in the spirit in which they're offered – which is to say, *caveat emptor*. Always research and/or try out software for yourself before purchase.

THE BASICS

There are six types of application I consider essential, and which enable any writer to work more easily and efficiently.

1. Writing software
2. Note-taker
3. Calendar
4. Task manager

It's a set-up

5. Spreadsheet
6. Local and cloud backup and archiving

In earlier chapters, I discussed *how* to use these applications as part of *The Organised Writer* system. Now let's look at *which* applications you should think about using.

WRITING SOFTWARE

Almost every writer starts out using a simple word processor, and for most of us that first application was Microsoft Word, part of the company's Office suite. Word is ubiquitous in the publishing world, and has become a de facto standard. There's no denying its benefits, the most obvious being its reliable cross-compatibility between platforms; if I'm on a Mac and you're on Windows, we can send each other Word documents, edit them, track changes, make comments – then send them back to the other person fully confident that everything will work as intended. Even versions of wildly different vintage are mostly compatible, with 20-year-old Word documents still readable on modern versions – albeit likely with some loss of formatting, but the text will be present and correct. Finally, Word's omnipresence means that no matter who you're working with, anywhere in the world, you can send them a .doc file and be very confident they can work with it.

However, Word also has one very big problem: it's not a good working environment for writers.

That's a slightly contentious statement, and you may disagree; perhaps you love Word, never have any trouble with it, and it's never prevented you from working efficiently. If that's the case, by all means continue. But Word, like all such linear word processors, is little more than a glorified typewriter. Those of us who work in a non-linear fashion, or operate across different media, can benefit from something more flexible. Enter the relatively new field of writing applications, designed to help you organise your notes and research in the same environment in which you draft your manuscript.

The pre-eminent application in this field is Scrivener, which is the software I use and recommend for almost any writer. Unlike Word, Scrivener is designed to let you work in non-sequential order without friction... or, if you really do prefer to work in a linear manner, you can do that perfectly well, too. The only assumption it makes is that you'll write more effectively if you can easily see your notes and research while you're writing, and keep them all contained in a single document. No matter what your writing habits are, I believe that's a sentiment most authors can get behind.

(Disclaimer: Scrivener users may notice that the 'Graphic Novel Script' template included with the software is attributed to me, as I was the first professional comics writer to use the application and worked with the developer to create the template. I receive no compensation for its inclusion, and happily pay for the software like everyone else.)

Scrivener's success has signalled a minor revolution in software for writers, and now there are many applications that allow you to outline, plan, hold research and notes, and write in a non-linear way, all in the same environment. Ulysses, Storyist, and Wavemaker are some of the better-known alternatives. All of these applications have free trial periods, so try them out and find the one that suits your working style best.

It's important to note that even a fully featured 'writing environment' often isn't enough by itself. For example, much as I dislike using Microsoft Word, I keep a current copy because of its universal compatibility; when I finish a manuscript I import the draft into Word, and the resulting document is what I send to my editor. There's a similar issue with screenplays, where applications such as Final Draft and Movie Magic Screenwriter have become industry standards, and upstart apps like Highland and Fade In are making inroads. Again, I write such scripts in Scrivener; but when it comes time to turn it in, I export the script to Highland, and submit a PDF of that document because it's what the client expects to receive.

You may think, 'Well, then why not just write in those applications to start with?', but that's my point; I find writing in Scrivener so much more pleasant that it's worth going through some import/export nonsense at the end.

Ultimately, you must evaluate your writing software and decide if it works well enough for you. You may find a different application suits you better; you may even decide you'll stick to Word, after all. But do take some time to investigate your options. My working life was forever changed, and for the better, when I threw off the shackles of linear word processing. Yours might be too.

OPENOFFICE (OO)

OO is a free, open-source clone of Microsoft Office, and is fine if you'd be equally happy working in Word, but can't afford/don't want to purchase it. However, it's important to note two things. First, while OO is a fairly mature and stable piece of software, it's not without quirks and bugs; and while it gets very close to 100 per cent compatibility with Microsoft Office, it's doubtful it can ever fully achieve it. If that compatibility is crucial to you, stick with the real thing. Second, OO may be free, but the price of software in general continues to fall. At time of writing almost every good modern writing application is less than £/$100 for a single-user licence. For a professional writer, investing such a relatively small amount in reliable software that will help you work more effectively is surely worth it.

NOTE-TAKER

With your primary writing software in place, you're ready to look at a few other essential applications, and first among equals is a good note-taker.

Cast your mind back to Chapter 3, and the vital importance of being able to easily take notes, and you'll understand why this is so. You should try to use a note-taker that's both cross-platform, and syncs across those platforms. What do I mean by that? Well, a good example is the Notes app on the Mac/iOS platform; it's available on every Mac and iPhone, and its contents automatically synchronise between them so that if you make a note on your iPhone, by the next time you open up the notes on your Mac it will already be there.

So if you're a Mac and iPhone user like me, Notes is probably all you need, and best of all, it's free. If you use a different computer and/or phone, however, you'll need something else. Microsoft OneNote also works across Mac, Windows, and mobile platforms, and if you're an Office user you may already have access to it. For non-Office users, Simplenote also works and syncs across all platforms, though it has fewer features. If you're very comfortable with Google's services, Google Keep is a free online service that works through a web browser on your computer, and mobile apps on your phone.

CALENDAR

I use the built-in Calendar application on my Mac and iPhone, because it does everything I need – makes appointments, blocks out time periods, sets reminder alarms – and syncs reliably. Some prefer more powerful applications, especially those with natural language-processing such as FantastiCal and BusyCal; I think they're overkill, but if you find yourself frustrated by the default calendar's simplicity, you should give them a try.

Windows comes with a built-in Calendar application that can be set to sync across your devices, and Office users can also use the Outlook calendar suite.

TASK MANAGER

As I mentioned in Chapter 2, my task manager of choice is Things for Mac and iPhone, which syncs across both platforms. Things is extremely simple in its approach to task management – too simple for some, as the developers' considered pace of development frustrates those who wish for constant updates and new features. Not me, though. My preference is for tools that do what they need to do well, simply and reliably, without over-complicating matters.

Things isn't available on Windows, but there are many other apps in this space, and many are cross-platform; Trello is web-based so works anywhere, while Wunderlist and Todoist are both available for Mac, Windows, iOS, and Android.

SPREADSHEET

I record my accounts in Numbers, another default Mac application. I simply don't need anything more powerful to record my revenue/expenses and calculate totals. As I have Microsoft Office, the much more powerful Excel is always to hand, but light usage such as mine really doesn't need it – and I find Numbers more user-friendly and intuitive.

If you're an Office user on Windows, you might as well stick with Excel. If you don't have Office, OpenOffice has its own Excel equivalent, or Google's Docs service includes Sheets, its online spreadsheet maker. For more business-dedicated use there's also Zoho Books, part of an online suite.

LOCAL BACKUP

A horrifyingly large number of people still don't back up their computers at all; if you're one of them, I implore you to get into the habit.

MacOS has an automatic local backup option, called Time Machine, built right into the system. To use it, just buy an external hard drive and plug it into your Mac; if Time Machine isn't already active, the computer will ask if you want to use it with this external drive. Click *Yes*, and off you go. Time Machine is simplistic as backup systems go, but *any backup is better than nothing*. Time Machine has saved my bacon several times over the years – normally when I've foolishly deleted a document thinking it was a copy, but in fact it was the original. We've all done it…

The other option, which you can use by itself or in addition to Time Machine, is to regularly 'clone' your computer's hard drive. Applications like SuperDuper and Carbon Copy Cloner can be scheduled to automatically make a complete copy of your hard drive whenever you like (most people set it for 3am, when the computer is otherwise sitting idle). The advantage of cloning software is that it doesn't just protect against a file going astray, it protects against your entire computer going haywire. You have an entire copy of the drive, with everything where you expect it to be, ready for transplant onto a replacement computer. Some of these applications even allow you to start up your computer from the external hard drive clone, and continue your work as normal. This should be a last resort, though, as by definition it means you no longer have a safe backup.

If you're on Windows, Acronis True Image is reliable and user-friendly, though licences require a purchase; if you're more tech-savvy, both DriveImage XML and Clonezilla are free to individuals.

CLOUD BACKUP

Local backup is quick, easy, and convenient. But it remains local, which makes it vulnerable to any localised disaster. A house fire won't just destroy your computer, it'll also destroy your local backup. This is why I (and most other tech-minded people out there) recommend also using a *cloud backup* service of some kind.

I say 'of some kind' because there are two things to consider. You've probably heard of Dropbox, Apple's iCloud, Microsoft's OneDrive, and several other similar cloud services, but they're not true backups in the sense I mean. Those are syncing services, which allow you to synchronise files between your computers over an internet connection, so your desktop and laptop always have the same versions of your documents (as long as the computers in question are online). This is incredibly useful, and I use Dropbox myself all the time. But if you're working directly on those files, they're not a true backup – because as soon as you make an edit, every version on your other computers is also changed. Overwrite a file when you didn't mean to? Tough luck, because now the overwritten version is the one in the cloud that all your other computers draw from.

That said... my technology-writer friends will give me stern looks for saying this, but Dropbox (or a similar service) is all most writers need, as long as you use it alongside automated local backup. Dropbox itself keeps prior versions of your files for a few weeks, so if you do make an error, as long as you spot it in good time you can revert to an older version. I have a paid Dropbox account, because I use it to hold much more than writing – design files, musical compositions, trailer videos, and more – but if you're a 'pure' writer dealing solely with small files like text documents and PDFs, any free cloud syncing account will likely have enough space to hold all of your work.

Nevertheless, you may also want to invest in a true cloud backup solution, such as Backblaze, CrashPlan, Arq, or one of the many others now available. These services work by installing a small application on your computer that runs in the background, continually backing up data from your hard drive to the company's servers via your internet connection. The beauty of these solutions is that you don't have to think about or do anything; the backup just works automatically, all the time.

Most of these services offer simple file restoration, i.e. the ability to download older versions of a file if you delete one by mistake, or make an overwrite error. Many also offer *full-drive* restoration, so if you have a catastrophic failure you can download (or in some cases, they will literally mail to you a hard drive containing) the entire backup of your computer.

I use Backblaze, as their one-size-fits-all offering suits my needs – but any good service will cost you money, so you should research what they offer and read reviews before taking the plunge yourself.

ARCHIVING

Archiving differs from backup because, similar to the archives of your paper documents, it concerns digital files no longer being worked on but which you must be able to access if necessary.

> **MIGRATING ARCHIVES**
>
> I used to burn CD-ROM copies of all my archive files, as optical discs were at the time an order of magnitude cheaper, and more reliable, than hard-drive storage. But hard drive storage is now as robust as it is cheap, and optical media is fast disappearing, so I recently spent a weekend 'repatriating' the files on all those discs back onto external hard drive storage. No doubt in ten years' time I'll be moving them all again, this time onto something like holographic memory sticks.

There are many ways to digitally archive files, depending on what kind of setup you already have. The important thing is that you have some defined location to store old documents, and move your projects to it when they're finished. Regardless of your chosen method, you should also make sure this archive is included in your regular backups.

If you have a Dropbox account with plenty of free space, you can move all your completed projects there, knowing Dropbox will keep a copy in the cloud; if you'd rather keep the backups at hand, you could make copies onto an external hard drive while maintaining the versions on your computer; or advanced users might even prefer to keep the archives on a network-attached storage (NAS) server connected to a cloud backup service. One reason I use Backblaze is that in addition to my computer itself, the service also backs up any physically connected hard drives – such as the large-capacity USB disk I have wired to it. When I archive a project, I simply move its folder to the external hard drive; this frees up space on my main computer, while ensuring there's still a backup copy in the cloud.

OTHER SOFTWARE

That's it for the essentials. The following suggestions are therefore optional, and not all are even about writing your manuscript, but they're applications I can't imagine working without.

Voice chat
Technically this is a whole field of software known as 'VOIP' (Voice Over Internet Protocol), but you probably know it better as Skype, which is the dominant application. There are however many others, and which you use will depend largely on who you're chatting to; some clients will ask you to use a specific conference call suite such as GoToMeeting or Zoom, others will be happy sticking to Skype, and some may ask if you have an iPhone so you can FaceTime. If you're unsure about any of this, I suggest you download Skype (it's free, and works on most computers and phones) and try it out. Don't worry about other applications unless and until someone wants you to use them.

Timeline creator
Not all authors will want or need a timeline creator, but if you're a writer of science fiction, fantasy, or historical fiction, you may already make timelines manually – be it with index cards, sheets of paper taped together, a whiteboard on the wall, whatever. Sometimes those simple ways are the best, especially in a collaborative environment. If you want something a little less unwieldy, or more personal, take a look at timeline software.

I use Aeon Timeline, an application that was designed from the outset for fiction writers. It's intuitive, very flexible, and available for both Mac and Windows. I was an early beta tester and have been using it since it launched to keep track of many stories and series, especially those with a rich fictional history such as *The Fuse* or *Wasteland* – but it's also been useful for stories where plot timing is crucial, such as *The Coldest City* and *The Exphoria Code*.

Character-finder and text snippets

There are two small utility-like applications I've come to rely on completely in my day-to-day work; character finders, and text snippets.

A character-finder is an application that allows you to locate and insert those hard-to-find characters – è, ć, ġ, Ø, ™, ¶, and so on – without spending five minutes playing finger-Twister on your keyboard, trying eight different modifier keys before you finally give up and look online. The one I use is called PopChar, an always-on application that lives in the menu bar of my Mac (it's also available for Windows) and can be accessed at any time with a single click, allowing me to find crazy diacritics or obscure emoji with ease. I've been using PopChar for more than twenty years, and continue to do so almost every day. It's one of the first things I install on any new computer.

Text snippet applications also save time, but in a different way. You use them to store blocks of text which you find yourself typing again and again, such as your email address, a standard sign-off, your mailing address, today's date, etc. These blocks are then automatically inserted in place when you type a certain abbreviation.

For example, mine is set up so that when I type *ajemail* it automatically replaces that made-up word with my email address. Most of these applications can also use variables; when I type *dt* followed by a space, it replaces that sequence with today's date, drawing the information directly from the computer system. It's possible to get very elaborate with these applications; some people have entire stock email replies stored, enabling them to reply to standard enquiries with a few keystrokes. I don't do anything that complex, but I've still come to rely heavily on the aspects I do use.

My preferred application in this area is Typinator (from the same developer as PopChar), which is Mac-only, though many friends and colleagues use TextExpander on both Mac and Windows. Other, similar applications include aText and TypeIt4Me (Mac), or Phrase Express and Breevy (Windows).

Launcher

In its simplest definition, a 'launcher' is software that allows you to open applications via your keyboard rather than clicking on them with a mouse or trackpad. On Macs, the Spotlight interface is a very basic launcher that does just that; you activate it with a key combination, type in the first few letters of the application you want to launch, then hit Enter and, hey presto, the application launches without having to lift your fingers from the keyboard.

Most launchers can do so much more. Even Spotlight can be used to perform simple calculations – launch it, type *2 + 2*, and the solution *4* will appear before your eyes – but many dedicated launchers can also move, copy, or rename files; look up contact details; perform online searches; control your computer's audio; convert images between file formats; and much more besides.

On the Mac, the three heavy hitters in this space are Quicksilver, Launchbar, and Alfred. Each has its own quirks, specialities, advantages and disadvantages, and it's therefore impossible for me to guess which is right for you. I'm a Quicksilver user, and have never been able to 'get into' Launchbar; but I have good friends who will say the exact opposite, and are baffled that I use Quicksilver. Then there are people for whom Spotlight itself is enough. It really is a matter of personal taste and sensibility. But if the idea of being able to perform powerful actions just from your keyboard – and without having to be a computer coder – appeals to you, check out the launcher applications you could be using. Quicksilver is another application I install immediately on any new computer, and I can barely imagine trying to get by without it.

On Windows, Launchy is a free and popular app that resembles Quicksilver, while Keybreeze (which has free and paid options according to the features you require) more closely aligns with Launchbar. Both are very much their own thing, though; on every platform, your choice of launcher is extremely personal.

Password manager

The headlines these days are full of data breaches. It seems that every other week millions of accounts and passwords from some service or other are hacked to be sold on the black market, and there doesn't seem to be a thing anyone can do about it.

Of course, there is one thing we can all do, and that's use a different password for each of our online accounts. That was easy when all we had was email, Amazon, and AOL Instant Messenger, but these days it's not so simple. Most of us now have dozens of online accounts, and trying to use a different password for each one (particularly if we also follow the advice never to write those passwords down) can be extremely taxing. On the other hand, not doing so leaves us vulnerable; if you use the same password for Facebook, Twitter, and Amazon, it only needs one of them to leak for hackers to gain access to the others.

This is where the password manager comes in – a secure, encrypted application that not only generates strong passwords you can use, but more importantly *remembers them for you*. The best known of these, and the one I use, is 1Password; so called because I need only create and remember one good, strong password to unlock all the others stored in its encrypted database. 1Password allows me to easily use a new and different password for every online account I have. Even if someone discovers my Twitter password, that password can't be used to log in to any other accounts; and because my password manager app stores all these different passwords for me, I don't have to struggle to remember them. Which is just as well, as I have hundreds.

Using a password manager requires you to place complete trust in both the application and its developers, of course. You're relying on it to work reliably, and not do anything nefarious with your information, so it pays to use established software from a reputable developer. Other well-regarded apps in this field include RememBear, LastPass, and Dashlane; they and 1Password are all available for Mac, Windows, iOS, and Android.

PDF editor

PDF editors have two main uses for an author. If you receive proofs in PDF format, you can make annotations directly onto the file; I find this particularly valuable on my iPad, where I can use an Apple Pencil to jot notes, strike words, mark as stet, and so on, right onto the pages. I can then either share that file directly with my editor – who may opt to do the same thing – or write them up using the annotated file as reference.

A PDF editor also allows you to complete forms and 'sign' contracts sent to you in PDF format, without needing to print and/or scan a paper version. As someone who regularly signs a dozen or more NDAs, let alone contracts, every year I gladly pay for that ability alone.

I use PDFpen on my Mac, and GoodReader on iOS, but there are many such editors on the market. Which one you use will depend on your own tastes and needs.

You can of course also use Adobe's Acrobat software, which is available on both Mac and Windows, but it's much more powerful than most of us require. Other Windows options include Nitro Pro, part of a paid online suite, and PDFill PDF Editor, a more basic app with free and paid options.

Scanner driver

If you bought (or already have) a scanner, it probably came supplied with driver software. Hopefully that software works with your computer… but that's not a given. Even if it works now, you may find your scanner lasts for many years longer than its drivers are updated. The manufacturer of my scanner hasn't updated its drivers since 2010, and as a result it stopped working with modern Macs in 2012, even though the scanner itself is fully functional.

I therefore use and recommend an application called VueScan, available for Mac and Windows (there's even a Linux version), which allows you to keep using that venerable scanner with your modern computer. VueScan has many advanced features that allow you to do things like create multi-page PDFs directly from scans, and you may find those more useful than I do; all that matters to me is being able to scan documents without buying a new scanner every two years. For that, VueScan works flawlessly.

Calculation app
Like many writers I'm practically allergic to mathematics, so easy-to-use calculating software is a godsend. Those of you who are more numerically-minded might want to check out an advanced calculator such as PCalc on the Mac/iOS, SpeedCrunch on Windows, or RealCalc Scientific Calculator on Android.

If you prefer dealing in words, though, an application called Soulver allows you to do calculations using natural language, such as '£500 – 15% *discount*' or '20% *of £1,650*' – ideal for working out sales taxes and tip amounts. It's also multi-line, and automatically calculates the sum of all items; just paste line amounts of, say, fees or expenses into a document and the total will appear automatically at the bottom. Soulver also has many more advanced features, and can handle quite complex mathematics; my usage is so rudimentary it barely scratches the surface, but it makes that usage so easy my purchase was easily justified.

Soulver is only available on the Mac and iOS, but Windows users can download a very similar app called OpalCalc.

Email
All modern email clients have basically the same features; if you're already comfortable with your existing software, carry on. If you're dissatisfied with the default email application on your computer, though, take a look at what's on offer these days. Even if you use a webmail service like Gmail, it's a fairly simple matter to access the account through an application rather than the web interface, if you'd prefer.

(On my Mac, I actually do use the Gmail web interface as it's sufficient for my needs. On iOS, I use Gmail's own app.)

Whatever you use, recall what I said in Chapter 2 about using filters/rules and labels/categories to process and categorise your incoming emails. Setting these up in advance can save you hours of boring administration and email filing in the future, as well as ensuring only important mail makes it to your inbox.

Travel software

Finally, if you travel for work there are some applications worth adding to your smartphone, to keep you informed on the road and make journeys easier.

You should certainly install any relevant loyalty apps for airlines, hotels, car services, and so on. In many cases you can now download your tickets to these apps without even needing to create an online account, which is very handy. I rarely use physical boarding cards for planes any more.

I also recommend using a travel itinerary app, which you can load up with details of where you're going and your schedule while there. I use a service called TripIt, because it syncs between the web and a mobile app – I can enter details into a standard web browser, and have everything ready on my phone when I leave. TripIt's superpower, however, is its ability to extract information from emails. If I book a flight, train, or hotel, I can just forward the confirmation email to a private TripIt address and the details will appear automatically in my account. I can also modify those details through the web interface, or enter something entirely by hand if I prefer. There are several services that do the same thing; I use TripIt because it was one of the first, and I'm very familiar with it. If you're just starting to use an itinerary tracker like this, check around to see which one suits you best.

Download timetable and/or tracker apps for the public transport services at your destination. If you're visiting London, grab an app with Tube maps and routes; if you're off to Paris, get the Metro app instead; for New York, download a subway app; and so on. Google has become increasingly good at handling requests for public transport details, so if you can't find a dedicated app, Google Maps may suffice to get around on a metro or to check train times. But a dedicated app will normally be more reliable. If you're catching a plane, there are several flight-tracking apps available for your phone;

my favourite is simply called Flight Tracker. Far beyond merely tracking flights, these apps will also alert you to gate changes, delays, and so on – sometimes even before any official announcement is made.

> **DO YOUR RESEARCH**
>
> Wherever you're going, be sure to know their policies regarding personal technology, bringing computers into the region, online privacy, etc. Always check before you travel.

Finally, remember that your smartphone has a camera, and use it to snap photos of things you need to recognise or remember. In the past I've used mine to take pictures of landmarks, signs in a foreign language, the licence plate of a hire car, even the number of my hotel room after I check in.

Taxonomy

Having an organised file system on your computer won't by itself make you a more efficient writer; indeed, I know one very successful scriptwriter who uses his computer's desktop as his file storage area, creating a seething chaotic mass of documents in seemingly random order. I break out in hives just to look at it, but it seems to work for him…

So I won't insist that you must adopt an organised file taxonomy on your computer; but if you want to, here's a very simple method.

Both Mac and Windows these days like to keep a bunch of system folders – your applications, downloads, system preferences, music library, and so on – in the 'root' directory of each user account. I recommend not messing with any of that; modern systems are very good at taking care of themselves, so leave them to it.

It's a set-up

Instead, in that same root directory you should create a single ur-folder and place inside it everything you work on – every project, every Word doc, every reference PDF, the lot.

I call my ur-folder *Archive*, partly so that it sits near the top of the root folder, but you could call it *Work* or *Writing* or anything else. Within my *Archive* I've created a number of sub-folders, to divide up the different types of work I do and other subject matter.

Archive		
Applications →	1 Writing →	
Archive →	2 Podcasts →	
Desktop →	3 Finances →	
Documents →	4 Design →	
Downloads →	5 Travel →	
Films →	6 Household →	
Music →		
Photos →		
Podcasts →		

The number prefixes ensure these folders appear in the same order every time I open the *Archive*, with the most frequently accessed at the top. The folder titles are self-explanatory, and of course you may not need so many. They all follow similar principles, so let's look inside the *Writing* folder.

Archive > 1 Writing		
1 Writing →	01 In Progress →	
2 Podcasts →	02 Awaiting Publication →	
3 Finances →	03 In Development →	
4 Design →	04 Story Reference →	
5 Travel →	05 Publisher Reference →	
6 Household →	06 In Limbo →	
	07 Cons, etc →	
	08 PR Stuff →	
	09 Finished →	
	10 Other People →	

More sub-folders, again numbered to keep them in my desired order. When I drill down into *In Progress*, I then find my current project folders.

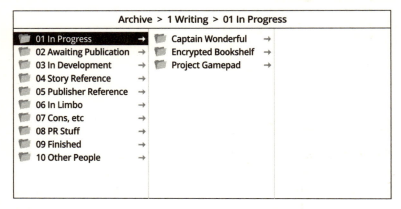

Within each project folder are its relevant digital files. I don't number individual files, but I do use a 'Z' prefix for infrequently-accessed folders, to keep them at the bottom of the list.

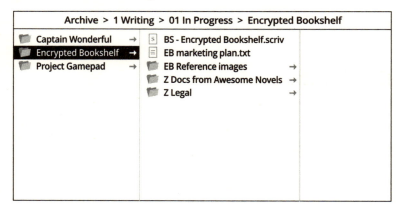

Let's look at another one. All my accounting records are in *Finances*, with the main folder containing the current year's files.

It's a set-up

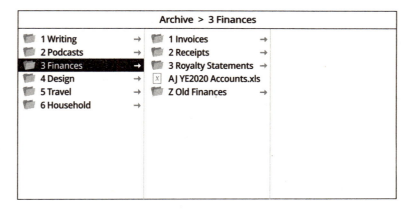

The *Old Finances* folder at the bottom contains archives filed by their financial year. *YE* is for 'Year Ending', so *YE2018* contains all the files for the financial year 2017–18; the UK tax year ends in early April, so dividing records by financial rather than calendar years prevents confusion and allows for consistency when locating relevant records such as invoices or receipts.

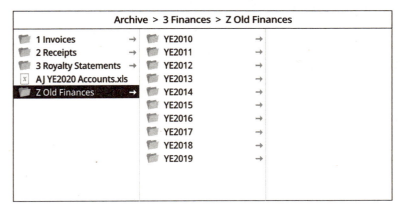

There's more, of course, but if you want to adopt a more organised taxonomy, that's enough to get you started. It's another of those areas where personal taste and habits really matter (hence my friend with the hives-inducing desktop).

Don't be afraid to experiment; if digital file management is something you struggle with, give a system like this a try. It could be one more thing that helps you on your way to becoming an *Organised Writer*.

Gadgets

These are all *strictly* non-essential. Nothing listed here is necessary to write a masterpiece... but they all make my life and work much easier.

SMARTPHONE/TABLET

It's not quite true to say all modern phones are alike, but they're certainly closer in functionality now than when they first appeared. I use an Apple iPhone, and I also carry an iPad when I travel, because I'm very comfortable inside the ecosystem. More importantly, as a Mac user syncing everything up between my computers, phone, and tablet is very simple. It's possible to sync a calendar, notes, to-dos, and so on between Android devices and Macs, but it requires a certain base level of technical knowledge and a reliance on third-party apps whose ability to access the ecosystem is temperamental at best. For me, that's not worth the hassle. Also, Scrivener has an iOS application, and while I don't use it a lot I'm grateful for it when I do.

On the other hand, if you're a Windows user, it's generally easier to accommodate an Android device and make it sync reliably – a lot of third-party software is designed to help you do just that, or you can always use Google's suite on an Android phone and access the data through your Windows computer's web browser.

BATTERY PACK

Smartphones have been a boon to mobile productivity but they've also given us a whole new set of worries, mostly concerning battery life. Readers of a certain age will remember when mobile phones, owing to their simplicity, could go a week on a single battery charge, but those days are long behind us. Even though battery efficiency increases all the time, so do the power demands of our devices. More than a decade after the original iPhone was released, most of us still struggle to get more than a day's use out of our smartphones.

Thus, when travelling I carry a battery pack; a small, rechargeable battery into which you can plug your phone and charge it on those occasions you just can't find a power outlet. Battery packs come in all shapes and sizes – I use one which is roughly the same size as my phone, thus enabling me to 'stack' them on top of one another, or even drop them side by side into a jacket pocket, for convenience. Whatever style you prefer, if you use a smartphone you should add a battery pack (and accompanying spare charging cable) to your travel kit.

TRAVEL TRAY

Like packing lists, this may earn you a roll of the eyes from friends or family. I don't travel without one, ever since a trip to Tokyo convinced me to give them a try.

> ### HAPPY TO HELP
>
> Given the Japanese fondness for order and tidiness, you might assume I saw someone there using a travel tray and was thus inspired. Ah, if only.
>
> I was hired to write a videogame for a Tokyo-based developer, so travelled to Japan for the first time. As it was a business trip, and Japanese business culture is notoriously formalised, I took several collared shirts. But halfway through the trip I had some spare time for tourism, so donned a T-shirt and left my shirt collar points on the desk of my hotel room. I returned to find the maid had seen the points, assumed they were bits of waste plastic, and 'helpfully' threw them out with the rubbish… at which point I realised that if they'd been in a tray, she wouldn't have assumed they had no purpose.

Using a travel tray is enormously reassuring once you make it a habit. Whenever I remove my watch from my wrist, my wallet from my coat, even my glasses from my head, they go in the travel tray. Keys, travel tickets, room key, phone charging cable, anything small and easy to lose goes in there. I don't have to search my room for such items, worry they might be lost, or wonder where I put them when filling my pockets to go out. I know they're in the tray.

If you've never seen a travel tray, prepare to be underwhelmed; it's simply a piece of flat fabric (easy to pack and travel with) that 'pops up' into a tray, usually via press studs or Velcro, though sometimes with flexible side struts. The better models also have slim pockets stitched into the sides, to hold items like a key card. I use a Maxpedition model, and after nearly a decade of continual use it's as good as new.

NOISE-CANCELLING HEADPHONES

As I mentioned in Chapter 4, I always recommend noise-cancelling (NC) models to anyone who needs headphones. Just a few years ago NC headphones were expensive and extravagant, but the price continues to fall. I wear Bose QuietComforts (generally regarded as the market leaders), which I find very comfortable and reliable.

Let me emphasise that if you work at home and don't travel much, you don't need NC headphones. But if you work in a coffee shop, or frequently travel by air, rail, or sea – any form of transport where engine noise creates a drone – you should consider buying a pair.

PRESENTATION GEAR

If you regularly deliver presentations with a slideshow on your laptop, there are a few items that can help things go smoothly.

First, buy your own 'clicker' rather than relying on venues to provide one for you. The freedom of movement and expression a good clicker affords during talks is invaluable; using one that you know works reliably with your own computer and software, with a shape you're used to feeling and manipulating in your hand, means you're not wrestling with unfamiliar technology before or during the presentation. I use a Kensington model, the catchily named *33374*. Not only is it reliable and comfortable, but in a stroke of design genius its USB adapter slides securely into the clicker's main body when not in use.

Next, carry a small bag of adapter cables to hook your laptop up to the projector. The world of projectors and presentation video boards is broad, and relying on venues to have the right cable to connect their hardware to your computer is at best unwise. I have a selection of cables I pack along with my clicker, one for each connection type of VGA, DVI, and HDMI. After all, would you rather have the cables with you and not need them... or vice versa?

> **TAKE YOUR OWN CABLES**
>
> Don't rely on people to know their own equipment. At times I've spoken in advance to a venue's technicians, and have been confidently assured their projectors and cables are all compatible with my needs – only to discover upon arrival that what they told me was sorely mistaken. It pains me to say it, but don't trust anyone; take your own cables.

Finally, it's a good idea to have a copy of your presentation on a USB thumb drive, in case of computer failure (or in case the venue insists you use their laptop). I carry two versions; one is a copy of the original animated presentation, which I can use if the venue has the same software. The other is a 'flattened' PDF, exported from the original but without animations or sound. This is a version of last resort – at the very least I should be able to plug the drive into any computer and display a PDF.

Summary

OVERALL:

- Take a weekend to organise your working space so that everything you need is to hand and can be easily located.

HARDWARE:
- Place your filing cabinet/drawer no more than two steps from your chair.
- Position desk trays within reach on your desk.
- Archive boxes can go anywhere within the room.
- Sort souvenirs from tools.
  - Keep souvenirs on display, necessary tools on desk or in drawers.
  - Items that are neither can be discarded.

PROJECT FOLDERS:
- Make manila folders and job sheets for every project.
  - File relevant project documents accordingly.
  - Don't be afraid to discard old and irrelevant creative documents.
- Determine whether the folder belongs in a desk tray, your filing cabinet, or an archive box.
- Make standard generic folders for yearly recurring non-creative items such as invoices and bank statements.
- Ensure you have spare folders, keep them handy, and don't be stingy using them.
- Make digital equivalents of project folders and inboxes.

CALENDAR AND TASK MANAGER:
- Add appointments, projects, and tasks as they come to you; get into the habit of doing this every time you become aware of a new appointment or task.
  - Make recurring calendar reminders for regular tasks and appointments, e.g. paying your credit card bill.
- Remember to add personal and family items too.

CHAPTER 8

Conclusion: Living as an organised writer

(×) A *disorganised writer* is what you were before you read this book.

(✓) *The organised writer* is what you will become when you put the system into practice, and look back on being disorganised with mild disbelief.

Tomorrow is the first day of your new life.

It's an old aphorism, somewhat trite, and often overused. That doesn't mean it isn't true. You read this book to change your habits, make your working practices more organised, and cope better with your workload.

Now that you've reached the end, I recommend you go back to the start and read it again. Having seen the whole, you'll have a new perspective on the earlier chapters. Then follow the directions in Chapter 7 to set up your work environment, and begin putting the system into practice.

For the first few weeks you may want to keep the book on your desk, or in a drawer within easy reach, so you can easily refer to it. Over time, as the methods and practices become natural habits, you'll need to do that less often. When you find yourself consulting the book less than once a week, put it on a shelf, take a deep breath, and return to your desk without a safety net.

Whether the book is on the shelf or not, after about a month take an afternoon to assess how closely you've been following the FASTEN principles.

- *Filing:* Are you keeping good records, and filing documents with ease?
- *Assistance:* Have you hired an accountant?
- *Say 'no':* Are you being mindful of how much work you take on?
- *Time:* Are you making effective use of your calendar?
- *Equipment:* Have you invested in the good quality tools you require?
- *Notes:* Are you reliably capturing your thoughts and transcribing them?

Perhaps most importantly, are you starting work every day with a clean mind?

As you conduct this assessment, you may realise you've forgotten to implement something from the book. Don't panic. Just relax, and resolve to include it in your work practices from here onward. Becoming an *Organised Writer* isn't something that happens overnight; it's a process, and what matters is that you approach it with a willingness to question and change bad habits.

That applies to how closely you follow the system, too; remember, *The Organised Writer* exists because none of the productivity systems I found were right for me. It would be churlish of me not to acknowledge that you might feel the same way. If you want to tweak and modify this system to make it work for your own circumstances, you have my blessing.

The Appendix has checklists if you need them. But after a while, you *won't* need them. You'll develop habits and practices that become second nature, and in time you may forget you're even using a system.

Afterword

'If you sit around waiting for the right moment to create, you will die waiting.'

There's that quotation again. It follows me around online like a zombie, refusing to die, occasionally found by someone new to be retweeted and Facebooked all over again. It's strange to think that of all the things I've written, those are the words which may outlive me.

Nevertheless, I stand by them. Every writer has a hundred ideas they haven't yet got round to writing, with more piling up every day. We're storytellers, and we want to tell as many stories as we can in what little time we have. We learn to resign ourselves to the inevitability that we'll never write everything we want to – if we could live twice as long, we *still* wouldn't have enough time – but that won't stop us trying.

That's why being an *Organised Writer* matters. It's not about cold, hard efficiency; it's about making the most of our time so we can tell more of our stories, and do so without driving ourselves to an early grave. Working smarter can improve not only our business practices, but also our writing.

Wherever you are, whatever you create, I wrote this book to help you do more of it. Let me know how it goes.

Acknowledgements

No book is written entirely alone.

Merlin Mann and David Allen paved the way for my first steps into the world of productivity; Merlin's *43 Folders* website is still online, and David's *Getting Things Done* remains a seminal work in the field.

My old friend and fellow author Benjamin Read wasn't the first to suggest *The Organised Writer* should be a book, but he was the one to convince me it might be a good idea.

I'm fortunate to have a group of thoughtful and incisive beta readers who regularly save me from disappearing up my own filing system. This time I'm especially indebted to Helene Wecker, Kieron Gillen, Lisa Schmeiser, and Candice Cardasis for their extensive and invaluable help. Alysoun Owen, my editor at Bloomsbury, cast an invaluable and insightful eye over the manuscript as she guided it to become the book you now hold.

Thanks and apologies are due to my agent Sarah Such, who did not explode when I told her I was pausing my next novel to write this book instead.

Living with a writer takes a certain, rather specialised set of skills, though the partners in question are often too modest to admit it. Marcia, mine own, is one of the most skilful.

Appendices

Summary checklists

This section reproduces the Summary sections from the end of each chapter in checklist form for your convenience. Feel free to photocopy them for your own use.

1. The FASTEN principles

- ☐ *Filing:* Keep good, clear records, and file documents in a simple, unified alphabetical system.
- ☐ *Assistance:* Delegate tasks to which you are not suited and hire an accountant.
- ☐ *Say 'no':* Be mindful of how much work you're taking on, and don't commit yourself to unrealistic deadlines.
- ☐ *Time:* Make effective use of your calendar to manage deadlines and make hard appointment reminders.
- ☐ *Equipment:* Invest in high quality tools you know you can rely on.
- ☐ *Notes:* Capture all your thoughts, ideas, and tasks immediately in the most convenient manner possible, then transcribe them when you're able to do so.

2. Clocking in (and out)

CALENDAR:

- ☐ Block out your work schedule for the next four weeks, with one project per day.
- ☐ Commit to a daily word count, not a set amount of time.
- ☐ Enter all your current hard appointment commitments, with date and time reminders.

EMAIL:

- ☐ Assess every new email in your inbox for its task contents, then do one of the following:
  - Read it, then archive it.
  - Deal with it now, then archive it.
  - Mark it unread, and deal with it later.
  - Delete it.
- ☐ Carry out a 'bottom-up' check of unread emails using the same criteria.

TASK MANAGER:

- ☐ Enter all projects – both work and personal – into your task manager, either as separate work projects or as miscellaneous Agenda & Admin items.
- ☐ Give each project one Priority/Today item each.
- ☐ Group related tasks to be carried out in a single sweep in a temporary to-do list.

3. Taking notes and making lists

NOTEBOOK:

- ☐ Carry a notebook and pen with you everywhere.
- ☐ Title and date all notes where relevant to an existing project.
- ☐ Don't forget to also note non-writing thoughts and tasks.
- ☐ Type up notes as soon as it's convenient.
- ☐ Transfer non-writing notes to a calendar or task manager.

LISTS:

- ☐ Make and print job sheets for your typical work projects.
- ☐ Write a master packing list for travel.

FILING:

- ☐ Everything goes in either desk trays, filing drawers, or archive boxes.
- ☐ In filing drawers and archive boxes, file all folders alphabetically.
- ☐ At the end of each year, the previous year's accounts go together in a separate, marked binder.

4. Five pages after breakfast

DAILY STRUCTURE:

- ☐ Set your phone to 'do not disturb' during normal writing hours.
- ☐ Set and make your daily writing quota.
- ☐ Deal with emails and phone calls.
- ☐ Do writing-adjacent revisions/outlining/research/etc.
- ☐ Finish work time with filing, invoicing, and office admin.
- ☐ Save social media and PR for the end of the day when you have time to spare.

5. From scribbles to script

WRITING STAGES:

- ☐ Make initial notes.
- ☐ Bullet-point outline the plot.
- ☐ Look for big problems, re-bullet as necessary (but don't worry about small problems).
- ☐ Write a treatment or pitch, if desired.
- ☐ Break down the story into chapters/scenes/pages as necessary.

- ☐ Write the Zero Draft, following the 'just write' mantra to keep going until it's finished.
- ☐ Rewrite, checking for word repetition and overuse.
- ☐ Put the manuscript aside for at least a week, then proofread it again.

6. Money matters

ACCOUNTS:

- ☐ Hire an accountant.
- ☐ Track your income and expenses with a simple spreadsheet.
- ☐ Send invoices as soon as the work is done.
- ☐ Block one to two hours each week to enter and check invoices, expenses, and bills due.
- ☐ Set recurring calendar appointments to remind you of filing dates.

7. It's a set-up

HARDWARE:

- ☐ Place your filing cabinet/drawer no more than two steps from your chair.
- ☐ Position desk trays within reach on your desk.
- ☐ Sort your souvenirs from your tools.
- ☐ Discard items you no longer need.

PROJECT FOLDERS:

- ☐ Make manila folders and job sheets for every project.
- ☐ Fill in a job sheet where appropriate and tape it to the folder.

Summary checklists

- ☐ Determine if the folder belongs in a desk tray, your filing cabinet, or an archive box.
- ☐ Make standard generic folders for yearly recurring non-creative items like invoices and bank statements.
- ☐ Ensure you have spare folders, keep them handy, and don't be stingy using them.
- ☐ Make digital equivalents of project folders and inboxes.

CALENDAR AND TASK MANAGER:

- ☐ Add appointments, projects, and tasks as they come to you.
- ☐ Make recurring calendar reminders for regular tasks and appointments.
- ☐ Remember to add personal and family items, too.

Job sheets

This section reproduces sample job sheets as detailed in Chapter 3, collected together for your convenience. You can download PDF versions from the website *http://organised-writer.com*

NOVEL JOB SHEET

JOB INFORMATION

TITLE   **PUBLISHER**

AGENT: **FEE:**   **CONTRACT?** ☐

---

1. Research ☐   2. Notes ☐

3. Plot ☐   4. Breakdown ☐

DRAFT

Zero Draft ☐   First (Rough) ☐   First (Polished) ☐

EDITORIAL

Sent to Editor ☐   Editorial revisions ☐ ☐ ☐

Copy editor revisions ☐   Galley proof checked ☐

PAYMENT   **ARCHIVING**

Advance ☐   Balance ☐   Archived ☐

DATE PUBLISHED

VIDEO GAME JOB SHEET

JOB INFORMATION

TITLE   **PUBLISHER**

AGENT: **RATE:**   **CONTRACT?** ☐

1. Research ☐   2. Notes ☐

3. Plot ☐   4. Breakdown ☐

#	DELIVERABLE	DRAFT	POLISH	SENT	FEE	PAID

Archived ☐   **DATE PUBLISHED**

SCREENPLAY JOB SHEET

JOB INFORMATION

TITLE _____ **COMPANY** _____

FEE: _____ **DEAL MEMO** ☐ **CONTRACT** ☐

1. Research .... ☐   2. Notes .... ☐

3. Plot .... ☐   4. Breakdown .... ☐

DRAFTS COMPLETED

Treatment ☐   **Treatment revisions** ☐ ☐ ☐ ☐ ☐

Zero Draft ☐   **First (Rough)** ☐   **First (Polished)** ☐

DELIVERED TO PRODUCTION

First draft ☐   **Revision Steps** ☐ ☐ ☐ ☐

PAYMENT

Signing ☐   **Treatment** ☐   **Delivery** ☐   **Revision** ☐
Steps: _____ ☐   _____ ☐   _____ ☐

Archived ☐   **RELEASE DATE** _____

GRAPHIC NOVEL JOB SHEET

JOB INFORMATION

TITLE   **PUBLISHER**

FEE: **WFH/CO**   **CONTRACT?** ☐

1. Research .... ☐   2. Notes .... ☐

3. Plot .... ☐   4. Breakdown .... ☐

DRAFT
Dialogue ☐   **Panel descriptions** ☐   **Polish** ☐

PUBLICATION
Sent to Publisher ☐   **Invoiced** ☐   **Paid** ☐

DESIGN
Story Art ☐   **Cover Art** ☐   **Cover Design** ☐
Interior Design ☐   **Backmatter** ☐   **Uploaded** ☐

Archived ☐   **DATE PUBLISHED**

TITLE		PUBLISHER		FEE		WFH/CO	CONTRACT? ☐

ISSUE No.																
Research																
Notes																
Plotted																
Page breakdown																
Dialogue																
Panel descriptions																
Polish																
Sent to publisher																
Invoiced																
Paid																

DESIGN								
Story art								
Cover art								
Cover design								
Interior design								
Backmatter								
Uploaded								
Archived								

PUB. DATE								

Further reading

Creativity and productivity:

Allen, David. *Getting Things Done* (Penguin, 2001)

Lamott, Anne. *Bird by Bird* (Pantheon Books, 1994)

Tharp, Twyla. *The Creative Habit* (Simon and Schuster, 2006)

Mann, Merlin et al. http://43folders.com

The craft of writing:

Bickham, Jack M. *The 38 Most Common Fiction Writing Mistakes* (Writer's Digest, 1992); *Scene & Structure* (Writer's Digest, 1993)

Block, Lawrence. *Writing the Novel: From Plot to Print* (Writer's Digest, 1979); *Telling Lies for Fun and Profit* (Quill, 1981); *Spider, Spin me a Web: A Handbook for Fiction Writers* (Quill, 1988)

Goldman, William. *Adventures in the Screen Trade* (Warner Books, 1983); *Which Lie Did I Tell?* (Pantheon Books, 2000)

McKee, Robert. *Story* (HarperCollins, 1997)

Noble, William. *Conflict, Action & Suspense* (Writer's Digest, 1994)

Yorke, John. *Into the Woods* (Penguin, 2013)

Various contributors. *www.writersandartists.co.uk*

The psychology of creativity:

Csikszentmihalyi, Mihaly. *Creativity: Flow and the Psychology of Discovery and Invention* (HarperCollins, 1996)

Doyle, Charlotte L. *Creative Flow as a Unique Cognitive Process* in Frontiers in Psychology (Frontiers Media, 2017), www.frontiersin.org/articles/10.3389/fpsyg.2017.01348/full

Livni, Ephrat. *Keyboards are overrated. Cursive is back and it's making us smarter* (Quartz, 2017), https://qz.com/1037057/keyboards-are-overrated-cursive-is-back-and-its-making-us-smarter

May, Cindi. *A Learning Secret: Don't Take Notes with a Laptop* in Scientific American (Scientific American, 2014), www.scientificamerican.com/article/a-learning-secret-don-t-take-notes-with-a-laptop

Mueller, Pam and Oppenheimer, Daniel. *The Pen Is Mightier Than the Keyboard: Advantages of Longhand Over Laptop Note Taking* in Psychological Science (Sage Journals, 2014), https://doi.org/10.1177/0956797614524581

Index

accountants 167–8, 169, 171
accounting period 170
accounts 104–5, 234–5
Acrobat 229
Acronis True Image 222
Adams, Douglas 21
adapter cables 239
admin tasks
  admin days 132
  calendars 31, 34
  multiple projects 44
  productive timeline 3
  record keeping 169, 170, 171
  task managers 62–3
  working to quantity, not time 68, 69
  writing on the move 143–4
Adobe Acrobat 229
Aeon Timeline 225
alarm notifications 32–3
alcohol 149
Allen, David 80
alphabetical system 103, 193
Android software 216, 236
Apple Pencil 229
appointments 27–32, 53–4, 61, 89, 90, 207–8
apps 84–5, 121, 236
archive boxes 194, 201, 205–6
archives 99, 102–5, 201, 205–6
archiving software 224–5
assistance 18
August, John 158
Austen, Jane 189
Awake, Mikael 70

Backblaze 223, 224
backups 146–8, 215, 221–3, 224, 225
banking 172, 175
battery packs 236–7
becoming an organised writer 1–9
  assumptions and caveats 5–6

book overview 7–9
clean mind theory 6–7
overview 1–3
productive timeline 3–5
being an organised writer 243
Billingham, Mark 68
bills 171, 172–3, 174, 176
blocking work time 27–35, 36–9
book reading 68, 142–3
brainstorming 141, 142
breakdowns, writing 156–7
breaks 44, 74, 120, 126
bullet journals 58, 89
bullet-point outlines 153–5
BusyCal 220

cables 239
calculating software 230
Calendar app 28, 220
calendars 27–42
  alarms/notifications 32
  bills 171
  blocking work time 27–35, 36–9
  dealing with problems 35–7
  digital and paper 28–9
  email 46, 53–4
  examples 30, 34, 35, 38
  how long will a job take 37–42
  making lists 89, 90
  overview 77, 240
  personal life 75–6
  software 220
  syncing data 28–9
  task managers and to-do lists 60–1, 207–8
cameras 232
cancelled work 185–6
capturing thoughts 80, 81, 82, 90
Carbon Copy Cloner 222
chairs 209–10, 211

character finders 226
chasing late payments 175–6, 183
clean environment 192
clean mind theory 5, 6–7, 42–3, 71, 119, 120, 123, 242
clickers 238–9
clocking in see calendars; time management
cloning software 146–7, 222
cloud services 58, 84, 146–7, 222–3, 224, 225
cognitive load 16, 55, 59, 146, 174, 190
comic series 100–1, 156, 157
comic writing 45, 92, 96, 98, 131, 156
commitments 65–7
company records 170
computers
  computer folders 204
  file taxonomy 232–6
  hardware 214–15
  internet
    blockers 121–2
  laptops 144, 145–6, 210
  making lists 89
  note taking 82, 84, 85–9
  writing on the move 144, 145–6
concentration span 44
contexts and sprints 22–3, 24, 27
corporate systems 4, 22
CrashPlan 223
creative flow see flow
creative muse 134
creative workers 4, 5, 6, 23, 70, 129, 165, 169
creativity 6, 19, 23–4, 44
crunch time 140
Czikszentmihalyi, Mihaly 23, 24

Dahl, Roald 189
daily writing quota
  after writing 126–8
  how long will a job take 39–42

Index

minimum
  quotas 124–6
multiple projects in one
  day 44
overview 149–50
questions 129–33
time off 129
working to quantity,
  not time 67–9, 123–4
daydreaming 117, 120, 143
day jobs 7, 131–2
deadlines
  blocking work
    time 27–35, 36–9
  crunch time 140
  dealing with
    problems 35–7
  how long will a job
    take 37–42
  job sheets 93
  learning to say
    'no' 65–7
  meeting 21, 27, 40, 43, 68, 124, 129
  missing 1, 2, 3, 36, 65
  multiple projects 43, 44
  productive
    procrastination 71
  re-negotiating 36
  using your calendar 27, 28, 29–30, 35–42
desks 144–6, 210–11
desk trays 102–5, 169, 176, 193–4, 200–1, 211
diaries 29
digital archiving 206, 224–5
digital bills 172–3, 174
digital calendars 28–9
digital expenses 172
digital file
  management 232–6
digital inboxes 204
digital notes 202–3
digital receipts 174
digital records 169, 174
digital signatures 215, 229
discipline 137
discounted rates 185, 186–7
distraction 13–15, 19–20, 23, 41, 65, 71, 85, 121
documents 102, 197–202, 206
do not disturb (DND)
  features 123

drafts 134, 135, 137, 139, 157–8, 159–61
dreaded tasks 70, 71, 72
drinking alcohol 149
DriveImage XML 222
drives 146–8, 215, 222–4, 239
Dropbox 146, 222, 223, 224
Dyment, Doug 109

early risers 130–1
editing 154
email 45–57
  after writing 117–19, 121–3, 128, 132
  benefits of 54, 57
  email clients 47
  examples 52–4, 56
  filters and
    labels 48–52
  Inbox Zero 46
  making lists 90
  managing emails 47
  multiple projects 45
  overview 45–8, 78
  problems with 54–7
  software 230–1
  task managers 63
environment *see* writing
  environment
environmental
  noise 145, 238
equipment
  FASTEN
    principles 18
  gadgets 236–9
  hardware 209–15
  setting up
    environment 191
  evening writing 131–2, 148
Excel 221
expenses 167, 171, 172, 177, *179*, *180*
external hard drives 215, 222, 224

Facebook 117, 118, 119, 121, 128
FaceTime 225
Fade In 218
family life 6–7, 37, 67, 69, 74–8, 81, 120, 208
FantastiCal 220
FASTEN prin-
  ciples 18–19, 242
file naming 62

file restoration 223
files and archives 102–5
file taxonomy 29, 146, 232–6
filing 18, 113, 206
filing cabinets 191, 193, 201, 211
filing drawers 76, 102–5, 176, 193, 203
filing trays 211
Filofax systems 29
filtering email 48–52, 54, 230
final draft 160
Final Draft
  software 218
finances *see* money
  matters
finishing projects 138, 139
first drafts 135, 139, 157
five pages after
  breakfast 117–50
'just write'
  principle 133–40
overview 117–20, 149–50
questions 129–33
words, not
  time 120–33
writing on the
  move 140–9
flagged emails 47, 51, 63
Flaubert, Gustave 9, 25
flight-tracking
  apps 231–2
floor mats 210
flow 13, 23–4, 44, 90, 125
focus 13–15, 19, 65, 81, 119, 128
folders
  archive boxes 205–6
  computer folders 204
  files and
    archives 102–5
  manila folders 197–202, 204, 205
  overview 240
  setting up environ-
    ment 197–202, 205–6
  spare folders 204
  standard
    folders 203–4
freelancing
  email 54, 55
  finding your price 184, 187

Index

job sheets 92
learning to say 'no' 65
money matters 165–6
productive timeline 3
full-drive
  restoration 223
future projects 200–1

gadgets 236–9
battery packs 236–7
headphones 238
presentation
  gear 238–9
smartphones/
  tablets 236
travel trays 237–8
getting organised
  FASTEN
    principles 13–20
  notes and lists 79–113
  overview 7
  time
    management 21–78
Getting Things Done
  (GTD) 4, 80
Gmail 29, 47, 230
GoodReader 229
Google 28, 29, 236
Google Docs 221
Google Drive 146
Google Keep 220
Google Maps 231
GoToMeeting 225
graphic novels 96, 98,
  99, 124, 183, 218
GTD (Getting Things
  Done) 4, 80

habits 25, 72, 80–1, 119,
  137, 190
hanging files 193
hard appointments 27–
  8, 32, 46, 51, 61, 90
hard drives 147–8, 215,
  222, 224
hardware 209–15
  computer and
    peripherals 214–15
  overview 240
  stationery 212–14
  working
    environment 209–11
headphones 145, 238
health 37, 120, 192
Highland app 158, 218
hindsight effect 39
holidays 74, 106–12, 208
hotels 148

iCloud 146, 222
ideal working day 26–7
imagination 19, 120
inbox 46, 48–52, 200
Inbox Zero 46
income records 177, *178*
index cards 157
initial notes 151
initial plot 151–3
inkjet printers 214–15
inner editor 138
inspiration 133, 134, 135,
  138, 139
internet blockers 121–2
interruptions 23, 24
intervals 23
interviews 52–3
investing time to set up
  system 72–4
invoices 174–6, 182–3
iPad 229, 236
iPhone 84, 216, 220, 225,
  236, 237

job sheets 91–101, 192,
  199
'just write' prin-
  ciple 133–40, 154, 158

Keybreeze 227
kill fees 185–6

labelling email 48–52,
  230
Lamott, Anne 157
laptops 144, 145–6, 210
laser printers 214–15
late payments 175–6,
  183
launchers 227
learning to say 'no' 18,
  65–7, 187
leisure time 31, 68, 69,
  74–8, 128–9
life hacks 70
lists
  to-do lists 60–1,
    207–8
  making lists 89–90
  memory distraction 17
  overview 113
  packing lists 106–12
living as an organised
  writer 240–2
local backups 221–2
luggage, and packing
  lists 106–12
lunch breaks 44

Mac Mail 47
Mac software 59, 216,
  217, 220, 221, 236
mail 90
making lists *see* lists
manila folders 197–202,
  204, 205
Mann, Merlin 80
manuscript
  writing 157–9
master packing
  list 110–12
mats 210
memory
  creative flow 24
  focus and
    distraction 14–20
  missing deadlines 36
  note taking 77, 79,
    81, 82
  off-loading tasks 17, 18
memory distraction
  14–17, 19, 20, 36, 77
Microsoft Excel 221
Microsoft Office 220, 221
Microsoft OneNote 87,
  220
Microsoft Word 217,
  218, 219
Miller's Law 15–16
minimum quotas 124–6
see also daily writing
  quota
money matters 165–88
  accounts and tax
    records 104–5
  finding your
    price 183–7
  hiring an
    accountant 167–8
  invoices 174–6, 182–3
  overview 165–7, 188
  record keeping 168–76
  spreadsheets 176–82
  turning down
    work 65, 67
morning working 130–1
Movie Magic
  Screenwriter 218
multiple projects 42–5,
  62, 92–4
muse 134

Nabokov, Vladimir 189
negotiation 36, 66
network-attached storage
  (NAS) servers 224
Nitro Pro 229

Index

no, saying 18, 65–7, 187
noise-cancelling (NC)
    headphones 145, 238
non-work notes 89
non-writing tasks 8,
    127–8, 130, 132
notebooks
  desktop 211
  making lists 89, 90
  note taking 76, 82–3,
    84, 86
  overview 112
  stationery 213
  task managers 58
  unused notebooks 195
  writing initial
    plot 152–3
Notes app 84, 87, 203,
    220
notes to self 158
note taking 79–113
  digital notes 202–3
  FASTEN acronym 19
  files and
    archives 102–5
  job sheets 91–101
  making lists 89–90
  notebooks 82–3
  organising your personal life 76
  overview 79–83, 112–13
  packing lists 106–12
  software 219–20
  using your
    computer 85–9
  using your phone 83–5
  writing on the
    move 141–2
  writing process 151,
    152, 154
notifications 32–3, 123
novel writing 29–30,
    67–8, 96, 124, 126, 155–7
Numbers app 221

Office 220, 221
off-loading tasks 17, 18,
    36, 94, 96, 160
OmniFocus 60
One Bag method 109
OneDrive 146, 222
OneNote 87, 220
1Password 228
online banking 172, 175
OpalCalc 230
OpenOffice (OO) 219,
    221
optical media 224

organised writers
  becoming an organised
    writer 1–9
  being an organised
    writer 243
  dos and don'ts 13, 21,
    79, 117, 165, 189
  living as an organised
    writer 240–2
outlining 129–30, 153–5
Outlook 28, 47, 220
overcommitment 28, 65,
    66, 73
overdue invoices 175–6,
    183

packing lists 61, 106–12,
    111
page counts/quotas 68,
    118, 124–6
  see also daily writing
    quota
panic method 71
pantsers 99
paper-based systems
  calendars 29
  job sheets 91
  note taking 82–3, 89,
    152–3
  record keeping 173–4
  task managers 58, 60
paperless projects 202
paper records 173–4
password managers 228
payments
  bills 172–3
  expenses 172
  late payments 175–6,
    183
pay or play
  agreements 186
pay rates 183–7
PDF editors 229
pens 212–13
peripherals 214–15
personal life 31, 37,
    74–8, 208
phones see smartphones
physical records 169,
    173–4
pitches 155–6
plot 151–3, 154, 155
point-of-view
    (POV) 156, 157
pomodoros 4, 23
PopChar 226
portable hard
    drives 147, 215

presentation gear 238–9
pricing work 183–7
printers 214–15
priorities 61–3
problems, dealing
    with 35–7, 45
problem time 38, 39
procrastination 70–2,
    136, 189
productive timeline 3–5
productivity 65, 66, 73,
    79, 80
productivity systems 4,
    22, 27, 41, 44, 46
projects
  folders and documents 197–200, 240
  job sheets 91–101
  multiple projects 42–5, 62, 92–4
  task managers 62, 64
proofreading 26, 27, 29,
    126, 127, 143
publication
  dates 99–100

quantity, working
    to 67–9, 123–4
Quicksilver
    launcher 227
quota, minimum 124–6
  see also daily writing
    quota

race to the bottom 187
rates of pay 183–7
reading books 68, 142–3
receipts 172, 174, 176
record keeping 168–82
  digital bills 172
  digital expenses 172
  files and
    archives 102–5
  filing drawers 176
  invoices 174–6, 182–3
  overview 168–76, 188
  paper records 173–4
  spreadsheets 176–82
rehearsal, and
  memory 15, 16, 17
reimbursable
    expenses 177
relaxation 68, 69, 77,
    121, 208
remittance advice 175,
    183
repetition in
    writing 160

262

Index

research for writing 129
revisions 39, 125–6, 127, 134, 135, 139, 158
rewriting 86, 125–6, 135, 154, 158, 159–61
room service 148

saying 'no' 18, 65–7, 187
scanners 215, 229–30
scheduling
 blocking work time 27–35, 36–9
 email 55
 how long will a job take 37–42
 multiple projects 42–5, 62, 92–4
 personal life 74–7
 record keeping 170
scratch documents 87
screen breaks 120
screenplays/screenwriting 98, 100, 124, 142, 156, 158, 183, 218
'scribbles to script' process *see* writing process
scriptwriting 68, 124, 125, 126
Scrivener 60, 124, 133, 218, 219, 236
searching 29, 88–9
self-criticism 138–9
serialised content 100–1
servers 99, 224
set-up and environment 189–240
 focus 13–14
 gadgets 236–9
 hardware 209–15
 investing time to set up system 72–4
 overview 18, 189–91, 239–40
 relaxing 208
 setting up process 190–208
 software 215–32
 taxonomy 232–6
shoebox applications 87
shopping lists 61, 110
short stories 156
short-term memory 16, 19, 24
shower conundrum 69
Simplenote 220
Skype 225
sleep 129, 132

smartphones
 avoiding distraction 121, 123
 battery packs 236–7
 calendars 28
 cameras 232
 as gadgets 236
 making lists 89–90
 note taking 76, 83–5, 87
 phone calls 32, 71, 123, 132, 144
 software 216
 task managers 58
 social media 41, 117–19, 121, 122, 127, 128, 228
soft appointments 28
software 215–32
 archiving 224–5
 basic essentials 216–17
 calculating software 230
 calendars 220
 character finders 226
 cloud backup 222–3
 email 230–1
 launchers 227
 local backup 221–2
 note-takers 219–20
 overview 215–16
 password managers 228
 PDF editors 229
 scanner drivers 229–30
 spreadsheets 221
 task managers 220–1
 text snippets 226
 timeline creators 225
 travel software 231–2
 voice chat 225
 writing breakdown 157
 writing software 60, 157, 217–19
solid-state drives (SSDs) 147
sophomore slump 136
Soulver 230
souvenirs 194–6
Spotlight 227
spreadsheets 169, 174, 176–82, 221
sprints 22–3
standing desks 120, 210
stationery 212–14
story ideas 14, 19, 79, 83, 89, 90

Storyist 218
stress 1–2, 15, 65, 68, 71, 168
subconscious 69
sunk cost fallacy 73–4
SuperDuper 222
syncing data 28–9, 84, 85, 220, 222
systemic memory 79

tablets 144, 236
taking notes *see* note taking
talking to the duck 118
task managers
 definition 60
 to-do lists and calendars 60–1, 207–8
 email 46, 47
 examples 63–4, 64
 making lists 90
 organising your personal life 75
 overview 78, 240
 priorities 61–3
 productive procrastination 71
 software 220–1
 using 57–64
taxonomy 29, 146, 232–6
tax records 3, 104–5, 166, 167–8, 170, 235
telephone calls 32, 71, 123, 132, 144
 see also smartphones
TextExpander 226
text snippets 226
Things task manager 59, 62, 220–1
thinking time 25
thought capturing 80, 81, 82, 90
timeline creators 225
Time Machine 221
time management 21–78
 blocking work time 27–35, 36–9
 dealing with problems 35–7
 definition 24–5
 FASTEN principles 18
 getting smart with email 45–57
 how long will a job take 37–42

Index

investing time to set up system 72–4
learning to say 'no' 18, 65–7, 187
multiple projects 42–5, 62, 92–4
organising your personal life 74–8
overview 21–5, 77–8
productive procrastination 70–2
using a task manager 57–64
using your calendar 27–42
working day 26–7
working to quantity, not time 67–9, 123–4
time off 42, 68–9, 73–4, 77, 128–9, 196–7
time tracking 24–5
Todoist 221
to-do lists 17, 22, 60–1, 63, 93, 138, 207–8
tools 194–6
to-read pile 142, 143
transcribing notes 87, 88, 90, 112–13, 151, 152
travel
  admin tasks 143–4
  avoiding writing 141–3
  calendars 32
  dos and don'ts 146–9
  overview 150
  packing lists 106–12
  simulating your desk 144–6
  software 231–2
  task managers 61
  writing on the move 140–9
travel trays 237–8
treatments and pitches 155–6
Trello 221
TripIt 231
turning down work 18, 65–7, 187
TV screenwriting 98
Twitter 117, 118, 119, 128, 228
typewriters 215
Typinator 226

ubiquitous capture 80
Ulysses 218
unread emails 47, 48, 51, 55, 57

unsolicited emails 55
unwinding 131
USB drives 224, 239

vacations 74, 106–12, 208
valuing your time 66, 67, 187
videogames 26, 100, 140, 142, 183, 186
voice chat software 225
voicemail 84, 123
voice memos 84
'VOIP' (Voice Over Internet Protocol) 225
vomit draft 157
VueScan 229–30

Wavemaker 218
Windows
  calendars 28, 220
  email 47
  smartphones 236
  software 216, 220, 221
  writing software 217–19
Word 217, 218, 219
word counts 41–2, 67–9, 120–33
word processors 215, 217, 219
word repetition 160
working day 26–7
working space 9, 13–14, 72–4, 209–11, 239
  see also writing environment
workload 65–7
work time blocking 27–35, 36–9
writer's block 70, 133, 135, 136
writers' guilds 167, 183, 187
writing
  becoming an organised writer 1–9
  being an organised writer 243
  five pages after breakfast method 117–50
  focus and memory 16, 19
  'just write' principle 133–40
  living as an organised writer 240–2

overview 7–8
time
  management 23–5
  working to quantity, not time 67–9, 120–33
writing on the move 140–9
writing process 151–61
writing environment 189–240
  gadgets 236–9
  hardware 209–15
  investing time to set up system 72–4
  overview 189–90, 239–40
  relaxing 208
  setting up process 190–208
  software 215–32
  taxonomy 232–6
  working space 9, 13–14, 72–4, 209–11, 239
writing on the move 140–9
  admin tasks 143–4
  avoiding writing 141–3
  overview 140–1
  simulating your desk 144–6
  travelling dos and don'ts 146–9
writing process 151–61
  breakdown 156–7
  bullet-point outline 153–5
  initial notes 151
  initial plot 151–3
  manuscript 157–9
  overview 117–20, 161
  rewriting 159–61
  treatment/pitch 155–6
writing quota *see* daily writing quota
writing software 60, 157, 217–19
writing speed 67
Wunderlist 221

Yojimbo 87

Zero Draft 157, 158, 159
Zoho Books 221
the zone 13, 23, 40, 121
Zoom 225